marriage and family enrichment:

NEW PERSPECTIVES AND PROGRAMS

Edited by

HERBERT A. OTTO

ABINGDON
Nashville

MARRIAGE AND FAMILY ENRICHMENT: NEW PERSPECTIVES AND PROGRAMS

2

Copyright © 1976 by Herbert A. Otto

Library of Congress Cataloging in Publication Data

Main entry under title:
Marriage and family enrichment.
   Includes bibliographical references.
   1. Family—Addresses, essays, lectures. 2. Marriage counseling—Addresses, essays, lectures. 3. Group relations training—Addresses, essays, lectures.
I. Otto, Herbert Arthur.
HQ734.M386   362.8'2   75-30743

ISBN 0-687-23620-7

MANUFACTURED BY THE PARTHENON PRESS AT NASHVILLE, TENNESSEE, UNITED STATES OF AMERICA

Dedicated to David and Vera Mace,
pioneers and innovators in
the marriage and family enrichment movement

CONTENTS

marriage-centered programs

national and regional programs and other resources

Contents

Preface

THE MARRIAGE AND FAMILY ENRICHMENT MOVEMENT IS ONE of the most promising contemporary developments to appear on the scene. The vitality and strength of this movement are evident both from its growth rate and from the creativity of the pioneers in this field. The thrust of the movement is to strengthen marriage and family life through what are basically preventive programs.

This book represents a first effort to survey this bourgeoning new field in order to furnish resources as well as some direction to the interested professional and lay person. All but three of the chapters are original contributions written specifically for this volume. The programs selected are representative of the field, but owing to space limitations detailed descriptions of a number of additional pioneering programs could not be included. Reference to some of these programs can be found in the introductory chapter and in the Appendix.

I would like to take this opportunity to thank the group of pioneers in the field who gave of their time by filling out an extensive questionnaire. This volume is a direct outcome of this initial study, conducted by the writer. I would also like to thank the Rev. Russell and June Wilson and Dr. David M. Fulcomer, for creative ideas and suggestions. Finally, permission by the Russell Sage Foundation and the National Council on Family Relations to use copyrighted material is very much appreciated.

H.A.O.

La Jolla, California

Chapter 1

Marriage and Family Enrichment Programs: An Overview of a Movement
Herbert A. Otto

ALMOST UNNOTICED BY THE PUBLIC AND LARGE SEGMENTS of the professional community, a new movement has made its appearance, and has achieved a lusty stature in only a few years. The growth of the marriage and family enrichment movement has been prodigious, and it is still in its infancy. Marriage and family enrichment is based on the growth ethos and the human potentialities hypothesis. These are, briefly, that all persons and all relationships are functioning at a fraction of their potential and that, *in every couple or family, there is the potential for growth in the relationship as well as the possibility of personal growth, leading to a more fulfilling togetherness.* It is a further hypothesis that *every union, or family, can be strengthened through the periodic regeneration and renewal offered by marriage and family enrichment programs.*

The need for relationship enrichment and personal growth is often not recognized by couples, and this can lead to a subtle and insidious debilitation of the relationship over a period of time. It is very possible that a significant proportion of extramarital affairs are a move of desperation as the individual unconsciously seeks for ways to achieve personal growth and actualize more of his potential

11

through a new relationship. Such affairs could well be called enrichment affairs. Enrichment programs may offer a more viable alternative in such situations. There is also every reason to believe that at this point in the history of human knowledge we are not yet fully aware of the many complex and intricate dimensions and potentialities present in a relationship between two individuals. In this sense marriage and family enrichment programs are an exploratory step in the right direction.

There is widespread recognition by specialists from diverse disciplines that the institutions of marriage and the nuclear family are beset by grave problems and difficulties. A number of authorities, for example, believe that in the very near future more than three out of five marriages will end in divorce. Some latter-day prophets encouraged by the rising divorce rate have already proclaimed the death of the family.[1] It is clear that the Western institutions of marriage and the family, at this point, are in particular need of help. To a considerable extent the rapid growth of the marriage and family enrichment movement appears to be in response to this need.

The knowledge now exists which can help couples to achieve a more fulfilling marriage and family life, and many tested marriage and family enrichment models and methods are now available. This knowledge, gathered over the past two decades especially, comes from the fields of communication, human sexuality, conflict resolution, humanistic psychology, family sociology, small group dynamics, and affective education. It is the purpose of this book to bring some of these models to the attention of those interested, in the hope that this will lead to the development of even more effective programs and further expansion of the field.

Notes on the Origins and Beginnings of a Movement

Marriage and family enrichment programs are group programs and with few exceptions utilize group interaction plus dyad interaction. The "T-group" and "sensitivity training" movement and research of the late forties and the fifties furnished the base for the proliferation of group work that followed. Sensitivity training then gradually merged into "encounter" and the human potentialities movement. The advent of the human potentialities movement, in the early to late sixties, saw within a relatively short period of time the establishment of over two-hundred Growth Centers in this and other countries. These growth centers offered, and continue to offer, workshops and weekend group experiences, usually led by professionals, designed to help people who are functioning well (the non-patient population) to function even better. First and foremost, however, *the human potentialities movement created a widespread acceptance of group experiences and intensive group programs.* It became the "in" thing among the educated segment of the United States public to have participated in a group marathon or workshop.

At the same time steady progress was being made in other areas: the field of human sexuality, family life education, and family sociology. Research in the field of human sexuality had a particular impact and contributed to the increasingly open communication about sexual matters characteristic today. In the area of actualizing human potential, humanistic psychology and affective education added to our understanding of the importance of values, the self-actualizing processes, and feeling-centered small group methods. Contributions from these diverse streams are today traceable in many of the marriage and family enrichment programs.

Among the early pioneers in the field must be mentioned David Mace's work in marriage enrichment with the Society of Friends (Quakers), begun in 1961.[2] The same year marked the writer's research and work with groups which focused on the building of family strengths.[3] (The program was called the Family Resource Development Program: The Key to Family Enrichment.) This was followed by the development of the Family Fun Council[4] in 1966 (a one-day celebrative-type program for churches and communities, designed to strengthen family life) and the More Joy in Your Marriage programs (1966). In 1965 Leon Smith (see chapter 20) began his nationwide Marriage Communication Lab program as a part of the Board of Discipleship of The United Methodist Church.

Unquestionably others, as yet unknown to the writer, were also conducting programs in the early sixties. As these come to my attention it is hoped that references to their work can be included in a subsequent edition of this volume. The conference called by Dr. William Genné, coordinator of the Committee on Marriage and the Family of the National Council of Churches, must also be mentioned. The conference, the first of its kind, took place in Indianapolis in December of 1973 and was attended by about thirty delegates of various denominations who were conducting marriage and family enrichment programs or were interested in such programs.

The following definitions of marriage and family enrichment programs were developed. They are, with minor additions, the definitions used in the national survey of the movement reported later in this chapter.

Marriage enrichment programs are for couples who have what they perceive to be fairly well-functioning marriages and who wish to make their marriages even more mutually satisfying. (The programs are *not* designed for people whose marriages are at a point of crisis, or who are seeking counseling help for marital problems.) Marriage enrichment programs are generally concerned with enhancing the *couple's* communication, emotional life, or sexual relationship; with fostering marriage strengths, personal growth, and the development of marriage and individual potential while maintaining a consistent and primary focus on the relationship of the couple.

Family life enrichment programs are for parents who have what they perceive to be a fairly well-functioning family and who wish to make their family life even better. (The programs are not designed for people whose family relationship is at a point of crisis or who are seeking counseling help for family problems.) Family enrichment programs are generally concerned with enhancing the *family's* communication and emotional life—the parents' sexual relationship, personal growth, and child-rearing practices, as well as parent-child relationships—with fostering family strengths and the development of family and individual potential while *actively involving the children as an ongoing part of the program.*

Forces Which Foster
the Growth of the Movement

Some major factors and a host of others foster the growth of marriage and family enrichment programs. First, there is the increasing recognition by couples that marriage and family life as it exists *can be improved and enriched,* and that a group or workshop experience can be an exciting and enjoyable adventure. Second, the ongoing momentum of the human potentialities movement is continuing to provide a climate in which group experiences, classes, or weekends are not only a part of the social climate but are the "acceptable thing" to do. (It is of interest in this connection that most participants in growth center events are "trendsetters," i.e., professionals from the upper- or middle-income brackets.) Furthermore the younger generation, which has been exposed to this climate for some years, seems to contain more risk-takers willing to try new programs. As important, if not more so, is the fact that wide segments of society, including hierarchic and influential segments, are aware that marriage and the family are in particular need of help and support in this time of transition. As a result there has been a mounting interest on the part of churches and major denominations. This can only be expected to expand in the years to come.

There is also a widespread recognition by members of the helping professions that a large proportion of marriages and families are "subclinical."—subclinical in the sense that they have problems with which they need help and that they are functioning much below optimum despite the couple's love and dedication to each other and their commitment to continuing the union. The vast majority of these families will not seek help, because the problems are of the low-level debilitating kind, never severe enough to precipitate a major crisis for which help must be sought. Recognition of the presence of this subclinical stratum in turn has convinced many professionals of the necessity for preventive programs such as the enrichment movement, which is essentially preventive in nature.

Finally, owing to the impact of sex research there is today more open communication about human sexuality than there was five or ten years ago. This has created a more receptive climate for marriage and family enrichment programs, which, by implication, will also deal with this subject. The institutions of marriage and the family as well as male and female roles are in a state of transition. In many people knowledge of this fact creates a state of "positive anxiety" which makes them more receptive to marriage and family enrichment programs. More open communication between the sexes is one outcome of this process. The additional impact of women's liberation has caused more women to be outspoken and assertive than ever before. This has meant that women are increasingly finding the courage to tell their partners that they believe their relationship will profit from an enrichment experience. It has been my observation that men in general appear to be more conservative and frozen in the status quo. (Women often outnumber men two or three to one in growth groups I have conducted.) Women are the risk-takers in our culture, and the risk-takers are increasing in number. There is every indication that the current conjunction of social forces favors the growth of marriage and family enrichment programs.

Some Sources of Resistance
to Marriage and Family Enrichment

Resistance to these new programs begins with the inbuilt resistance of the individual to growth and change. Growth involves change, and change is linked with the appearance of the new. With very few exceptions people tend to avoid the new because they have become habituated to the status quo in themselves and others close to them.

Aside from the individual's inner resistance to personality growth (or the actualizing of his/her potential), another factor needs to be taken into consideration, namely, the tendency of two people who spend much time together to become enmeshed and "frozen" in deeply ingrained habits of interaction. This very often results in a form of routinized living together that is almost totally lacking in dynamic components and dominated by "keeping things the way they are." As a result, both individual personality growth and the actualizing of potentialities present in the relationship are impeded.

To some degree this process makes inroads into most marriages. Enrichment programs perform the invaluable service of helping to dissolve this bind so that the partners have renewed motivation to develop the possibilities inherent in their relationship. The difficulty lies in helping partners who have become very used to "the way things are" to have a new vision of the possibilities for greater fulfillment in their union. This is a point of considerable resistance. (The resistance to change appears to be even more marked in family units than in married couples.)

A number of additional factors contribute to the resistance to marriage and family enrichment programs.

1. Although people will agree that problems, difficulties, and disagreements are part of every marriage and family relationship, and in this sense "normative," most people are ashamed of this facet of life together. They feel the need to present a facade of "we never have any problems" to the world and are afraid that this unreal facade will be penetrated if they attend one of the new programs. Closely related to this is what David Mace calls "privatism," i.e., the notion that marriage and family life are very private and personal and you don't talk to anyone else about what goes on.

2. It is also clear that problems and difficulties in a marriage or family are often insufficiently resolved or worked through. This leads to a cumulative buildup of emotional residues or affective forces. Over the years this reservoir of imagined or real slights, resentments, and hurts creates inner pressures and insecurities and subtly undermines and threatens the relationship. One or both partners may then feel that the relationship is more fragile than it should be and that it is best not to subject it to the uncertainties of a workshop or program dealing with couple relations. This is the "let sleeping dogs lie" syndrome. It is my observation that even in "good" marriages where the partners love each other, like being together, and wish to continue the union, *affective residues from the past are often so strong that the partners have difficulty being aware of the range of strengths, positive factors, resources, and possibilities present in the relationship.*

3. In some persons today's role-conflicts and change, the generation gap, the influence of women's liberation—in short, the phenomena of institutions in transition—generate a sense of insecurity. Insecure persons are not likely to risk the growth offered by new programs.

4. Finally, conformity pressures ("We can't be different from the Smiths next door") are very much operative. Many people still believe that attending a marriage or family enrichment program will be interpreted by others to mean that their relationship is beset by problems and difficulties for which they have sought help. This

touches on one of the key issues facing this new field: the presentation of family enrichment programs in an educational context, so that first and foremost they are perceived by the public as operating from a health-centered rather than a pathology-centered model.

A Nationwide Survey of the Movement— Findings and Conclusions

From November, 1973, through May, 1974, the writer conducted a survey of marriage and family enrichment programs in the United States and Canada. Only a summary of the results is presented here, since a detailed report has been published elsewhere.[5]

The definitions used as a base for the survey are essentially those found on pages 13-14 above.

It is important to recognize that in spite of some differences marriage enrichment and family enrichment programs have more similar goals and aims than they have dissimilar ones. Accordingly, data from both types of programs is presented without differentiation.

A total of thirty professionals hailing from fifteen states participated in this survey. Thirteen of these indentified themselves as ministers or priests, six as educators, three as sociologists, two each as marriage counselors, social workers, and YMCA directors, and one as a psychologist. One person did not identify her professional affiliation.

Slightly more than 75 percent of the respondents stated that they had originated the programs they were conducting. Over two-thirds of the respondents mentioned specific authors, as well as books or materials, that they used as resources. The writer's books were mentioned six times; references to Thomas Gordon's Parent Effectiveness Training and a Transactional Analysis book occurred four times. Finally, the books of George Bach, Howard Clinebell, and Virginia Satir were each listed three times. Also mentioned three times were materials on human sexuality. Communication training and materials on values were mentioned twice. An additional twenty-one single references to various authors and materials were made.

The distribution of the years in which the programs were first conducted is revealing. David Mace, Leon Smith, and the writer directed their first marriage and family enrichment groups during the period 1961–65, while the Roman Catholic Marriage Encounter groups began in 1967. Nine respondents had conducted their first programs in 1970, six in 1971, seven in 1972, and five in 1973.

Eleven facilitators stated that fewer than one hundred couples had participated in their respective programs. Thirteen professionals listed between one hundred and five hundred couples, and three noted that between a thousand and two thousand couples had attended their programs. One respondent listed a total attendance of three thousand to thirty-five hundred couples (Minnesota Couples Communication Program), and one an attendance of seven thousand couples (Methodist Marriage Communication Lab). One person estimated that the Catholic Marriage Encounter program had had an approximate attendance of four hundred thousand at the time of the survey.

It was found that almost 80 percent of the respondents were training other couples as group facilitators. Ninety percent of the respondents indicated that their programs were conducted by either husband-wife teams or man-woman teams.

The use of a variety of group techniques or ways of working with a group were reported. Twenty-seven of the facilitators used "group discussion," and twenty-three utilized "structured experiences." Twenty-one facilitators listed the use of "two-person experiences," while fourteen facilitators noted "nonverbal experiences." The use of "sensitivity sessions" was reported by eight respondents, and six facilitators listed "encounter sessions." Lectures were used by twenty-one facilitators, and eight respondents noted the use of films. Whereas twenty-three of those reporting stated that an average of 53 percent of their total program time was spent in the area of couple or family communication, only sixteen facilitators listed an average of 14 percent of total program time spent in the area of sexual relationships.

Based on the reports of nineteen of the thirty facilitators, marriage and family enrichment programs appear, for the most part, to take place during a weekend. Seven group leaders conducted a class in addition, and four a combination of classes plus a weekend. An average of fourteen hours were devoted to activities other than eating and sleeping during a weekend. Of those reporting the use of weekends, 85 percent used residential or overnight facilities. The size of weekend groups varied from four to five couples (six facilitators reporting this number) to six to eight and six to ten couples (five facilitators reporting for each category). Classes tended to be much larger, averaging ten to fifteen couples. Most classes met in church facilities and private homes.

Charges per couple for the marriage or family enrichment program varied widely. Three respondents indicated that they made no charge. Three stated that they charged from five to ten dollars per couple, and two facilitators listed a fee of fifteen to twenty-five dollars (plus room and board). Four noted that they charged thirty-five to fifty-five dollars plus room and board, and six recorded that their charge was sixty to seventy-five dollars. Other respondents pointed out that their charges varied, "were set by the sponsoring organization," or followed a formula such as "charge for room, board, and meals, plus one hundred to three hundred dollars per leader couple."

Twenty-two facilitators stated that they used evaluation forms or questionnaires, or "subjective written feedback," while only three respondents referred to specific research projects. Six respondents noted that they did not use evaluation, and two left this item blank.

On the basis of limited data it would appear that Canada is about three years behind the United States in the development of such programs. (An exception is the Banff Conference for Couples, a regional conference of about 130 couples, which in 1975 was in its seventh year.) It is clear, too, that the marriage and family enrichment movement is of comparatively recent origin, since 90 percent of the respondents first conducted their programs in 1973 or later. Survey respondents are fairly evenly divided into those who conduct marriage enrichment programs and those who conduct family enrichment programs, with some conducting both.

The survey and subsequent data revealed that approximately 420,000 couples have attended the programs reported by the respondents. The number of facilitators who have come to the attention of the writer in the course of this research project must be likened to the tip of the iceberg. It is my estimate that approximately twice that number (840,000 couples) have attended marriage and family enrichment programs to date.

The programs currently being conducted are *eclectic* in nature: they utilize varied techniques and draw on a considerable number of diverse sources, resources, and materials. About 80 percent of the programs have certain common elements, such as the use of group discussion, two-person structured experiences, and lectures. It is possible to range contemporary programs on a continuum using the amount of structure built into the program (or lack thereof) as the main variable. Using this paradigm, on one end of the continuum would be the Roman Catholic Marriage Encounter program, where there is maximum structure with group interaction restricted to feedback; at the other end of the continuum would be the programs utilizing mostly or entirely sensitivity or encounter sessions.

A very rapid proliferation of programs seems to be taking place. Between the end of the survey in May 1974 and September of that year over a dozen facilitators came to my attention who were beginning new programs. Several couples have written in stating that they have organized leaderless marriage enrichment groups. One person, the coordinator of a family enrichment unit in Charlotte, North Carolina, sent in a report on an "Experience for Families"[6] which is available at cost. The tape cassette field is also undergoing a growth spurt with two new programs[7,8] announced since the beginning of the survey.

The Family Cluster Movement

The family cluster movement deserves special mention. This appears to have been a spontaneous movement dating back to the mid-sixties. The first reference to the family cluster concept seems to occur in the late Frederick Stoller's essay entitled "The Intimate Network of Families as a New Structure."[9]

Dr. Margaret M. Sawin and the writer are two persons who have played focal roles in the growth of this movement. Dr. Sawin started two family clusters in the spring of 1970 at the same time that the writer was interviewing family clusters in California. The family cluster is a circle of three to five families with generally similar aims, goals, and values, meeting regularly and sharing specific family functions and services, i.e., joint child care and/or rearing, joint purchasing of groceries, etc. Each family maintains its own home as a base.

Dr. Sawin's model of the family cluster focuses on religious nurturing and has thus far been organized largely under church auspices. She states: "The source of religion is human experience itself. Religious behavior is meeting critical life experiences creatively, living in healthy relationships with others, and making worthy moral judgments. Religion is changing rapidly because mankind's experiences are changing rapidly. As such, religion is the emergent arising out of reflection on the meaning of these experiences as they become open to growth and change .... Religious nurturing today is the opportunity for the development of relevant meanings for experiences in this world of rapid change, interpreted with an existential stance within the context of caring and support."[10]

The writer's model has as its basic thrust "to strengthen the family, to foster personal growth and the self-actualizing processes in a celebrative and life-affirmative way. Commitment to the unfolding of family potential and to personal growth in this context is one of the basic means at man's disposal to give more love and caring to himself. The Family Cluster provides a framework which allows for the organic growth and development of love and caring so that members *by loving themselves more are more better able to give to others*. This perhaps is the greatest contribution this concept can make to the quality of our living. Finally, the Family Cluster offers everyone an opportunity to become participants in the wonder and joy of fostering growth in ourselves and others, our family, our friends, our environment, our world."[11] Family clusters appear to be a fairly widespread phenomenon in the United States. In a recent report,[12] for example, one thousand of the Unitarian fellowships and churches in the United States were found to have family clusters. For further information on family clusters see the Appendix.

Marriage and Family Enrichment and the Future

Marriage and family enrichment programs are by no means restricted to the United States, although this country is without doubt the leader in the field at this time. Judging by my correspondence and informal communications with colleagues, there is a worldwide interest in this movement. It is clear that within a few years it will be global in scale.

An assessment of programs at this point in their development clearly indicates that certain shifts and improvements in program aims and content can and will be of benefit to the continued high-level growth of the movement. The convening of a national conference on marriage and family enrichment (possibly sponsored by all organizations currently active and involved) to examine some of the major issues facing the movement is perhaps one of the most productive next steps that could be undertaken.

Although resistance to the concept of enrichment on the part of couples is still prevalent, it is on the decline. The best way to reach such couples is through an "enabling agency" or person inspiring trust and confidence. Enrollment in an enrichment program is most productively facilitated through a couple's relationship with a trusted person who recommends, sponsors, or leads such a program. From the writer's point of view, the church and the minister are in the best position to help couples take advantage of their opportunity to "make a good marriage even better." Primary consideration needs therefore to be given to encouraging more extensive denominational involvement in this movement on a national and local level. Such involvement needs to be on both the seminary training and the clergy training level. Next, growth centers could be encouraged to include more offerings of marriage and family enrichment (or couple enrichment) programs in their catalogs. Family service societies and mental health centers could also be encouraged to sponsor such groups, since marriage and family enrichment falls within the framework of preventive programs. It is also very important that family life educators teaching courses in colleges and high schools be reached to ensure, as soon as possible, that the marriage and family enrichment concept is included in the course content of classes now offered.

Present-day medical science widely recommends that we have an annual physical checkup as a means of prevention. In a similar manner, an annual assessment and evaluation could be made available to couples interested in developing and improving their marriages. The goal would be to identify, strengthen, and develop family potential before crises arise, with the main focus on helping a family achieve an even more loving, enjoyable, creative, and satisfying relationship. The plan of a Marriage and Family Potential Center was developed in 1967 and 1968 by a colleague, Dr. Lacey Hall, and the writer.[13] A major thrust of such marriage and family potential centers, which need to be established on a nationwide scale, would be to offer enrichment—the latest findings on how couple and family relationships can be made even more satisfying and fulfilling. It is indeed gratifying that with a somewhat different emphasis, but with a focus on prevention, Dr. Clark Vincent has organized a Marital Health Clinic which has now begun operations under the auspices of the Bowman Gray School of Medicine in Winston-Salem, North Carolina.

It speaks for the confusion of our times that conservative administrations, which might be expected to support traditional values, have perhaps done least for marriage and the family. One would expect such administrations to furnish massive federal support for programs designed to help marriage and families beset by problems. A network of federally supported marriage counseling clinics making marital and premarital counseling services available throughout every state in the Union could accomplish much toward reducing marital unhappiness and divorce, as well as reducing the cost of child welfare care, etc. For similar reasons marriage and family enrichment programs also deserve federal support. Unfortunately it would appear that the advent of such a program of federal funding must await the arrival of a more receptive administration.

Some areas which merit further attention by leaders in the marriage and family enrichment field can be distinguished. There is evidence that the couples teams conducting programs are striving for a high degree of professionalism. Efforts which are under way by ACME and other organizations to codify leadership training standards need to be continued. It is encouraging that in 1975 the Council of Affiliated Marriage Enrichment Organizations (CAMEO) was formed. This organization will also concern itself with leadership training standards. Since the highly structured nature of many of the programs encourages the utilization of trained natural leaders, special efforts need to be made to seek out and utilize such leadership resources. Through the efforts of Dr. Sawin and others in the group known as Family Clustering, a number of training laboratories for persons interested in leading family groups are held each summer. Information can be obtained by writing to Family Clustering (see the Appendix). ACME also offers leadership training. Finally, it may be of value to establish graduate-level training courses for facilitators of enrichment programs under the auspices of institutions of higher learning.

Since an increasing number of married students are enrolling, marriage enrichment courses could well be offered by colleges and universities in the near future. Extension departments of colleges and universities could offer marriage and family enrichment classes on a year-round basis. As the movement gains momentum, other adult education programs will be interested. Other "special publics" need to be reached. Already marriage enrichment programs designed exclusively for ministers are offered (see the Appendix). There have been several experiences with clergy families, carried out by Dr. Sawin through denominations. The writer is presently in the process of preparing marriage enrichment programs for physicians and attorneys.

The movement could well benefit from a series of articles in the national press and from leaders' participation in television and radio programs. Making the public aware of the concept of marriage enrichment and of the fact that such classes and programs are available remains a paramount issue. In this respect the Catholic Marriage Encounter movement seems well ahead of the field, even to the point of issuing decals to be affixed to rear windows of automobiles, acclaiming attendance at one of the programs.

It is of interest that among the U.S. denominations, The United Methodist Church has two marriage enrichment programs. One is directed by Dr. Leon Smith (see chapter 20) and the other by Mrs. Virginia Law Sheel with Dr. Carl Clarke as consultant (see the Appendix).

Publicity and public education by satisfied participants remains one of the most effective ways to break down suspicions about these programs. As Howard Clinebell correctly points out in chapter 21, "Because the growth model is so new to most people, they tend to view even this affirmation with suspicion, assuming that marriage enrichment is really therapy in disguise." The enrichment model inherently has a theme of affirmation—"Come and build on your strengths to make your marriage even better." We need to stress this and to point out that this new movement offers education, not therapy. In the final analysis the quality of the program is the best guarantee of the continued growth of the movement.

In order for a high program quality to be maintained, a number of additional areas need further attention. Only slightly more than half of those participating in the writer's survey stated that they were working with couples in the area of sexual relations. Yet Masters and

Johnson have concluded that four out of five marriages need help in this area. The writer's research[14] also supports this conclusion. Hopefully more facilitators will include work in the area of sexual relationships as the movement expands further.

Judging by informal conferences with colleagues following the writer's survey of the field, there is now some evidence that more professionals are in the process of conducting marriage enrichment programs. A need seems to exist for professionals to conduct more enrichment programs which can be attended by the whole family, however.

There would also appear to be a need for more follow-up programs or a "phase two" of the current offerings and classes. Owing to the cultural emphasis on "the new," many couples do not wish to repeat a program they have already attended, although they will express a desire for more enrichment and will ask about the availability of a follow-up program. Some national denominational organizations have already moved in this direction (see chapter 18), and others are planning to do so. Some growth centers (such as High Point Foundation, Altadena, California) are already offering follow-up programs open only to couples who have attended a previous marriage enrichment workshop. In the fall of 1975 the writer completed a book tentatively entitled "Marriage Enrichment"—a book of experiences designed for "home use" by interested couples. It can be used as a supplement to marriage enrichment programs as well as a base for the design of follow-up programs. Finally, *the need for more research and studies about the effectiveness and outcomes of programs (over and beyond workshop evaluations) remains pressing.* It is encouraging that the Jewish Marriage Encounter program (see chapter 12) is in the process of completing such a research project.

The major focus of the marriage and family enrichment movement is the improvement of marriage and family life, not via an outside agency but by the couples themselves. It is of interest in this connection that as early as 1967, at the biennial meeting of the Family Service Association of America (FSAA), Richard Farson issued this challenge: "As professionals in family service agencies we are going to have to find ways of involving nonprofessionals in our work. But I do not mean simply training subprofessionals to do in a diluted form the same kind of work we do. I mean this: *The greatest resource for the solution of any social problem is the very population that has the problem.* . . . And yet our national goal is to create more professionals to solve our social problems. It is a hopeless task; it is an embarrassing and empty task. The greatest resource, the real resource, is the people themselves . . . . One experiment involves developing networks of families in the community that can be helpful to each other—because it has been found in therapeutic groups of couples that couples are very good for each other." It is indeed promising that there is currently in the FSAA a strong and growing interest in preventive programs and in what can be done to enrich marriage and family living.

Marriage and family enrichment programs are by and large eclectic, in the sense that they utilize a variety of methods, approaches, and materials drawn from diverse disciplines and fields. There appears to be a tendency on the part of facilitators to continue to upgrade their programs, to search out new elements, and to incorporate the best from other programs into their own. It can be expected that the eclectic paradigm of the marriage and family enrichment program, modeled in this country, will rapidly spread to Europe and other continents. There is every indication that this new movement is in the process of making a significant contribution to marriage and family life, both in the United States and in other parts of the world.

The Scope and Aim of This Volume

An effort has been made in this volume to provide a comprehensive sampling of marriage and family enrichment programs currently offered by leaders in the field. These programs fall naturally into two groups: family-centered programs and marriage-centered programs. A variety of programs are offered under both headings, including those with relatively little structure as well as highly structured programs. National and regional programs are listed under a separate heading. Only one example of an ongoing national denominational program of family classes has been included (chapter 6). This program was selected because it would appear to be one of the most up-to-date and comprehensive programs currently available. One contribution was included on facilitator training (chapter 20), as this area will be of increasing importance in the years ahead. Finally, the concluding chapter on audio-visual materials contains information for anyone interested in developing leaderless groups and programs. With the exception of three (chapters 2, 15, and 16), all papers are original contributions written for this volume.

It is the aim of this book to offer an overview of a newly emerging field and to explore some of its possibilities. Another major purpose is to offer resources and fresh ideas, approaches, and methods to those conducting enrichment programs who are interested in making their programs even more effective. For those starting out in the field this volume will offer a range of resources and possible frameworks. It is also clear that an increasing number of group facilitators will want to develop a follow-up program or "phase two" for couples who would like to repeat the marriage enrichment experience. The demand for this type of program will grow steadily with the years. This volume can serve as an excellent base for those interested in designing such a follow-up program.

Additional Marriage and Family Enrichment Resources

Since one of the main contributions of this volume is to furnish a wide selection of resources, a brief annotated compendium of additional materials and resources has been placed in the Appendix. In a number of instances leaders in the field and researchers have agreed to make rough copies of original articles and monographs, as well as reprints, available at nominal cost. In other instances materials will be sent for the asking.

In order to make available a variety of aids and new approaches, contributors to this volume have been asked to make materials they use in their programs available to interested professionals at nominal cost. Most authors have included this information at the end of their respective chapters. Through a happenstance, one team of contributors included almost all the materials used in their program as an appendix to their chapter (see chapter 17). Since this gives the reader some very specific examples of the types of aids used in enrichment programs, it was decided to include this chapter as originally submitted.

Marriage and family enrichment and *relationship enrichment* is the wave of the future. It is the hope of the editor that this volume will foster and enhance the ongoing growth and development of the movement.

Notes

1. David Cooper, *The Death of the Family* (New York: Pantheon Books, 1971).
2. David and Vera Mace, *We Can Have Better Marriages* (Nashville: Abingdon Press, 1974).
3. Herbert A. Otto, "The Personal and Family Resource Development Programs—A Preliminary Report," *International Journal of Social Psychiatry*, vol. 8, no. 3 (Summer, 1962), pp. 185-95.
4. Herbert A. Otto and Ann W. Kilmer, *The Family Fun Council* (Salt Lake City, 1967). A Xerox copy of this monograph can be obtained for $1.00 (postage included) from H. A. Otto, % Holistic Press, 8909 Olympic Blvd., Beverly Hills, Calif. 90211.

5. Herbert A. Otto, "Marriage and Family Enrichment Programs in North America—Report and Analysis," *The Family Coordinator*, vol. XXIV, no. 2, pp. 370-75.

6. Ted Bowman, "Enrichment Weekend for Total Families—Summary and Evaluation, 1973." Copies of this report can be obtained for $1.00 from Mr. Ted Bowman, The Family Enrichment Center, 301 S. Brevard St., Charlotte, N.C. 28202.

7. Gregory T. Leville, *Making Marriage Work*. Cassettes and written materials, $50.00, from Dr. Gregory T. Leville, Family Service of Philadelphia, 311 S. Juniper St., Philadelphia, Pa. 19107.

8. Sally Edwards, *Creative Problem Solving in the Family*. Cassette program, $6.99, from Successful Marriage Cassettes, Box 1042, Kansas City, Mo. 64141.

9. Frederick H. Stoller, "The Intimate Network of Families as a New Structure," in Herbert A. Otto, ed., *The Family in Search of a Future* (New York: Appleton-Century-Crofts, 1970), pp. 145-60.

10. Margaret M. Sawin, "The Family Cluster—A Process of Religious Nurturing," unpublished MS. (See Appendix, p. 267, for more information.)

11. Herbert A. Otto, *The Family Cluster—A Multi-Base Alternative* (Beverly Hills, Calif.: Holistic Press [1971], 1975). Obtainable for $3.50 from the publisher (see n. 4, above).

12. "Clusters for Caring," *Human Behavior*, June, 1975, p. 9.

13. Herbert A. Otto, "Has Monogamy Failed?" *Saturday Review*, April 25, 1970, pp. 23-25.

14. Herbert A. Otto and Roberta Otto, *Total Sex* (New York: Peter H. Wyden, 1972).

Chapter 2

The Family Growth Group: Guidelines for an Emerging Means of Strengthening Families*

Douglas A. Anderson

CURRENTLY EMERGING IN MANY REGIONS OF THE UNITED States is a promising mode of family education variously referred to as the "family growth group," "family cluster," or "family enrichment" program. The family growth group may be defined as a program involving three to five families who meet together regularly and frequently for mutual care and support and for the development of family potential.

Such a program has at least three unique advantages as a means for strengthening families:

1. The family growth group goes beyond most traditional family life education programs by involving the whole family together as a unit in the experience. Reuben Hill and Joan Aldous are critical of most family life education programs for teaching individuals instead of being designed for families as groups (1969, 934). David Speer, who views traditional family life education programs as sterile and superficial, calls for innovative programs that combine the new understanding of the family as a growing and changing system with the new resources of awareness-expanding techniques (1970). Clare Buckland maintains that all family members need to participate together in what has been known as "parent" education, parent education becoming family education and being conducted in family learning centers. When all family members participate, "the interactional effects characteristic of human systems will accelerate the behavioral change in the intended direction" (1972, 158).

2. The family growth group provides a supportive network of families to strengthen the family unit. In a society that fragments the family and that isolates families from extended kin and other families in the community, there is increasing need for programs that give families a sense of community and belonging. The family growth group gives the family an opportunity to participate in deep

*From *The Family Coordinator*, January 1974, pp. 7-13. Copyright 1974 by National Council on Family Relations. Reprinted by permission.

sharing within an intimate network of families (Stoller, 1970), in caring for and helping other families as well as being supported and aided by them, in learning by observing other families interact, in undergirding one another in the child-rearing task, particularly through providing alternative adult role models, and in exchanging attitudes and values while also exploring together new value system possibilities.

3. The family growth group facilitates family change and growth by focusing upon the development of family potential. Family potential can be understood as those latent resources within every family for changing and growing, loving and caring, communicating, resolving conflict, adventuring, creating, and experiencing joy. The family growth group, focusing more upon growth than upon problems, provides opportunities for families to increase their awareness of their unique strengths and resources and then to actualize these dormant capacities in family living.

The Study

While family growth or enrichment programs utilizing these advantages have recently been multiplying, often they have developed in isolation from each other. As a result, these programs have lacked a unifying theoretical framework to guide their development and a set of widely accepted criteria for selecting and evaluating program goals and methods. The purpose of this study was to attempt to overcome this lack of formulating guidelines for the theory and practice of the family growth group, paying particular attention to one setting for this program—the local church. The search for these guidelines included (a) a review of the literature; (b) an examination by means of reading, interview, and observation of a number of innovative programs of both family enrichment and multiple family therapy, a very similar modality in the field of psychotherapy; (c) the rating by ten family education professionals of a tentative set of guidelines drawn from these programs; and (d) a synthesis of the literature, interview responses, and rater responses into a proposed set of family growth group guidelines.

The remainder of the present paper will illustrate some of the variety of programs that were studied and then summarize the proposed guidelines arrived at through the final synthesis. It is hoped that these guidelines will be tested and improved upon by family educators through ongoing experience with the family growth group modality.

Varied Programs

The varied nature of family growth groups can be seen by surveying a number of current programs.

Margaret Sawin inaugurated a program of "family cluster educa-tion" in January, 1970, in First Baptist Church, Rochester, New York, of which she was teaching minister (Sawin, 1972). Family clusters of four to five family units meet weekly for a two-hour intergenerational educational experience of enhancing family communication, ex-amining beliefs and values, and deepening relationships with other families. Families remain in "cluster" over an extended period of time. Six of Sawin's families have been cluster members for three or more years.

Clusters are led by co-leaders, at least one of whom is an experienced leader.

A typical cluster meeting opens with the families sharing in a "bag" supper and relaxed conversation. A physical sport or game follows. For the second hour of the meeting the leaders involve the families in a learning activity, utilizing the experiential learning philosophy of enabling participants to have an experience and then reflect upon it. Varied activities are utilized, such as finger painting, Tinkertoy building, fantasy, "fishbowl" observations, discussions in dyads or simulated family groupings, parties, audio-visuals, and simulated games. The central activity develops one facet of a theme the cluster has chosen to pursue over a ten-week period, such as communication, power in the family, sexuality, prayer, or death and its meaning. In planning for the meeting, the co-leaders follow the "emerging design" principle, planning on the basis of observations of the intrafamily and cluster group dynamics of the last meeting and the expressed interests and needs of the members.

Peggy Papp, a family therapist at the Nathan W. Ackerman Family Institute in New York City, inaugurated in January, 1972, a program of family growth groups in the community (Papp, Silverstein, and Carter, 1972). These groups are designed for "well families" to discuss everyday family problems and concerns and to form a supportive sharing community for otherwise isolated nuclear families. Early detection and prevention of family pathology is another purpose of the program.

Leaders are therapists from the institute. Groups of four families meet weekly in homes or churches.

The group leaders utilize some of the techniques of family therapy, especially family sculpting, along with more content-oriented educational techniques, including lectures and focused discussions. The knowledge from the field of family therapy of how family systems operate is communicated to the participants, who are encouraged to apply this knowledge to their own families.

Herbert Otto, chairperson of the National Center for the Explora-tion of Human Potential in La Jolla, California, advocates his widely known family cluster model (Otto, 1971). The cluster is a group of three to five families, without an outside leader, who meet regularly in a climate of intimate sharing and caring to actualize individual and family potential. This climate is created through the members participating together in a number of small group exercises, such as Otto's "Depth Unfoldment Experience." Other exercises focus upon the discovery of individual and family strengths.

While the cluster families live in their own homes, they may share together various family functions, such as communal buying and meals and joint child-rearing.

Carl Clarke, a marriage and family counselor, in 1972 developed with United Methodist Church leaders a Family Enrichment Weekend program. This program represents an adaptation of an earlier marriage enrichment program developed by Clarke (1970) and of procedures developed by Herbert Otto. Clarke's carefully structured program is designed for the participation of a group of families over one weekend in a camping or retreat setting.

The program aims to facilitate family members in affirming the value and worth of one another through expressing positive feedback. One exercise employed is to have all members of a family take turns sitting opposite each other in dyads sharing positive feedback by completing a series of statements, including, "I feel loved and appreciated when you . . ." and "I feel joyful when you . . ." Other exercises help family members to increase awareness of their family's unique beginnings and of their latent resources.

Jonathan Clark, director of the Graduate Program in Emotional Disturbance at the Boston University School of Education, in 1971 developed a program of Therapeutic Family Camping, in partnership with a team of other professors and graduate students (Clark and Kempler, 1971). While this program was designed for disturbed families, Clark believes it has rich promise for "normal" families as well.

A group of usually four families are brought together for a weekend in a camp setting with a team of leaders. The weekend focus is on teaching the families to observe themselves and to observe alternative interpersonal styles in other families. A central technique is to designate a family member as official "observer" of his family for an event, such as a meal. Afterward he discusses his observations with a staff member and then with his family, who respond to his observations. The unstructured camping environment away from routine enables family members to gain a new perspective on their lives and to try out new behavior.

Clark believes that the most effective format for this type of program is to have two or three weekend programs spaced two weeks apart and involving the same group of families. This permits both intensity of experience and opportunity for the families to "process and ingest" the experience. Additionally, leadership team members visit the families in their homes for a meal between the weekends to reinforce the use of the observational model back home.

Anne Lee Kreml, an ecumenical minister in Johnson County, Kansas, has developed a Family Actualization Model for participation of a small group of families in eight two-hour weekly workshops sandwiched between two weekend family laboratories in a retreat setting (Kreml, 1970). The central purpose of this program is to enable families to actualize their potential by understanding and working through family conflict. A series of exercises is designed to enable family members to creatively resolve conflict, leading to increased caring and deepened relationships.

A carefully trained leader helps family members by leading them through experiential learning events and in reflection upon their meaning. The leader serves as a model by being able to face conflict openly when it occurs and to work through it creatively.

Guidelines

Guidelines for the family growth group were drawn in the study from a number of programs, including those discussed above. The guidelines focused upon four areas: (1) goals, desired outcomes for participating families; (2) means, methods that may be employed to accomplish these goals in the areas of leadership, group formation, and program development; (3) evaluation, procedures for determining whether or not the goals have been accomplished; and (4) setting, considerations specific to sponsorship by the local church.

Goals

Among the goals that need to be developed in a particular program are stated assumptions about characteristics of the "ideal" family as the outcome goals of the program. Such a normative goal was phrased in the guidelines in terms of a systems model of the "fully-participating family." This model was summarized in one of the guidelines:

> To help families become more open human systems, through (a) family members participating more fully in each other's lives through a free flow of communication within the family, including a rich interchange of information, values, and emotions; (b) families participating in surrounding human systems, including caring for other families in the community and working to change growth-blocking societal structures and institutional policies; and (c) families enabling their members to participate more fully on the level of transcendental systems

through fulfilling their goals in trusting partnership with the Divine Participant and Source of all growth.

Other goals that need to be formulated are those that relate to the specific needs of families who participate. For example, goals for quite isolated families would emphasize the provision of an ongoing, intimate support system of other families, while goals for less isolated families would focus more upon stimulating growth through developing family potential.

Means: Leadership

The role of group leaders was stressed in these guidelines, noting that the group tends to reflect the personalities, leadership styles, and personal values of its leaders. A male-female leadership team is preferable, for the leaders are very influential in modeling the behaviors specified by program goals, especially intrafamily communication patterns. Leadership selection should include careful attention to the personal qualities of a potential leader, including enthusiasm for the family growth group model, differentiation as an individual, ability to create an atmosphere of mutual trust in a group, creative imagination, basic confidence in the potentiality of families to change and to be a resource to themselves, and a readiness to live and interact with families at close range.

Thorough training of leaders is necessary and should include: (a) training in such human relations skills as group facilitation and observation and methods of designing and conducting experiential learning exercises for intergenerational family groups, (b) cognitive learning about the operation of family systems and about family and individual development, (c) opportunity for trainees to achieve a fuller understanding of their own family backgrounds and current family relationships, (d) practice in reflecting upon the relationship of family growth to life meanings, (e) the experience of co-leading a family growth group with an experienced leader, and (f) participation in a family growth group with one's own family—or a simulated family within a training laboratory.

Means: Group Formation

In recruiting families for the groups, potential participant families should be visited in their homes by the co-leaders at a time when the whole family can be present. Leaders should clarify their own personal goals as well as the growth-oriented nature of the program. Each selected family should form a contract with the leaders and with the other families, in which there is a clear mutual understanding of expectations and responsibilities.

Groups should include entire family units and would be enriched by also including members of more than two generations, one-parent families, childless couples, single individuals, and families with exceptional or handicapped children.

The format of the group should be tailored to the unique needs and goals of the participating families. It may include some combination of intensive, growth-triggering programs (as a weekend or weeklong workshop in a camp setting) and ongoing weekly programs that enable the integration of change through practicing new learnings in everyday family living. Other possible alternatives include a three- to six-hour meeting every other week, an all-day meeting once a month, or a series of two or more weekend programs. A single-weekend program is insufficient without follow-up meetings to allow the experience to be integrated into the family system.

Means: Program Development

After the group of families has participated in trust-building experiences, family members should be encouraged to choose and specify growth objectives for themselves, based upon coming to an awareness of how they are presently operating as a family, what they desire to change, and what broad goals of growth are available.

The families should be enabled to utilize their own interests, needs, and resources in designing and carrying out a flexible program in cooperation with the leaders who are following the emerging design principle. It is important that the families view themselves as participants in, not subjects of, the process, coming to the awareness that the resources for growth and problem-resolution lie within themselves.

Activities should be selected in which members of different generations all can participate at their own developmental level and which foster intergenerational dialogue and interaction.

Subgroupings of the total group may be structured that stimulate families to observe and learn from one another, such as interchanges of members of one family with members of other families. Activities may be designed that stimulate each family to examine its value systems and to test them out against alternative values that may be held by other group members.

Evaluation

Through self-monitoring questionnaires, each family may periodically evaluate its progress in relation to its own objectives. Observations of a family by other families and by the leaders may be given to the family in the group setting, noting especially any changes in the operation of the family system.

More objective evaluation data can be obtained by "before and after" administration of such instruments as family actualization scales from humanistic psychology (Kreml, 1970) and nonverbal research techniques from family therapy, including picture-selection procedures (L'Abate, 1972b) and conjoint family drawings (Bing, 1970).

Evaluation of program events and exercises is essential to improving the program and enriching the families. An integration of research and program-provision is optimal. However, to avoid manipulation of the families, evaluation must be done primarily for the benefit of the families, not for the advantage of the researcher.

Setting of the Local Church

The local church is a natural context for family growth groups because the church has access within its membership to entire families and all generations, and deals generally with a nonclinical population. Further, the church has valuable contributions to make to the family growth group because of its four unique functions as a sociocultural subsystem (Pattison, 1972):

a. As a valuing center, the church has experience in assisting families to clarify and explore life meanings and values, including the developing of a normative view of the family from a theological perspective.

b. As a lifelong learning-growth center with values and traditions related to human growth, the church can enable family members at all stages of the life cycle to develop their latent intrapersonal, interpersonal, and spiritual resources.

c. As a sustaining-maintaining center the church can enable families to care for one another within intimate nourishing communities.

d. As a reparation center with rich experience in restoring relationships, the church can enable families to resolve conflict through a reconciliation model for forgiveness.

A family growth group program sponsored by a church must avoid attempting to impose a narrowly specific core of values upon families. It should rather aim to create a climate of spontaneity and freedom in which families can grow spiritually in self-chosen directions.

Randomization in denominational and socioeconomic background of the families in the group is preferred to having all families from the same church and locale. Sponsorship by an ecumenical agency may encourage randomization.

The church should offer its family growth group program to the total community and work in close cooperation with other community agencies.

The church needs to develop a corps of trainer-consultants to train lay and clergy family growth group leaders and to provide them with a support system of ongoing consultative resources. Quality training and consultation are essential to optimal family growth group practice.

Conclusion

Family therapist James Framo speaks for many family practitioners when he states his conviction that "the family is the most vital, lasting, and influential force in the life of man. Such social contexts as the community, neighborhood, school, work, and friendship networks can never approach the unique and powerful effects of the family, due to the deep emotional and blood ties, the family's personality-forming influence, and the special rules . . . which apply to family relationship" (1972, 272).

The family growth group is a most promising instrument for undergirding this most vital human institution and enabling it to develop its full potential for influencing persons in growth-oriented directions.

Resources

Bing, Elizabeth. "The Conjoint Family Drawing." *Family Process,* 1970, 9, 173-94.

Bockus, Frank M. "The Church's Role in Creating an Open Society." In Howard J. Clinebell, Jr., ed., *Community Mental Health: The Role of Church and Temple.* Nashville: Abingdon Press, 1970.

Buckland, Clare M. "Toward a Theory of Parent Education: Family Learning Centers in the Post-Industrial Society." *The Family Coordinator,* 1972, 21, 151-62.

Clark, Jonathan, and Kempler, Hyman. "Therapeutic Family Camping: A Rationale." *The Family Coordinator,* 1973, 22.

Clarke, Carl. "Group Procedures for Increasing Positive Feedback Between Married Partners." *The Family Coordinator,* 1970, 19, 324-28.

Clinebell, Howard J., Jr. *The People Dynamic: Changing Self and Society Through Growth Groups.* New York: Harper & Row, 1972.

Framo, James L. "Symptoms from a Family Transactional Viewpoint." In Clifford J. Sager and Helen Singer Kaplan, eds., *Progress in Group and Family Therapy.* New York: Brunner/ Mazel, 1972, pp. 271-308.

Hill, Reuben, and Aldous, Joan. "Socialization for Marriage and Parenthood." In David A. Goslin, ed., *Handbook of Socialization*

Theory and Research. Chicago: Rand McNally & Co., 1969, pp. 885-950.

Kreml, Anne Lee. "Understanding Conflict in the Normal Family: An Educational Model for Family Actualization." Unpublished M.A. thesis, Chicago Theological Seminary, June, 1970.

L'Abate, Luciana. 1972*a.* "Family Enrichment Programs." Unpublished mimeographed paper, Georgia State University, June, 1972.

————. 1972*b.* "The Laboratory Evaluation of Families." Paper presented at a Symposium on Group Testing Approaches at the Annual Convention of the American Psychological Association, Honolulu, Hawaii, September, 1972.

Laqueur, H. Peter, Wells, Carl F., and Agresti, Miriam. "Multiple-Family Therapy in a State Hospital." *Hospital and Community Psychiatry,* 1969, 20, 13-20.

Mead, Margaret. "New Designs for Family Living." *Redbook,* October, 1970.

Otto, Herbert A. *The Family Cluster: A Multi-Base Alternative.* Beverly Hills, Calif.: The Holistic Press [1971], 1975. [See p. 27 n. 11.]

————. *The Utilization of Family Strengths in Marriage and Family Counseling.* Beverly Hills, Calif.: The Holistic Press, 1972.

Papp, Peggy; Silverstein, Olga; and Carter, Betty. "Family Sculpting in Preventive Work with 'Well Families.' " *Family Process,* June 1973, 12, 197-212.

Pattison, E. Mansell. "Systems Pastoral Care." *Journal of Pastoral Care,* 1972, 26, 2-14.

Satir, Virginia. *Peoplemaking.* Palo Alto, Calif.: Science and Behavior Books, 1972.

Sawin, Margaret M. "Religious Nurturing Through Family Clusters: A New Model for Christian Education." Unpublished mimeographed paper, Rochester, New York, 1972.

Speer, David C. "Family Systems: Morphostasis and Morphogenesis, or "Is Homeostasis Enough?' " *Family Process,* 1970, 9, 259-78.

Stoller, Frederick H. "The Intimate Network of Families as a New Structure." In Herbert A. Otto, ed., *The Family in Search of a Future.* New York: Appleton-Century-Crofts, 1970, pp. 145-60.

family-centered programs

Chapter 3

The Family Enrichment Weekend

*Russell L. and
June N. Wilson*

JACK AND MARY ANN AND THEIR CHILDREN, KATHY, BILL, AND Anne, were huddled cross-legged on the floor. The children were looking intently at their parents. Kathy had just asked her mother and dad how and when they met for the first time.

"You kids remember how we met, don't you?" Jack asked with a "surely you do know, don't you?" look on his face.

The children's faces reflected their total lack of information. Not one of them could recall anything about the unique and exciting events which surrounded Jack and Mary Ann's first introduction to each other and their wartime romance.

In the next few minutes Jack and Mary Ann related their first meeting, a blind date arranged by Mary Ann's roommate with a young serviceman who was then home on leave from duty. Something of their joy and excitement was communicated as they told the children about their first date and the remaining evenings of Jack's leave that they spent together. Mary Ann's face was radiant with the joy of memories as she shared with the children how deeply she and Jack had felt about each other and how much they had enjoyed being together. Jack filled in the details of their wedding, which took place when he returned from the service several months later.

The Traberts were "playing detective," which is the first activity in the Family Enrichment Weekend. The children were looking for "clues," and Jack and Mary Ann were responding by telling them about their introduction, their courtship, their marriage, and the circumstances surrounding the birth of each of their delightful children.

The occasion was the first Family Enrichment Weekend. The "Wesley Weds" (the church school class which we attend) were sponsoring the weekend at a youth camp twenty miles from Des Moines.

It all began when Jan Boelter, the program chairperson of "Wesley Weds," asked us to lead a weekend experience for class members and their children. "We want something that will help our families— something that will draw us closer together and help us to communicate better," Jan said. "We don't want to just go to a camp and goof around and have recreation; we've done that. We would like to have some growing experiences with our children."

We received the invitation with mixed feelings. We were pleased that our friends in the class had asked us to lead. That was a good stroke. It would be good to experiment with total family programming. However, we both felt some apprehension about accepting. We had worked with couples and small groups for several years, but the program resources we had available for total families could be counted on the fingers of a little girl's hand. After a day or two we called Jan to say we would accept the invitation. Then we began to search for ideas, activities, experiences, and other possibilities for a growthful and helpful weekend for those families. The extra push motivated us to search the field and see what options were available.

A few days later, Russ had the good fortune to meet Nancy, a graduate student from Iowa State University who was working on a master's degree in family environment. Russ asked Nancy if she could help, and she lent him a large file of papers and handouts from several classes. The first opportunity to review those papers came on a Sunday afternoon in July, when we were sitting in the backyard of our home relaxing and reading. In that file of papers Russ discovered outlines of a number of activities which were developed by Dr. Herbert Otto[1,2] while he was directing a family research group at the University of Utah. The experiences were designed for families with children. In his research, Dr. Otto found that these exercises helped families learn to communicate better. They also helped family members identify and affirm one another's strengths. One exercise was designed to help family members plan and work together on projects of mutual interest. The "developing family strengths" experience in and of itself was experienced by families as strengthening. Wow! What a serendipity!

The more Russ studied the exercises the more excited he became.

He interrupted me to share the material. I immediately saw the possibility of their application to the family weekend we were attempting to design. Discussing the Otto activities started a flow of ideas. The "playing detective" experience in which the Traberts were participating emerged along with other possible ingredients for the weekend. During the next hour or so, we experienced one of those rare periods of inspiration when ideas flowed easily and each of us built on the other's contributions. The result was a rough—very rough—draft of a design for the weekend with the couples and their children.

Over the next several weeks we worked on the schedule, tested out some ideas with our daughter, Kirstin, who was then ten year old, and perfected the design for the late September weekend.

Twelve families attended, with children ranging in age from four to sixteen. Camp Wesley Woods was a beautiful setting. The leaves were beginning to turn. The huge stone fireplace with a glowing fire provided a perfect center around which to conduct the activities. After the session on Saturday night the group built a big fire outside and toasted marshmallows and sang camp songs with children, young persons, moms, and dads joining in. The weekend came off much better than we could ever have hoped.

We asked for written evaluations from each person who participated. The responses were very positive and tremendously encouraging. Parents unanimously affirmed that it was a helpful experience for their families. Their responses convinced us that we should continue to perfect the weekend experience for other groups.

Several weeks later, Virginia Law Shell, then director of family worship of the United Methodist Board of Evangelism in Nashville, came to Des Moines for a speaking engagement. With several persons, Russ arranged to have lunch with her to discuss the Marriage Enrichment Weekend her department was sponsoring.

After lunch, Virginia and Russ returned to his office. She had a lot of contacts around the country, and he wanted to learn from her what other United Methodist conferences were doing in family ministries. In the course of the conversation, Russ shared with her the delightful experience we had had with the Family Enrichment Weekend. She wanted to know more about it, and as they discussed the components of the weekend she became excited about the possibility of offering the Family Enrichment program as an option to local churches. Virginia suggested that we get together with Dr. Carl Clarke, the author and designer of the Marriage Enrichment Weekend,[3] and a few Marriage Enrichment leader couples to review and critique the family program. That sounded great to us, so Virginia arranged a meeting between Dr. Clarke, herself, two other couples, and ourselves, to critique the family program and test its applicability as a possible companion program to the Marriage Enrichment Weekend. Dr. Clarke's response was enthusiastic, and he granted permission to use the "sharing seats" exercise from the Marriage Enrichment Weekend, a tremendous experience for family members. The group offered many helpful suggestions and ideas. We were delighted with the group's response and Virginia's interest in promoting the Family Enrichment Weekend throughout The United Methodist Church.

We continued to test the design with other groups. A tent-and-trailer-camping group at St. John's United Methodist Church in Davenport, Iowa, invited us to lead a weekend with their families. Except for a windstorm and torrential rain that struck during the Friday night session, it was a great weekend. The written evaluations of that group were both positive and helpful. St. Paul's United Methodist Church in Bryan, Texas, a church with many faculty members from Texas A & M, invited us to conduct a weekend there. That group felt the need for a somewhat more structured worship experience at the end of the weekend, and several of their creative members, including young persons, helped design the corporate worship which is now included as the closing experience of the weekend. A weekend at Woodbine, a small, rural town in southwestern Iowa, proved to be a unique experience. The activities, meals, and family cluster discussions were held in a huge apple-processing shed on the orchard farm of the Davis family. Camping families parked their campers in the orchard. That program, with many rural families participating, assured us that the experiences were helpful for rural church families as well as for urban groups.

To date, an estimated 350 families have participated in the weekends. Additional programs are scheduled in Texas, Missouri, Wisconsin, New York, and Indiana, and nearly thirty weekends are scheduled in Iowa. The Council on and the Iowa Conference of The United Methodist Church Ministries endorsed the program in 1973 and encouraged local churches to sponsor weekends for their families. Funds were included in the 1974 and 1975 budgets to underwrite the cost of training leader couples in Iowa and provide support for the program.

Content of the Weekend

Included in the Friday-evening-through-Sunday design are five basic units of activity. Each unit is opened with a few camp-type choruses or songs. Song sheets are provided. Each unit is introduced with an "imagination center" which brings even the smallest children into brief dialogue about that particular subject.

Each unit includes an activity in which the whole family participates. On Friday evening "playing detective" gets each family involved in a discussion of the family's history. Later each person makes a "mini-collage" telling something about his or her family. Each unit is concluded with a brief time for sharing in two- or three-family clusters.

Sponsoring groups are encouraged to plan campfire activities after the sessions on Friday and Saturday nights. Children and youth are urged to bring their guitars and other instruments to play and sing during the campfire time.

The Saturday morning unit includes reading the "Warm Fuzzy Story," and two of the Herbert Otto exercises. One phase concentrates on individual family members' strengths, and the other focuses on the total family's strengths and potentials. Lists generated in these discussions are then shared in the family clusters.

A brief (one-hour) unit on Saturday afternoon involves each person in clay sculpturing symbolizing his good feelings about his family or an occasion when he really had fun with his family.

Free time on Saturday afternoon allows each family to hike, swim, snow slide, or whatever they enjoy doing together.

Many groups plan a cookout or cooperative meal on Saturday evening with all the families sharing the meal together.

The Saturday evening unit is introduced with a slightly more serious mood. A couple are selected to demonstrate "sharing seats," and then each family is instructed to find a more or less private place to participate in this activity. A campfire or other group fun time concludes the unit.

On Sunday morning individual families find appropriate places out under the trees, on a hillside, or wherever they choose, to participate in their own "creative family worship" using the "family treasures" they brought with them. After their worship, the families gather for the "developing family strengths" unit. Guidelines are given to each family for preparing an action plan for developing family strengths. The plans are then shared in the family clusters.

An informal worship experience symbolically brings the activities and experiences of the weekend together and offers them to God. Families who wish to do so may make a commitment to God and/or to one another as a result of the weekend.

A total group meal usually concludes the program on a warm and festive note.

We are presently in the process of preparing a follow-up packet of activities which the families can do at home, since many parents have indicated that they would like to have additional exercises for their families.

Schedule of the Family Enrichment Weekend

Friday Evening Session

6:00	Evening meal (optional)
7:00	Get-acquainted activities
	Group singing
	Imagination center
	Activity I—Playing detective
	Making "mini-collages"
	Sharing in cluster groups.
9:00–10:00	Gather around the campfire

Saturday Morning Session

8:15	Breakfast
9:00	Brief worship
	"Warm Fuzzy Story"[4]
	Imagination center
	Activity II—Discovering your family members' strengths
	Relaxation and refreshment break
10:15	Activity III—Discovering your total family's strengths
	Sharing in cluster groups
11:30	Adjourn for lunch

Saturday Afternoon Session

1:00–2:00	Activity IV—Clay sculpturing
	Sharing clay sculptures
2:00–7:00	Free time for family activities, recreation, etc., and dinner

Saturday Evening Session

7:00	Group singing and worship
7:15	Activity V—Sharing seats experience
9:00	Campfire fun

Sunday Morning Session

8:15	Breakfast
9:00	Creative family worship
9:30	Imagination center
	Activity VI—Action plans for developing family strengths
	Sharing action plans in clusters

10:30	Break
10:45	Family worship and celebration
11:30	Lunch and dismissal

Assumptions of the Family Enrichment Weekend

1. Every family has the potential to grow and become more loving, caring, supportive, creative, and joyful. We not only believe that they have the potential to grow, but we also feel very optimistic about the things we see happening to families as the result of Family Enrichment Weekends, and other growth-producing total-family experiences. We are firmly convinced that family members can learn skills and develop attitudes which will help make their family life a more rewarding and meaningful experience.

2. The Family Enrichment Weekend is designed for normally healthy families who want their family life and relationship to be better and more rewarding than they are now. It is not a therapy program for sick families.

3. We assume that children learn most of their religious and spiritual values from their parents and others in the family. A child, for example, experiences the love of God through the love of his father and mother. Children learn to value themselves primarily because their parents and other family members value them. The Family Enrichment Weekend provides an opportunity for family members to "be together" for a whole weekend, and to demonstrate loving and caring, fundamental Christian values, by listening to one another, identifying one another's strengths, and providing positive feedback about what they enjoy and appreciate about one another.

4. Persons grow best when they are being loved, valued, respected, praised, and recognized as persons of worth. The content of the experiences in which family members participate during a weekend, and the leadership style, are designed to foster expressions and affirmations of how much they value and regard one another. The inevitable result in most families is a deeper sense of closeness and belonging.

5. Very few families have the opportunity, or take the opportunity, to identify their individual strengths (what they like about one another) or their total family strengths. In the Family Enrichment Weekend, families have opportunities to identify these strengths and potentialities and to share them with other families. As family members identify, discuss, and share their strengths and potentials, they find that this experience is strengthening and bringing the family closer together.

6. Families are often accustomed to planning together and working together on vacation trips or holiday outings, and these

skills can be utilized to help them develop other potentialities. A family may wish to become a more creative family or a more artistic family. The same planning and collaboration that is used in planning a trip can be used in developing artistic ability or other family strengths.

7. It is extremely important for family members to be together. "Being together" in this sense means much more than being in the presence of one another and talking to/listening to each other. It means being consciously and deeply aware of one another, and experiencing one another on a deep feeling level. The weekend is not a family "encounter" weekend, but it provides exercises which help many families to experience one another at a deeper level than they normally do.

8. Both parents and children can learn from observing the members of other families relating to one another. In sharing clusters, family members have the opportunity to observe other families. It is also important, we believe, for all members of the family to share the responsibility for the family's growth and progress and for the growth and development of individual members of the family.

9. Parenting is a difficult and complex role, and parents need to be affirmed as persons of worth and value in the context of the family. Being a son or daughter, brother or sister, is also a demanding role, and children and youth need to be affirmed in the context of the family. The Family Enrichment Weekend introduces family members to models for affirming one another within the family circle.

Objectives of the Family Enrichment Weekend

1. The overall objective of the Family Enrichment Weekend is to provide church families with a growth-inducing experience which children, youth, and parents can participate in together. There is certainly a place for church-sponsored family weekends, camping trips, and outings which are basically recreational in nature, but we feel there is also a place for a family-oriented program which offers growth opportunities to the participants.

2. A second objective is to get families away from home, work, school, and telephone so that they can get in touch with one another. Parents often remark that the weekend was a pleasant and refreshing opportunity to enjoy being together with their children.

3. Throughout the weekend the facilitator couple/family try to exemplify a quality of caring for the children, the young adults, and the parents which will be supportive of their own loving and caring for one another. For example, the facilitators listen carefully and intently to the children during the "imagination center" sequence so

as to demonstrate that careful and intentional listening to a child is an expression of loving and valuing that child.

4. A further goal is to provide a setting and a flexible structure which will help family members communicate freely, identify the things they like and value about one another, and express their positive feelings for one another.

5. A number of authors have called attention to the fact that many children in our mobile society have a very weak self- and family image. Several of the activities in the Family Enrichment Weekend are designed to reinforce the participants' sense of family identity.

6. Family members usually know much more about their weaknesses, conflicts, and limitations than they do about their potentials and what they have going for them. One aim of the Family Enrichment Weekend is to help family members identify their strengths and open up new avenues of mutual cooperation and support.

7. Another objective is to give families an experience with the power of positive feedback. When persons give feedback to one another about how they experience one another's positive behavior, the positive behavior is reinforced.

8. "Creative family worship" is included in the weekend to help families recognize some of the many occasions for spontaneous worship and celebration which grow out of their daily experiences.

9. The final objective is to create in the family an atmosphere of mutual acceptance and openness in which persons can share their feelings, concerns, and frustrations and know they are going to be listened to, understood, and accepted.

Additional Information

The Family Enrichment Weekend may be conducted in a variety of settings. Youth camps, retreat centers, tent-n-trailer parks, and church fellowship halls are acceptable locations. No special facilities are necessary, but it is essential to have an enclosed building or shelter where total group activities can be conducted.

The experience is designed for families with children. Families with children and youth from ages five or six years through fifteen or sixteen years seem to benefit most from the activities. Smaller children are welcome to be with their parents, but baby-sitting services must be available when young children become restless. Older youth and young adults are welcome to attend, and many have enjoyed participating with their families.

With minor adaptations, the Family Enrichment Weekend could be used with any church group. Families from other denominations have attended and felt quite at home. Among the trained leader couples/families is a Lutheran family whose members are some of the program's most enthusiastic supporters.

Several couples/families, both clergy and lay, have been trained to lead Family Enrichment Weekends. In a few cases the husband or the wife has some experience or background in group leadership, but in most cases they are selected because they possess the following qualities:

1. They have a stable marriage and family relationship.
2. They can relate easily with one another, with their children, and with groups of persons.
3. They are able to relate to children and youth on an open, warm, and loving level.
4. They are actively participating in their own church.
5. They are willing to commit two or three weekends per year to leading the weekend programs.

The first step in the training includes attending a weekend with their family as participants and experiencing the program. As a second step, the couple and their older children and young adults attend a training weekend. Several hours are spent with the trainees reviewing the assumptions, objectives, leadership style, and contents of the program. The *Leader's Manual*[5] provides adequate direction for the leader couple to lead a group through the weekend. Leader couples agree to contribute their leadership as a "gift of love" to the families, but their travel, meals, and lodging are paid by the sponsoring group or church.

Observations Related to the Family Enrichment Weekend

Perhaps it will be helpful to consider some of the observations we have made which relate to the development of the Family Enrichment Weekend.

One observation is that in many church families, parent-parent, parent-child, and child-child frustrations, conflicts, and miscommunications (or lack of communication) erode the sense of caring, loving, mutual support, and joy. Church-related families, including ministers' families, are experiencing marital and family tensions and traumas just as their neighbors are. Church families need support and nurture, and the churches can, if they are willing to do so, provide growth-producing programs and opportunities which are tremendously helpful to both parents and children.

A second observation is that the churches have created a credibility gap for families that is wide enough to fly a 747 through. More often than not, Christian family life has been interpreted in such idealistic and lofty terms that no family could achieve that ideal even if they thought they wanted to. We both remember a Mother's Day sermon that portrayed the Christian mother as a perfect woman, ideal wife, impeccable mother, and a revered saint. That image doesn't exactly fit with reality for us. Mothers, including those in the church, have their limitations, their weaknesses, their shortcomings—they're human. The gap exists between the saintly image and the human frailities which all mothers share. Many other examples of churchly unrealism could be cited. The point is, we think that if the churches could accept parents and children where they are and as they are, they would be more effective in helping families grow.

Thirdly churches are in a key position to perform a much-needed service, and at the same time to render a valuable ministry, by providing person-centered and family-centered growth opportunities such as the Family Enrichment Weekend. Some churches are beginning to see themselves as personal and family "growth centers" for their members, and in addition to the more traditional programs are offering such options as Marriage Enrichment Weekends, Family Enrichment Weekends, Values-Clarification labs, Parent Effectiveness Training classes, Human Potential experiences, sex education seminars, family communication classes, and ongoing family clusters. We think these growth-producing events for parents and families are meeting a great need and should be included in every church's program for families.

Fourthly, when members of church families have a positive and growth-inducing experience with a Marriage Enrichment Weekend, a Family Enrichment Weekend, or one of the other good programs, they often feel much more positively about themselves, about their families, and about the church. When they discover that the church can offer programs which help couples and families work out their problems and develop stronger ties, their confidence in the church will be increased.

Notes

1. Herbert A. Otto and John Mann, eds., *Ways of Growth* (New York: Grossman Publishers, 1968).
2. Herbert A. Otto, *Group Methods to Actualize Human Potential: A Handbook* (Beverly Hills, Calif.: The Holistic Press, 1970, 3d rev. ed., 1973). [See p. 108 n. 2.]
3. Carl Clarke, *Group Leader's Guidebook for Conducting a Marriage Enrichment Weekend*, copyrighted 1972 by Carl Clarke, Ph.D.
4. Claude M. Steiner, "A Modern Fairy Tale" condensed into the "Warm Fuzzy Story" and printed in the *Leader's Manual—Family Enrichment Weekend*, by Russell L. and June Wilson, 1973.

5. Russell L. and June Wilson, *Leader's Manual—Family Enrichment Weekend* (Des Moines, Iowa, 1973).

Resources

Persons interested in obtaining additional information about
scheduling weekends or being trained to lead Family Enrichment
Weekends should contact Russell L. Wilson, Coordinator of Family
Ministries, Iowa Conference, United Methodist Church, 1342 73rd
St., Des Moines, Iowa 50311.

Chapter 4

The Family Camp: An Extended Family Enrichment Experience
Ed Branch, Jr.

THE FAMILY CAMP IS DESIGNED TO BE A LIVING-LEARNING experience. The following are typical comments made by participants:

- —"It makes marriage fun again."
- —"We really worked, but it was enjoyable work."
- —"We not only had fun on our vacation, but we felt like we had accomplished something."
- —"I don't want to go away from my friends" (a child).
- —"We invested five days into our relationships and still had vacation time."
- —"It was nice being with people who enjoy one another."

Such comments indicate that there are a number of couples with basically good marriages who want to ensure the vitality of their relationship. David and Vera Mace in founding ACME seem to have touched upon an area of interest for today's marrieds (see chapter 15).

The idea of couples with basically good marriages banding together to be supportive of marriage and one another is a very exciting concept. Nearly everyone has been made aware of the problems confronting marriage in North America today. We have not been made as aware, however, of the benefits to be obtained from marriage. Marriage must be guarded as a very fragile relationship, but being fragile many times only serves to make something more precious, not less worthwhile. We have been told that marriage is in a very shaky condition today because it no longer has as many reasons for existing as it did when it was of an economic necessity. In other words, marriage today is not so much based on a need to be married in order to survive as it is on a desire to be married in order to be together. To me, wanting to be with someone instead of needing to be with someone is a much more appealing basis for marriage. However, if we like ourselves best when we are together, and are together because we want to be with one another, then it stands to reason we must discover new ways of being together to replace those which prevailed when married couples *had* to be with one another. This volume is testimony to the recognition of this need to discover new ways of being married and of cultivating the marriage relationship.

Going separate ways to work, separate ways to recreation, and when at home together watching television, is not conducive to a dynamic marriage relationship. This is especially true if real relationship time always receives the least priority. We have taken marriage for granted, but now, when it is no longer a necessity for survival, we must cultivate it just as we would a garden from which we hoped to obtain delicious fruits. We wish to keep it warm, moist, and fertile, and we try to dig out the weeds as they appear. However, constantly weeding and cultivating becomes oppressive if the fruits are not forthcoming or worthwhile.

The Family Camp is a way of shifting gears out of the workaday, television-watching, meaningless humdrum into which we may find ourselves slipping. It is an opportunity to try out a more dynamic family life. It gets us away from the home and work setting. This makes trying out new behaviors easier. And yet a Family Camp keeps us with our family group so that one or two of us are not doing some changing that might come as an unpleasant shock to others. The camp experience is set up to be fun. Far too often we've gotten the idea that work on family relationships has constantly to be a very serious, heavy encounter. Then, too, some studies indicate that participants of growth groups can change their behaviors for those growth groups but that many times the change does not carry over to a back-home setting. *Since the changes that might occur in the Family Camp occur with the family members present, the behaviors should have a better chance of being carried back home.*

When I talk about changes occurring, this does not mean that I think we are going to straighten out family problems. Mary Ette (my wife) and I believe that change cannot help but occur in family life, because we look at family life as a dynamic, unfolding process. We are interested in people having more awareness of the potential for change, and especially more awareness of their abilities to enact changes which they may desire for their relationships. We operate from a developmental model. We see problems as just something that exist in life, and believe that people can learn to be more effective problem-solvers. An effective problem-solving process creates experiences which encourage people. They feel good about themselves. When this happens to a whole family, the process promotes a feeling of liking themselves best when in the other members' presence.

Several years ago, I was approached by the Catholic school system in Edmonton to do in-service training with teachers in their family life education program. Having been a summer camp worker and director through my growing-up years, and having directed my own camp for years, I suggested that they encourage the teachers to come with their families to a camp setting. They picked up on the idea and funded the camp, which turned out to be so successful that people requested another experience the following year. Following that year, participants requested another experience and began to plan reunions during the year. The University of Alberta's Family Studies Department decided to pick up on the program, and we have been offering it as a course since the summer of 1973 for people who wish to take it for university credit.

In 1972, Mary Ette, the children, and I went to Idaho and participated in a camp with Virginia Satir. This was not only a validating experience for us as a family, but it also confirmed for us the belief that fancy camp facilities are not necessary for a good Family Camp experience. Many families today have a tent, tent-trailer, or camper of some type which they are only too happy to use for their sleeping accommodations. Large enough facilities for eating and meeting are therefore the main requirements, and are much easier to obtain at a reasonable cost than facilities that would also be suitable for housing the participants. In fact, in the Idaho camp we met in a barn. In our camps around Edmonton, we have rented church camps at very reasonable prices. One way Mary Ette and I have run our camp is to have all meals included in the cost. This way no one has to interrupt their participation in order to prepare or clean up food. Our program is very full, and we find that mealtimes with everyone sitting down together are an important part of the total experience. At this time plans are underway to set up a HYPHEN centre in Florida on a beautifully wooded lakefront acreage. The name HYPHEN represents the interpersonal process, the communication bridge between I and Thou. Our first program was conducted there in 1975. But camps can be run quite easily in any location where fifteen couples wish to have one.

Generally camp begins with supper on the opening day and closes with lunch on the final day. For example, if a camp started with supper on a Friday, it would terminate with lunch the following Wednesday. Usually a camp session includes a weekend, and frequently we have used long weekends. People who must arrange time off from work in order to attend can more easily arrange two or three extra days than four or five. The following outline is a typical camp day:

Schedule

8:00	Breakfast
9:00–11:30	Morning program
	(adults and children separate)

12:00	Lunch
12:30–3:30	Families relax and play
3:30–5:30	Afternoon program (adults and children separate)
5:45	Supper and relax
7:00	Family leisure enrichment (families together)
7:30–8:00	Free
8:00–10:00	Evening program (adults and children separate)
10:00	Snack

The morning session is from 9:00 until 11:30 and is devoted to the Minnesota Couples Communication Program (see chapter 16). When Mary Ette and I took Sherod Miller's MCCP leadership training course, we decided that the program was similar to what we had been thinking and doing in communication training, but that it had some ideas which we had not arrived at. Therefore we became certified as leaders and have incorporated the program into our work.

The afternoon session generally runs from 3:30 until 5:30 and is devoted to group discussion of related readings which participants have usually read prior to arrival at camp. From 7:00 until about 7:45, there is generally a family activity planned. This can be anything from making a family mobile, as described in Virginia Satir's book *Peoplemaking*, to a communication game using blocks. From 8:30 to 10:30 or 11:00, there is the marriage enrichment session which at times also incorporates sexually explicit materials. While communication skills and the communication process are the core of our program, content may vary. For example, in 1973 the focus was on parenting and the marriage relationship. The 1974–75 focus area was sexuality and communication in the family. The times in between the workshop sessions are devoted to relaxing, boating, swimming, game-playing, what have you. While the adults are in session, the children are cared for. There are things for them to do and people to aid them in the doing, but they are not regimented into activities.

Our camp in 1973 was nominated for the "Creative Programming Award" of the Western Canadian Colleges and Universities Summer Sessions. It was also evaluated by a student at the University of Alberta in research for his master's thesis. He reported in his findings that there was a lessening in alienation for the participants, an increase in ability to live in the present time, and an increase in inner-directedness, all at statistically significant levels. At the present time other aspects of our program are being researched, and I have recently completed a research study indicating what has been believed for some time: namely, that *self-esteem is significantly related to the perceived amount of loving behaviors in the marriage relationship.*

Our leadership might be defined as the setting up of stimulus events related to what we call "positive experience theory." This is based on learning to give and receive positive experiences more frequently. Positive experiences promote the development of both giver and receiver and are of two types. The first is what I call a positive-positive. It takes place in a "life situation environment" that is conducive to development, and the way a couple relates in that life situation environment makes the most of the good situation. The second type is negative-positive and occurs when a couple works through a "sore spot" into new understandings together. It is a strengthening experience. The two experiences could be compared to the fast, soft growth of spring and the slow, hard growth of summer. The above theory is described further in *I Want to Be Used.* Other treatments of this concept may be found in Landsman's paper "Positive Experience and the Beautiful Person" and Otto's Minerva Experiences as described in *Group Methods to Actualize Human Potential.*

Our approaches make use of didactic input, group discussion, and experiential learning. We use books, handouts, charts, films, slides, tapes, games, and a video-tape recorder when it is available. The program is not designed for marriage therapy, and occasionally when couples have gone through our program looking for a type of therapy they have reported that at times they felt lonely or left out. However, one such couple had an experience which enabled them to say that this was a much more hopeful approach to marriage than just trying to cope. People preparing to be family life teachers, "single again" persons, priests, and nuns have also participated in camps. They have reported benefits from experiencing family life in such a setting instead of merely reading about it. They also reported that at times (e.g., marriage enrichment time) they felt somewhat lonely or left out, even though they had an activity in which to participate.

The camp setting offers an avenue for an extended family enrichment experience. It is longer than a weekend retreat, and at the same time it allows for a sense of extended family and community. Children are not isolated from the adult world. They can see adults working and playing. And they are able to make contact with Mom and Dad at almost any time. Also, they not only become friends with children at camp but frequently develop close relationships with other adults.

The Family Camp is a unique opportunity for parents to model marriage as they would like to picture it to their children. In our fast-paced world, children see very little marital behavior. They see a lot of parenting behavior, that is, mothering and fathering. As mentioned earlier, North American culture is in a period of marital flux. Men and women are learning to live in a marriage as a *process* and not as a *final state* that you achieve by riding happily off into the sunset. Whereas change generally snaps or shatters something which is in a fixed state, a process orientation helps keep relationships flexible and expectant of change.

Keeping marriages vital requires tender loving care. The Family Camp is time out from today's fast-paced urban living. It is an extra opportunity for parents to be involved with their family and to demonstrate that they are interested enough in their marriage relationship to want to work at it. This is a new type of modeling behavior which children have not often had the opportunity to observe. Not only that, but it takes some of the emphasis away from parenting, which can put children too much in the center of the family. I believe that the center of the family is the marriage relationship, around which the children revolve. This centering of the family on the marriage actually helps prevent children from developing an unrealistic sense of power. If a child comes to view himself as the center of the family, he also feels responsible if the marriage malfunctions. I think we should help children understand that marital functioning or breakup is adult business. Marriages which do terminate would not then leave children feeling that somehow they are responsible.

Much of the role-modeling many of us had was of mothering and fathering behavior. Today an opportunity exists for partners to develop ways of role-modeling husbanding and wiving behaviors which may be helpful to their children's future role-making behaviors. Satir has pointed out that much learning takes place through relationships between parents and their children. However, she emphasizes that the greatest learning takes place from the child watching the relationship between the husband and wife.

The major message for the children from the Family Camp experience is not that Mom and Dad are working on their marriage relationship. *The major message is that a functional, gratifying man-woman relationship is something which Mom and Dad value and enjoy.*

Resources

We will be happy to try and answer upon request specific questions the reader may have concerning the planning of a Family Camp. Requests should be mailed to: Ed and Mary Ette Branch, The Hyphen Consultants, Ltd., 10022 103 Street, Edmonton, Alberta,

Canada. Food costs, etc., vary from year to year and with location. The forms used to obtain relevant data from participants prior to camp and my unpublished papers (listed below) may be obtained upon request for the cost of duplication and mailing (about $1.00). The "Two-to-One" game will be mailed upon request, at a cost of $7.50. *I Want to Be Used* is available from Celestial Arts Press, 231 Adrian Road, Millbrae, Calif. 94030.

Papers

Anderson, C. Master's thesis in progress re "Marriage Enrichment Program." University of Alberta, Department of Educational Psychology.

Branch, E. B., Jr. "A Local Family Life Education Council: Emphasis on Two Areas of Programming." Unpublished round table discussion paper presented at the 1973 Annual Meeting of the National Council on Family Relations in Toronto, Ontario.

———. "Self-Concept, Self-Disclosure, and Marital Satisfaction." Unpublished paper, University of Alberta, Spring, 1974.

———. "Vicarious Sex Education." Paper presented to the Alberta Association on Family Relations, May, 1974.

Clarke, Carl. "Group Procedures for Increasing Positive Feedback Between Married Partners." *The Family Coordinator*, vol. XIX, no. 4 (October, 1970), pp. 324-28.

Foote, Nelson N. "Matching of Husband and Wife in Phases of Development." *Transactions of Third World Congress of Sociology*, vol. IV (1956), pp. 24-34.

Landsman, Ted. "Positive Experiences and the Beautiful Person." Presidential address to the Southeastern Psychological Association, 1968.

Pashelka, M. Master's thesis in process re "Family Camp," University of Alberta, Department of Educational Psychology.

Books

Bandura, Alberta. *Principles of Behavior Modification* (see esp. chap. 3). Toronto: Holt, Rinehart and Winston, 1969.

Branch, E. B., Jr. *I Want to Be Used: A Way of Approaching Life.* Illustrated monograph. Millbrae, Calif.: Celestial Arts, 1974.

Miller, S.; Nunnally, E. W.; Wackman, D. B. *The Minnesota Couples Communication Program Couples Handbook.* Minneapolis: Interpersonal Communication Programs, 1972. [See p. 190 n. 2.]

Otto, Herbert A. "The Minerva Experience." *Group Methods to Actualize Human Potential: A Handbook.* Beverly Hills, Calif.: The Holistic Press, 1970. 2d limited ed. [See p. 108 n. 2.]

———. *More Joy in Your Marriage.* New York: Hawthorn Books, 1969. [See p. 108 n. 3.]

Otto, Herbert A., and Otto, Roberta. *Total Sex: Developing Sexual Potential.* New York: Peter H. Wyden, 1972.

Satir, Virginia. *Conjoint Family Therapy.* Palo Alto, Calif.: Science and Behavior Books, 1967.

————. *Peoplemaking.* Palo Alto, Calif.: Science and Behavior Books, 1972.

Schiller, Patricia. *Creative Approach to Sex Education and Counseling.* New York: Association Press, 1973.

SIECUS. *Sexuality and Man* (Sex Information and Education Council of the United States, Inc.). New York: Charles Scribner's Sons, 1970.

Other Publications

Branch, E. B., Jr. "Two-to-One," a couples communication game. Edmonton, Alberta: The Hyphen Consultants, Ltd., 1972.

Chilgren, R. A. (Director). *Program in Human Sexuality.* University of Minnesota Medical School, Minneapolis, Minn.

Chapter 5

The Care-Lab: A Family Enrichment Program

Kenneth G. Prunty

MANY PARENTS TODAY HAVE A LOW PROFILE OF THEM-
selves as persons and as parents. Though they know the truth of Earl
Nightingale's comment that in all history there is not a single case of
a child having been raised properly, they still would like to do it
more properly than they now feel they are able to do. Parents are
better parents when they feel good about themselves and when they
know how to really listen to and how to confront their children
without tearing down their self-esteem or tearing up the relationship.
With about one in three of our youth today having strong persistent
feelings of worthlessness and alienation from parents and friends,
there is much room for improvement, according to Merton Strommen.

In the church, where parents tend to be more uptight and
overcontrolling of their children's behavior, parent-child relationships may end up in even greater jeopardy. Parents in the church and
in society are often told to listen more, to be honest and open in their
relationships, but are seldom given the opportunity to develop the
necessary skills. Dr. Tom Gordon, developer of Parent Effectiveness
Training, has said, "Parents are blamed but not trained."

Whether the parents cared or not, really, is not as important as the
fact that the fourteen-year-old who wrote the words below did not
perceive any understanding or care.

> My parents are too busy to stop and lend an ear
> Too busy to try to understand the way I feel
> And maybe—just maybe—too busy to really care.
>
> It seems as though they're computers
> Programmed to say Yes or No and to talk all the time
> And never to listen.

How the Care-Lab Came to Be

When I began my work with the National Board of Christian
Education of the Church of God in 1964, with my own three children

entering the teen years, I quickly found myself in the throes of many of the problems described above. In seeking ways of enriching family relationships and also the relationships between teacher and student and young person and youth worker, etc., I became aware of the Dr. Thomas Gordon Parent Effectiveness Training program. This provided a model which had much to say to the kinds of concepts, skills, and life-styles that it seemed essential for more families to be able to model if gaps, hostilities, loneliness, and alienation in the family situation were to be bridged.

Familiarity with the Parent Effectiveness Training model enhanced the development of a program that has come to be known as Care-Lab. It is a twelve-hour enrichment training experience primarily for parents, teachers, and youth workers. Over fifty of the labs have been conducted throughout the United States and Canada during 1973 to 1975. More than twelve hundred people have participated in them. The labs, usually held on a weekend with a three-hour session on Friday night, six to seven hours on Saturday, and two or three hours on Sunday, are well received by local church groups.

The less than 5 percent dropout rate of lab participants is almost unheard of in most training experiences provided in local church settings. People have apparently perceived the concepts and skills dealt with in the lab to be helpful and useful in their parenting as well as in other relationships.

The Care-Lab provides participants with an awareness of those relationship styles—roadblocks—that cut off communication and meaningful relationships. It helps persons develop listening and leveling skills that enhance relationships, and provides the process and guidance to resolve needs and value conflicts.

The number of participants in Care-Lab groups has varied from fifteen to sixty. Most leaders would favor a group of twenty-five to thirty persons as being most effective.

Care-Lab leaders are persons who have group leadership skills, have taken the Dr. Thomas Gordon Parent Effectiveness Training, believe in, have internalized, and are able to model the concepts and skills of this program, and have participated in at least one Care-Lab and shared in the leadership of a lab before doing one alone. The leader is a facilitator and seeks to be a helping agent to participants, who must do their own learning. He avoids imposing concepts and skills on participants. He hopes to help them learn to use them, yet be free to reject them if they seem less than helpful to their situation.

There are certain hazards in an intensive weekend Care-Lab experience that call for special skills of acceptance, listening, and leveling. There is little time for cooling off if the struggle with the concepts and skills becomes heated. Thus, a lab leader must be in touch with his own feelings, and be able to accept the feelings of others and to reflect these in nonjudgmental and nonblaming ways. Leaders must also be able to provide leadership within the theological framework of a local church situation.

Below is a typical weekend Care-Lab schedule:

Friday Night

7:00–7:30	Worship and reflection on themes of self-worth, love, and grace
7:30–8:15	The problem of problem ownership
8:15–8:30	Coffee break
8:30–9:30	Experiencing roadblocks to communication
9:30–10:00	Discovering listening as an effective way to help persons solve their own problems

Saturday

9:00 A.M.	Worship and reflection
9:15	How roadblocks cut off communication and relationships
9:30	Presentation of the Active Listening model; illustrations of it through role-playing and practice in using it in triads
10:20	Coffee break
10:35	Continued practice of Active Listening skills in dyads and triads
11:30	Discussion of the value of Active Listening and problems in using it
12:00 noon	Lunch
1:00 P.M.	Why am I afraid to level with you when your behavior is causing me a problem?
1:30	How to level with love and confront with care
1:45	Practice in forming and using I-Messages in dyads and triads
2:45	Discussion of value of I-Messages and problems in using them
3:00	Coffee break
3:15	What are our conflicts, and how do we usually try to resolve them?
3:30	The risk in using power and authority and punishment and reward in resolving conflicts—win-lose *vs.* win-win
3:45	Presentation of a win-win approach called we-win

4:00	Practice of we-win process in dyads
4:30	Value of we-win approach and problems in implementing it
5:00	Adjourn for day

Sunday

2:00 P.M.	Sharing of experiences in the use of Active Listening, leveling skills, and the we-win approach
2:15	Our values and how we got them
2:45	The freedom to choose one's own values and the conflicts that follow
3:00	Ways to handle value conflicts
3:30	How values are shared: values are best taught and caught when you feel good about yourself and when there is warmth and congeniality between parent and child, teacher and student, etc.
4:00	Where can I go for additional help? What to do after a Care-Lab
4:20	Closing worship and reflection on themes of self-worth, love, and grace

An In-Depth Look at the Care-Lab Process

Now let's look at the Care-Lab in more depth—at the kinds of experiences and exercises that are designed to make the learning of concepts and skills as effective as possible.

The Care-Lab design assumes that it is better to teach persons how to fish than to give them a fish. The process works not so much at solving individual problems as at providing concepts and skills and the opportunity to practice them so that relational problems can be worked at outside, and after, the lab.

The lab begins on a congenial note with emphasis on getting acquainted and coming to accept the worth and values of each person. A physically close circle is formed in which persons affirm their worth as creations of God and their need to live with and relate to others. In this attitude of devotional reflection the group thinks about some of the data from Strommen's Youth Research studies which evidence the need for us to rediscover and experience our worth as persons.

Problem Ownership

Participants are presented with several situations in which they are asked to determine problem ownership. A problem is considered to be my problem when I am working on my needs and feelings and on what's happening to me. It is considered to be the other person's problem when he is working on his needs and feelings and on what's happening to him. Situations such as the following are presented on worksheets:

1. A neighbor worried about his financial situation comes over for a talk.
2. A nursery child cries when left in the nursery by his mother.
3. A teen-ager leaves records and clothes in the living room.
4. A neighbor mows his backyard with a power mower when you are trying to have food and fellowship on the patio with friends.

In the terms of the definition of problem ownership, the first two would be the other person's problem in that he owns the feelings and is working on what's happening to him. The last two are in the "my problem" category in that the other person's behavior is causing me a problem.

Participants work through a list of several such items, checking them as to who they believe owns the problem. Answers are discussed in dyads and triads to discover differences and to see if a consensus can be reached. The larger group then goes through the items to further develop the ways of determining problem ownership. Realizing that a problem belongs to another does not mean I don't care. It means I am now in a better position to be helpful.

A number of Care-Lab participants have indicated that they find this section of the Care-Lab especially helpful. Many parents tend to buy quickly into problems that belong to their children, or to deal with what is their own problem with a child's behavior as if it were the child's problem.

Ownership of problems has much to do with the kind of response that is appropriate and helpful. If the other person owns the problem, the feelings, and the needs, there is a particular skill—primarily the listening skill—that is most likely to be helpful. Listening is not a helpful response, however, when parents own the feelings and have the needs. Here the leveling-confronting skills are more appropriate and helpful.

How Do We Usually Respond to Another When He Has a Problem?

How do we let each other know we have a problem we are working on? How do we express our feelings and our needs? How do we indicate our desire for the help of another? Crying, sullenness, physical rigidity, slamming of doors, and banging of toys, are some of the nonverbal ways that are listed by a lab group. Loud talking, defensiveness, hostility toward others, and occasionally a verbal indication of "Hey, I need to talk to you" are other ways problem ownership is indicated.

How can we respond to another person when he is expressing feelings and owning a problem in dealing with his own needs? Most of us begin computing almost automatically. We feel compelled to find a solution to the other person's problem, or become analytical, seeking to discover why, when, where. Or we may become judgmental and try to find the "guilty" factor or person to blame. Or we may seek to divert attention from the problem by reassuring the person, cheering him up, or by running away from his feelings entirely.

In the lab a person is often asked to play the role of someone who has a problem he is working on—such as being worried about finances, disgusted with school, upset with a friend. The Care-Lab leader then responds to messages sent with a blaming response (*Judge*), a solution-oriented response (*Mr. Fix-It*), an analytical or probing response (*Dr. Psycho*), or with the evasive, diversionary techniques of the *Clown*.

Participants usually sense that these are not particularly helpful responses. They discover that it may feel good to try to solve another person's problem or to probe or to cast blame. But when you are the one seeking help you do not feel helped by these responses. These responses frequently block communication, stop others from talking, cause defensiveness, build resistance and resentment, and basically hurt the relationship. When a person shares a feeling, concern, or need and the other person seeks to fix it, the sender feels distrusted and put down.

Is Listening Really Helpful?

After experiencing the put-down power of the Dr. Psycho, Mr. Fix-It, Judge, and Clown responses, participants are eager to explore more helpful ways of responding to a person who is sharing a problem or concern. If these responses are not helpful, what is?

Dr. Paul Tournier, the Swiss psychiatrist, has said that if you listen to most of the conversations of the world—between nations as well as between spouses—they are for the most part dialogues of the deaf. The simple truth is that most times as friends and as family members we do not listen well to each other.

Care-Labbers often feel that listening is not enough. Some way or another, if I am really going to be helpful to another person, I have to do something more concrete than listen. Lab participants discover that listening, though seemingly simple, is one of the most beneficially helpful things that one human being can do for another.

A person has two ears and one mouth, and it could be that this says something to us about the proportion in which they were intended to be used.

A basic assumption in the Care-Lab is that we help another person most by really listening to him. This helps the other person to feel cared for, loved, understood, accepted, and helped.

What does a person need to be able to do in order to listen to another? What attitudes are needed? What responses are helpful? The necessity of opening one's earlids is obvious. Seeing the importance of trusting a person to find his own solutions, of accepting his feelings and affirming that feelings are okay, may be more difficult. Feelings express who I am at a particular moment. Feelings change, especially when they are accepted and listened to.

There is a real need for separateness from the other person. The listener must admit that the feelings and needs belong to the other person. Two persons do not occupy the same space, and separateness and some space in togetherness are essential. This is particularly difficult, of course, in the home situation, where parents tend to think every problem and feeling their children own is theirs as well. Sometimes, of course, this is true, but often it is not.

The need for the listerner to be trustworthy, to hold in confidence what he hears, is of the greatest importance. It is especially helpful for a child to feel that he can tell either of his parents what is going on inside him and to know that if he does not want it told to the other parent it will not be.

Ways to Listen

Lab members are helped to see that door-openers themselves are helpful ways of listening. When someone starts to air a feeling or concern, the listener can say, "It's okay. I have time to listen." Or, "I can't listen now, but how about just before supper?" Sometimes it is okay, if the parent cannot give the child his full attention, to suggest a later time for doing so. If the parent keeps the appointment the child learns that the parent can be trusted and that he is not seeking to escape from a listening-helping relationship.

The necessity of being still in order to listen is also emphasized. It is difficult to hear when one's mouth is expounding. Opening the ears and stopping the mouth are important parts of the listening process. It is also acknowledged in the Care-Lab that silence as a listening style has its limitations. The other person doesn't know for sure that you are hearing his words and feelings if you make no response. He does not know how you are decoding his messages.

Thus, ways of using the mouth in the listening process are affirmed in the lab experience. One is the use of simple sounds. An occasional "Yes," "Well," "Huh," "How about that?" etc., is helpful in letting the other person know that you are there with him by acknowledging what he is saying. These, of course, also have limitations even though they are often helpful. This writer's eighteen-year-old son once said to him, "Dad, if you 'yeah' or 'uh-huh' me one more time . . ." He was suggesting that his dad's simple sounds were not enough to convince him that his dad was really listening.

Listening is seen as really being fully present with the other person, as hearing the other person's words and feelings, sensing his message, humming the other person's tune. It is bringing our entire being—our own senses, feelings, and presence—into the here and now of the other person. It is paying attention to the other person; it is being with him, being together in the fullest possible sense.

The listening that is most of this quality is that which has been called "Active Listening" by Parent Effectiveness Training and a number of other related programs in recent years. It is listening to the other person so carefully that you are able to mirror, to reflect in fresh words, what you understand his words and feelings to mean. It is hearing the other person's song—words and music—and reflecting, mirroring, it so closely to the sender's message that there will be no reason for anyone to sing, "Look what they did to my song, Ma!"

At this point, lab participants get into groups of three and decide who is A, B, and C. A sends a message to B and C for two minutes about something that he feels very disturbed and concerned about—something that irritates him or aggravates him. At the end of the two minutes B and C share together, with A listening, what they understand A's words and feelings to be and to mean. B then becomes the sender, and then C as the exercise continues.

In this exercise persons usually discover how unused to listening they really are and also become aware of their tendency to want to be a Mr. Fix-It, a Judge, Dr. Psycho, or Clown. They also begin to discover something of what it means to really listen and to reflect their understanding of the sender's words and feelings.

The second time around, the A person sends another message. This time B is the listener, and he seeks to reflect, to give feedback, to A about what he understands A's words and feelings to be. C is an observer. He watches for any of the Dr. Psycho, Mr. Fix-It, etc., responses in B as B listens and responds. The observer is encouraged to be very picky-picky, to be supersensitive to the advice-giving, blame-making, and probling responses that are so easy for most of us to make when another is sharing his problems and feelings.

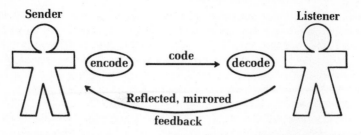

The Care-Lab leader seeks to model Active Listening to the responses that participants give. He seeks to be accepting and reflective of the feelings and concerns of participants as they struggle with the Active Listening style of response. He works with the group so that each person has an opportunity to be a sender and a receiver and an observer. Usually this section on Active Listening is closed with a large group role-play where the Care-Lab leader plays the role of a young person in a bus station who is considering leaving home because of the problems he has in dealing with his mother's rigidity after his father's death.

Problems in implementing the Active Listening as contrasted with other ways of responding to people's needs and feelings are shared. Values usually listed are: It helps the other person to feel cared for and better understood. It leaves him free to find his own solutions. It helps him get his temperature down and to regain control of his own life. It helps to build closeness in relationships, etc.

How to Level with Love

In the next phase of the lab experience, participants look at leveling and confronting skills. Two temptations are faced here realistically. One is that if someone's behavior is causing me a problem and he is, for example, a neighbor, an infrequent visitor in the home, or a high-status acquaintance, we may be inclined never to say anything at all.

The second temptation, which is especially troublesome with people we are close to in the family, is to level with the person, to confront him so brutally, and sometimes in such a bizarre fashion, that we literally tear up our relationship with the person and tear down his self-esteem.

Lab participants are encouraged to examine themselves when in situations where another person's behavior is causing them a problem. Am I just being picky-picky? Is it the wrong time of the month? Is my energy level low? Am I upset about something else? etc. If a person can modify himself and admit that the source of the problem is in himself rather than in the behavior of another, self-modification is encouraged. If the environment can be changed, we should do so. If the stereo is loud right where I'm sitting and by moving to another area I can greatly reduce the sound and the irritation it may produce, I'm under an obligation to change myself or the environment if at all possible.

Obviously, these changes are often not possible. Lab members discuss with their leader why it is so difficult for us to level with another person sometimes, and why at other times we do it so brashly and cruelly. We often assume that the other person knows what he is doing and that he knows how his behavior is affecting us. We often think that because we love each other in the family we can read each other's mind.

The Care-Lab helps us to see that any confrontation or leveling with another person is rightly concerned with what it does to self-esteem, to the relationship, and whether or not it will be effective.

Lab participants see that the usual kinds of responses used to confront fall into what are called "You-Messages" in Parent Effectiveness Training. These are put-down, solution-loaded messages that carry a great deal of naming, blaming, and shaming in them. The Dr. Psycho, Mr. Fix-It, Clown, and Judge responses are again experienced, as, for example, in the case of someone's feet on a freshly painted chair, when the owner might say:

—"Would you please get your feet off my chair?"
—"When did you first start putting your feet on people's freshly painted chairs?"
—"What's the matter with you? You know better than to put your feet on a chair that has just been painted."
—"Why don't you go home and rest your feet and come back when they're not too tired."

Again, in the home these messages often become more severe and damaging:

—"How many times do I have to tell you?"
—"Won't you ever learn?"
—"You can't ever do anything right."
—"You're the biggest slob I've ever seen."
—"You'll never amount to anything."
—"Who in the world would ever want to have you around?"

Effects on self-esteem as well as on the parent-child relationship are fairly obvious.

The I-Message of Parent Effectiveness Training and of Haim Ginott is presented as a way of confronting with less risk of hurting self-esteem or the relationship and greater chances of being effective. Most of us are willing to change our behavior if we do not have great needs we are meeting in it, if we have three kinds of information from the person affected by our behavior.

1. What he sees and hears me do.
2. The real effect of my behavior on him.
3. The feeling he has about it.

Two or three situations are read to the group to which they are to write I-Messages. One example: friends have come over for a visit. Your two small children are playing in the kitchen and dining area as they frequently do, but their joy, laughter, and loudness in playing make it difficult for you and your friends to visit.

A You-Message would be "All right, you kids, stop all the noise right now," or "Get out of the kitchen. You're making too much noise. Go back to your room and play."

Since most people are well practiced in sending such messages further practice is not needed in the lab. Thus, the lab group is to avoid like the plague anything that even sounds like a You-Message and move to writing and sending an I-Message.

Step 1 What I see and hear children doing: they are playing and talking loudly and joyfully.

Step 2 The real effect: we cannot hear and it is hard for us to carry on a conversation.

Step 3 The feeling: we want to be able to hear and talk, and are feeling upset because we cannot.

Putting this together in the form of an I-Message, parents might say to children, "Our friends are here and we'd like to be able to visit. We cannot when you are talking and laughing so loudly." In one real-life situation the child responded, "Is it okay if we play in our bedroom?"

What About Physical Punishment and Rewards?

Often during the leveling skills presentation and discussion the issue is raised whether or not another person can be trusted to respond to an I-Message without the threat or use of some form of punishment or reward. This same issue is a part of conflict resolution. It is here that the lab examines the use and effect of punishment-reward approaches. Are bribes, coercion, the withholding of privileges, or the threats of other punishments really effective? Are there alternatives that do less harm to self-esteem and relationships and are equally or more effective?

The risks involved in the use of power and the effectiveness of the power game are looked at carefully. When physical punishment and reward are employed by parents it often encourages children, and particularly teen-agers, to use the power that is in their hands. Participants face realistically the limitations of parental power and the reality of the power that is in the hands of children. Physical punishment and reward, of course, usually don't keep someone from doing something, but rather from talking about it or getting caught.

Power is ineffective in creating self-discipline and inner control. A neighboring family in this writer's childhood who fenced in their backyard to keep their children in are an example. The fencing was not such a problem, except that the hook on the gate kept on having to be raised as the children grew. A sensitive pastor in a small town in South Dakota observed that this family needed to get the hook off the gate and get the hook in the children. It was the values educator John McCall who noted at the 1972 Religious Education Association meeting in Chicago that the fences of control and morality are down. Whether this is good or bad is beside the point. Now persons in our world have to look inside themselves to find guidance, inner discipline, and control. "They look inside," McCall suggested, "and there's nobody home."

Lab members are challenged to see what it is they can do as parents to enable children to build the inner man and inner disciplines, to accept responsibility for their own behavior. The weaknesses of a win-lose approach are there for all to see. Are there alternatives?

Shortly before his death Dr. Haim Ginott was asked on a TV talk show how he would define discipline. He said, "Discipline is finding alternatives to punishment."

Is there a win-win approach that can serve as a viable alternative to the win-lose approaches so commonly used? Is there a way of resolving conflicts between parents and children that enables both to get their needs met?

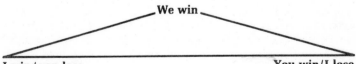

The lab uses a process for resolving conflicts similar to that of the Parent Effectiveness Training program: (1) Admit there is a problem—a conflict. (2) Define the problem in terms of needs. (3) List possible ways to resolve the conflict. (4) Evaluate the ways and solutions listed. (5) Choose the best solution and put it to work.

This process is practiced in role-play situations, first as a larger group and then in dyads. One person plays the role of the parent and the other that of the child. Active Listening and I-Messages are important to this process. Usually it begins with an I-Message from the parent which often brings out some defensiveness from the child which, of course, needs to be "active listened" to.

What About Value Conflicts?

Value conflicts are numerous in family situations today. Hair, music, dress, language, use of money, national policies, college, drugs, drinking, smoking, church attendance are only a few of the value conflicts experienced in many homes. Lab participants welcome the opportunity to think about ways to deal with such conflicts.

The process in the lab involves the definition of a value according to the criteria described by Sidney Simon. A value is the basis on which one shapes one's sense of worth and self-image. It is

—chosen freely from several alternatives with full consideration of the consequences

—cherished and publicly affirmed

—lived and acted out, not only once but repeatedly

In this process we discover that value choices are a very personal thing and that all of us want our freedom of choice respected. American society has placed a strong emphasis on freedom to choose one's own beliefs and values. Our heroes over the centuries have been those who have resisted the pressure to give up this freedom.

Respecting this freedom in the home is more difficult. One father in a lab stated sensitively, "Sure, I can respect the freedom of young people to make their own value choices. I won't judge them or blame them—as long as they are somebody else's kids."

The guidance and resources for dealing with value conflicts are less specific than other facets of the lab. The following guidelines are shared and discussed:

1. Accept and respect the value choices of others and yourself.

2. Define the conflict in terms of values. What do you as a parent value? What do your children value? What are the real differences? What are the commonalities?

3. Discuss possible ways the conflict of values can be lived with.

4. Get inside each other's values. "Active listen." Really hear each other and feel what the values mean.

5. Keep a warm, open relationship. Persistent hassling has a way of chipping away at a relationship and of cutting off communication. If a relationship becomes heated and hostile there is little chance for influence. Parents are encouraged to be more concerned about

having influence with their children than about controlling and restricting them.

6. Accept what you cannot change. Values are in a continual flux. Values are not static. They are always in process. Accepting the changeability of values is an important part of dealing with value conflicts.

Accepting and respecting the value choices of others, and particularly of children, is important. Keeping a sense of grace, hanging loose in the saddle, is an important attitude to maintain in dealing with the value conflicts in the home.

How Do We Teach Values?

How do parents communicate values to their children? How do we want the children and young people in our families to feel about their values? Which end of the continuum below is most ideal?

Candy Cocksure   **Calvin Cave-in**

List the words that describe the more ideal kinds of feelings we would like kids to have about their values. The words "positive," "confident," "open," "accepting," "conviction," "sensitivity" are among those listed in many Care-Lab groups.

There are several ways of teaching values. What are the strengths and weaknesses of the following approaches?
   —moralizing
   —modeling
   —laissez faire
   —consultant-clarifier
   —congenial relationships
   —exposing, talking about your values but avoiding imposing through coercion or bribery and avoiding deposing or putting down the values of the other person

Where to Look for More Help

The lab closes with information about getting additional help and further developing one's skills. Participants are provided with guidance in practicing Active-Listening and I-Message skills and in working at conflicts of needs and values. Within a week of the lab, participants are to read again through the packet of materials provided. They are to practice the listening, leveling, and conflict resolution skills with other persons, and within two weeks the entire group is urged to get together for a sharing time.

Participants are strongly encouraged to enroll in the Dr. Tom Gordon Parent Effectiveness Training program. (Information on where and when the course is offered may be secured by writing to: Effectiveness Training Associates, 110 S. Euclid Ave., Pasadena, Calif. 91101.) If that is not possible, they are encouraged to read Dr. Gordon's book, *Parent Effectiveness Training.*

What Do Evaluations Indicate?

Over a period of several months written evaluations were secured from participants. Printed below are some comments from evaluation forms:

"I feel I have been made aware of the fact that if I really care for someone I will want to listen to more than their words. I will want to hear what they are saying on the inside."

"My feelings are valid ones—I need to express them in ways that do not hurt my brother."

"It has 'disturbed' and stimulated me to new ways of understanding others. It has 'encouraged' me to keep trying! It has offered new (to me) intergenerational ideas and solutions with my family."

"I have found a way to relate to others. Before, I felt like there must be a better way but I didn't know what. It has helped me understand about values and that *example* is not enough; also to look at my own values."

"I gained a more polished form of what I have learned to be effective in my own experience."

Resources

Board of Christian Education. from Board of Christian Education, P.O. Box 2458, Anderson, Ind. 46011. *Care-Lab Packet.* $3.00
———. *Christian Leadership* educational journal. $2.25 per year.
Gordon, Thomas. *Parent Effectiveness Training.* New York: Peter H. Wyden, 1970.
Raths, Louis E. *et al. Values and Teaching.* Columbus: Charles E. Merrill Publishing Co., 1966.
Simon, Sidney *et al. Values Clarification: A Handbook of Practical Strategies for Teachers and Students.* New York: Hart Publishing Co., 1972.
Strommen, Merton. *Five Cries of Youth.* New York: Harper & Row, 1974.

Chapter 6

The Family Home Evening: A National Ongoing Family Enrichment Program

*Au-Deane S. Cowley and
Ramona S. Adams*

THAT THE DISINTEGRATION OF THE MODERN FAMILY HAS become an alarming social problem is a fact of twentieth-century life. Critics of the family have differed in their reactions to this disorganization, ranging all the way from those who are oriented toward the past and take the conservative view that, in order to survive, the family must conform to traditional family patterns, to those who are oriented to the future and seek to make radical changes in the family, either by destroying it altogether or by reconstructing it around new and completely different forms.

One specific reaction to the perils facing the modern family is reflected in the spiritually based programs designed to strengthen family life that have been developed by the Church of Jesus Christ of Latter-day Saints (Mormon). The focus taken by the leadership of this religious organization tends to fit somewhere in between a conservative call for a return to the patriarchal-dominated life-style of old and the far-out experimental family models found in many communities today. In an effort to build family unity around a semipatriarchal form where there is a respect for authority and a striving for the common good, coupled with an appreciation and respect for the individual needs of each family member, the LDS Church has instigated several programs, all with the same broad objective: to improve the quality of life within the home.

The programs instituted by this church have grown out of its philosophical and theological traditions. In order to understand these programs and to achieve a perspective on the importance they have in the lives of church members, one needs to put them into a historical context.

Amid the modern-day Babel where there are many differing and ever-changing "authorities" in child guidance and a growing number of family life "experts," the LDS Church programs offer a security to the membership that is both psychological and spiritual in nature, by providing a clear and distinct pattern of how to live in families. In this institution marriage is still conceived of as a religious sacrament, not a civil contract, and the family is viewed as an indissoluble unit whose bonds can and should endure, not only for all time, but for all eternity. The responsibilities of parenthood are held to be sacred obligations which should be given top priority in the life of every parent.

Harold B. Lee, a past president and prophet of the church, made this statement to his followers, emphasizing the church position that the calling of a father to preside over his family is one of the most important callings that a man can ever receive and is to be taken as seriously as a calling to any other church position. He said:

> Now, you husbands, remember that the most important of the Lord's work that you will ever do will be the work you do within the walls of your own home. Home teaching (in other members' homes), bishopric's work, and other Church duties are all important, but the most important work is within the walls of your home.[1]

It was another president and prophet, David O. McKay, who said, "No other success can compensate for failure in the home." These words have been quoted hundreds of times by the faithful in the church and are words that state unequivocally and succinctly the exalted place of family life in the philosophy of the Latter-day Saints. This commitment to family life prompted President McKay in 1965 to announce and formalize one of the most important programs in the Latter-day Saints Church today, known as the Family Home Evening. At that time he wrote:

> Earnestly we urge parents to gather their families around them, and to instruct them in truth and righteousness, and in family love and loyalty. The home is the basis of a righteous life, and no other instrumentality can take its place nor fulfill its essential functions. The problems of these difficult times cannot better be solved in any other place, by any other agency, by any other means, than by love and righteousness, and precept and example, and devotion to duty in the home.[2]

These quotes by modern-day church leaders are but echoes of the past counsel and commitment of earlier prophets. Since the founding of the church over a hundred years ago, when its first prophet, Joseph Smith, promised church members that if they would gather their children around them once a week and instruct them in the gospel their children would not go astray, family solidarity and enrichment has been a prevailing theme among leaders of the Latter-day Saints Church.

This theme has been given additional reinforcement in recent years by the development of carefully planned programs which stress the importance of family life among church members.

The single most important and unique family program in the church, and the one on which all other family programs focus, is the Family Home Evening program. Formally launched in 1965 by President David O. McKay, this program designates each Monday night as "family night," and no other formal church activities are allowed to be scheduled on that evening. All families in the church are encouraged to meet together as a unit on Monday evenings and to take part in activities and shared experiences that will increase family closeness and remind each member of his/her responsibility to the family organization.

Church officials have manifested their conscientious support for the Family Home Evening program in ways other than simply setting aside one night a week as family night. In addition, special church-developed materials are made available to parents as aids in providing guidance to their children. In doing this church leaders have repeatedly emphasized that, though they give special help and assistance in making family life programs available, the ultimate responsibility for the teaching of children resides with the parents.

In a message to parents in 1974 signed by the three members of the First Presidency of the Church, the following statement with respect to parental responsibility was made:

> No church organization can supplant the parents in discharging this obligation. The best the church can do is to give every aid possible so that the parents will be left without excuse in discharging this most sacred and vital work of building a solid foundation in the home from which their children can learn lessons that will strengthen them to resist the temptation of the world.[3]

To support parents in this task of child guidance, a fine set of Family Home Evening manuals has been developed and circulated by the church. Since the first one was circulated in January, 1965, eight different manuals have been developed. In 1974, the decision was made to repeat the first eight-year cycle of lessons with a fresh approach. Throughout these issues two basic themes are emphasized—"Love of God" and "Love of Each Other." Each year's lessons also have a yearly theme. For example, the 1974 theme was "Personal Commitment," and the year's lessons were organized into four basic units: (1) Commitment to Be a Good Member of the Family; (2) Commitment to Live as a Child of Our Heavenly Father; (3)

Commitment to Remember Jesus Christ; and (4) Commitment to Seek the Holy Ghost.

The clarity of the individual lessons within the Family Home Evening manuals makes them understandable even for very young children. Each lesson is accompanied by colorful illustrations and/or by cutouts, gamelike pieces, and charts, and other materials, such as suggestions for daily activities to help reinforce teaching objectives. The lessons contain a harmonious blend of revelation and psychology—a mixture of ancient scriptures and the most recent advances in social and behavioral science theory. Lessons utilizing communication theory, behavior modification techniques, and experiential learning are side by side with spiritually focused lessons based on religious scriptures and hymns. To give the flavor of these lessons some specific topics will be described.

In *Family Home Evening Manual 3*, 1974, one of the lessons is entitled "Communicating Our Feelings." This lesson has as its objective to "show your family members how to express their feelings in a way that will communicate more love." Exercises are outlined for involving the family in activities that will produce specific and easily expressed feeling responses. The individual nature of feelings is stressed, and specific stories are included to illustrate the effects within families when feelings are expressed honestly as opposed to communication which distorts or misconveys the original feelings of the message sender. Six specific questions to stimulate discussion and aid integration of the communication principles are included. Practice guides to aid family members in sending messages which express real feelings are also outlined. To complete instructions on communication skills subsequent lessons in this manual present theory, exercises, and illustrations on listening and receiving messages. Specific ways to develop the ability to show more "loving responses" within the family unit are given. These lessons are well organized and theoretically sound. They make it possible for all parents, without additional training, to become effective teachers of communication skills and techniques within their own families.

Besides lessons teaching how to relate to others, some of the lessons have been specially devised to focus on family unity and solidarity. One such lesson in *Manual 1*, 1972, is entitled "The Best Family Ever." This Family Home Evening begins with a family dinner where each member has a place card describing an outstanding quality or skill that he/she possesses. Family games and activities are outlined to emphasize the theme "This is the best family ever." This is followed by a brainstorming session where each family member suggests how the family could improve by completing a sentence beginning with "I wish our family would . . ."

Other lessons in the Family Home Evening manuals are slanted toward helping family members to be more nonjudgmental in their relationships with people outside the family circle. Lesson 36 *Manual* 3, 1974, is entitled "Judge Not by Appearances." Special cutouts of optical illusions are included which help reinforce one of the main concepts to be taught—"Appearances are often deceptive." A game plan for making judgments is followed for each of several illustrative stories to help family members learn to ask not only "what" people do but also "why" they do the things they do. Activities are suggested that span the next week and reinforce the concepts devised to help family members be more understanding, and hence more accepting, of others.

Many of the lessons have spiritual messages to teach. One example in the 1974 manual is Lesson 3 in *Manual* 3, entitled "How Great His Love." Hymns and discussions of scriptures describing God's love for his children get the Home Evening under way. Next, each family member is asked to make his own list of "everything he can think of that our Heavenly Father does to show that he loves his children." Stories are read and exchanged. Lists made by family members are then shared, and this sharing goes on throughout the next week during mealtimes. As another reinforcement of this lesson, a reminder is placed on the table each day as an evidence of God's love, e.g., a vase of flowers, a picture of nature, etc.

The variety of lessons available in the Family Home Evening manuals for use in developing or enhancing family integration, mental health of family members, social skills, and spiritual at-homeness within the family can be appreciated only when one becomes well acquainted with the manuals themselves. All the lessons describe the materials needed to teach the many concepts that are presented, and the lessons have been devised in such a way as to include family members of all ages. Often, different members of the family are given opportunities to develop leadership skills through a rotation of who is in charge of family evenings.

Some families have developed unique variations for their Family Home Evening. For instance, some enlarge the family circle to include the extended family, and these several related families take turns meeting weekly at each other's home. Such a practice, one family reported, helps to lessen the "overload" that suburban living places on the isolated, nuclear family. It also provides an opportunity for cousins, aunts, uncles, grandmothers, etc., to become real "significant others" who are intimately involved in the lives of their extended family members rather than merely semistrangers.

In some instances where family units do not include children, and others where families are missing grandparents, etc., unrelated "families" join together to enrich each other's family experience.

Such application shows that units other than the natural family can benefit from the use of these materials.

Whether a family chooses to meet separately or in conjunction with other families, which lessons are taught, and how Home Evenings are conducted are decisions that are left to the discretion of each family unit. The leadership of the LDS Church encourages families to individualize the lessons and to utilize them in ways that meet their own special needs.

Specific directions on how to use family time in an intentional way are described by one father of eight as "a real strength of the Family Home Evening program for my family." Commenting that being prepared to present structured family activities designed to accomplish specific goals had helped his family to develop more "closeness," this father remarked, "Our *Home Evening Manual* is the greatest help for developig family togetherness that we've ever had."

In addition to the manuals, several books have been written and compiled by church members to provide additional training for parents on how to conduct effective Family Home Evenings. These outline creative activities families can use to build a family history and a home atmosphere where each family member can feel loved and needed. (These books and some pamphlets listed under Resources at the end of this chapter.)

This Family Home Evening program has a unique support system to encourage and ensure its success. At many levels and through numerous auxiliary programs the church focuses on various ways to develop increased skill in family living. One example is the Sunday School program designed to encourage the participation of all members of the family. This program includes a series of lessons open to all adults who wish to learn more about effective family living. Entitled *The Family Relations Class*, this group of lessons aimed at helping members of the church to better conceptualize the purpose of family life, to develop stronger commitments to its structure, and to upgrade their personal knowledge and skills in dealing with the ever-increasing pressure on family interaction. The instructions in the preface of the teachers' supplement entitled *Parent and Youth* encourage Sunday School teachers to individualize their presentations "not only according to the class members, but to the children of class members as well." With this personalized approach, participants are then encouraged to take the information presented in class and make their own homes "vital educational institutions."

Many of the concepts and exercises developed for use in the Sunday School Family Relations Class could be used effectively by professional people working with families. First the major objective of each lesson is spelled out, then specific and detailed "learning activities" are described. Materials needed for making effective presentations are also carefully listed for each lesson. Some of the topic headings that might interest professionals working with families are: "The Home Influences and Behavior Control," "An Ideal Concept of Maturity," "Developing Faith and Knowledge in Our Children," "The Making of an Eternal Marriage," "Consideration in Developing Good Marriages," and "A Good Home for Youth."

In addition, the women's auxiliary of the church, known as the Relief Society, supports the family through a series of lessons focused on "mother education for mothers with children to age eighteen." The lessons are given at every third meeting of the month, simultaneously with the social relations course, and any woman who feels the need for developing better mothering skills may opt to attend these lessons. The 1974–75 lesson titles included the following: "Good Beginnings," "Developing Self-Discipline," "Parent-Child Conflicts," "Expanding Middle Years," "Moving into Adolescence," "Guiding the Adolescent," "Parental Counseling and Love," and "The Adolescent." These materials could be very valuable as a resource for professional people working with parent-child problems.

Sister Belle S. Spafford, president of the Latter-day Saints Relief Society, is very clear in stating her belief that mothers should receive competent training and experience in child-rearing. She has said:

> The mother of today must realize that "instinct doesn't furnish all the equipment necessary to meet her child-rearing problems, and mother love is not an adequate substitute for knowledge and efficiency." She must make a scientific approach to her task of child guidance. She must recognize that divine wisdom must be constantly applied in solving problems![4]

The lessons developed as a part of the Relief Society course of training are expected to help mothers gain greater knowledge, efficiency, and wisdom in the rearing of their children and are an acknowledgment that one way to enrich family living is to develop and enhance mothering skills.

To aid fathers, Priesthood lessons are presented each Sunday morning to the male membership of the church. These lessons stress the importance of family life and the father's responsibility to guide and direct his own family unit. The male priesthood bearer in the church is not only given the sacred task of ensuring familial success in his own family, but is also assigned specific families in his ward that he is to visit each month with his home-teaching companion. The home teachers are charged with the responsibility of reporting to the bishop any problems they find in homes they visit. In addition, they are to encourage, reinforce, and assist parents in developing family participation in the Family Home Evening program and other church activities. Many of the pamphlets listed at the end of this chapter are specifically designed for these priesthood home teachers as aids in developing the skills they need to motivate and stimulate family involvement. These pamphlets give specific instructions on skill development that would be valuable to anyone who teaches or works with families. They also outline programs that can be effectively used by any family to create more interesting learning experiences in the home.

Not only do the Sunday School, the Relief Society, and the Priesthood mount programs to support family life, but the group known as Aaronic Priesthood and Young Women, designed specifically to meet the needs of young people in the church, has developed a special program for young marrieds which outlines its objectives in the following words: "The Young Marrieds program is an educational, recreational, cultural and spiritual program designed to build closeness among groups of married couples in a ward; to strengthen, stabilize, and enrich marriages and to increase their interest in and devotion to their families and the Church."[5]

The lessons outlined for this age group contain material which is focused on family life and seek to show how it can be enriched and made a more rewarding experience. Examples of some of the lesson titles are: "Family Camping," "The Sacredness of Marriage," "Put Father Back at the Head of the Family," "Television and the Family," and "Seven Danger Signals of a Sick Marriage." Again, these lesson materials are detailed and can be a valuable resource for professionals working in the area of family life.

The development and enrichment of family life is considered by the Latter-day Saints Church to be a divine mission instituted and directed by God through his prophets. President Joseph Fielding Smith, speaking as a prophet of the church, articulated the importance of an eternal concept of family life for church members when he said:

> Marriage is considered by a great many people as merely a civil contract or agreement between a man and woman that they will together, "until death do you part."
>
> No ordinance connected with the gospel of Jesus Christ is of greater importance, of more solemn and sacred nature, and more necessary to the eternal joy of man than marriage in the house of the Lord. It is an eternal principle upon which the very existence of mankind depends. The Lord gave the law of marriage to man in the beginning of the world as a part of the gospel law. In the gospel plan, marriage should endure forever. If all mankind would live in strict obedience to the gospel and in that love

which is begotten by the Spirit of the Lord, all marriages would be eternal, and divorce would be unknown.[6]

It is clear that for the Church of Jesus Christ of Latter-day Saints the preservation and enrichment of the family unit is critical, and it has reaffirmed its commitment to this institution by developing the Family Home Evening program and giving it visible and undeniable support in every auxiliary group and at every level within the church organization. Its belief in the divinity of family life and the importance of strong families is more than a philosophic position to be verbalized. It is a vital matter that is backed by ongoing program development and accompanied by a specific designation of times and places where these programs can be carried out consistently and effectively. The enrichment of family life is not left to chance. The church leaders are clear in their expectation that church members will be responsible for instituting spiritually and educationally focused programs in their individual homes.

In 1964 Harold B. Lee, then president and prophet of the Latter-day Saints Church, gave the following admonition to the mothers and fathers of the church. He said:

> I say to you Latter-day Saints mothers and fathers, if you arise to the responsibility of teaching your children in the home, priesthood quorums preparing the fathers, the Relief Society the mothers, the day will soon be dawning when the whole world will come to our doors and say, "Show us your way that we may walk in your path."

Notes

1. Harold B. Lee, "Strengthening the Home," Pamphlet 032-8, 1973, p. 7.
2. *Family Home Evening Manual* (Salt Lake City: Corporation of the President of the Church of Jesus Christ of Latter-day Saints, 1965), p. iii.
3. *Ibid.* p. 2.
4. Belle S. Spafford, *Women in Today's World* (Salt Lake City: Deseret Book Co., 1971), pp. 214, 282-83.
5. *Young Marrieds' Manual* (Salt Lake City: Paragon Press, 1972), p. 1. (Compiled by a church-appointed committee to write lessons for this age group.)
6. Joseph Fielding Smith, "The Sacredness of Marriage," in *Make It a Good Home* (Salt Lake City: Paragon Press, 1972), p. 30.

Resources

Books

Belnap, Dean, and Griffin Glen. *About Marriage and More.* Salt Lake City: Deseret Book Co., 1969.

A realistic discussion of marriage and ways to support and enhance the marital relationship.

Bennett, Archibald F. *Family Exaltation.* Salt Lake City: Deseret Book Co., 1957.

This book focuses on theological and theoretical foundations for family living. The author discusses why families are important and gives special emphasis to the value of compiling family records.

Clarke, Harold Glen. *Families, Families and Families: How Do You Keep Them Together?* Provo, Utah: Brigham Young University Press, 1963.

An excellent chronicle of activities families can do together. Particularly creative are the suggestions made by Dr. Clarke on how familiar tunes can be modified with words to reflect specific family histories.

Hoole, Daryl V., and Ockey, Donette V. *The Art of Teaching Children.* Salt Lake City: Deseret Book Co., 1973.

A well-documented book on ways to teach children more effectively.

Knight, Hattie M., ed. *Family Unity Through Reading.* Provo, Utah: Brigham Young University Press, 1963.

This book discusses the value of reading with family members and gives excellent suggestions on ways to do this effectively.

Landau, Elliot. *Raising Fine Families.* Salt Lake City: Deseret Book Co., 1972.

Written by an outstanding and creative educator, this book is an excellent reference for those who are working with parents in an effort to create more congenial and productive parent-child relationships.

Paxman, Monroe and Shirley. *Family Faith and Fun.* Salt Lake City: Bookcraft Publishing Co., 1972.

A book published specifically to give helpful hints for Family Home Evening. An excellent reference.

Paxman, Shirley Brockbank, and Paxman, Monroe J., eds. *Family Night Fun.* Salt Lake City: Deseret Book Publishing Co., 1959.

Ways to build family tradition and promote solidarity. Specific ways to plan a family night program.

Taylor, Lucille, and Taylor, Harvey L. *Family Togetherness.* Provo, Utah: Brigham Young University Press, 1963.

Five pillars of family strength are outlined and discussed: counsel, prayer, partnership, participation, and play. An excellent resource book on ways to arouse interest and motivate family togetherness. Discusses ways to create family traditions and gives a list of standard play equipment and materials every family should have.

Manuals

Family Home Evening Manuals. Salt Lake City: Corporation of the President of the Church of Jesus Christ of Latter-day Saints, 1965–74.

Each yearly manual contains lesson plans and specific family activities and outlines to enhance the weekly family enrichment program.

Parent and Youth. Salt Lake City: Corporation of the President of the Church of Jesus Christ of Latter-day Saints, 1971.

A publication which focuses on specific concepts and activities that can be used to enhance parent-child relationships. (Cost $1.00.)

Relief Society Courses of Study. Salt Lake City: The Church of Jesus Christ of Latter-day Saints, 1974.

This publication contains pertinent materials focused on the development of increased skills for "mothering." The section devoted to specific descriptive materials for mothers with children to age eighteen is particularly valuable as an addition for those seeking to build a library of family enrichment materials. (Cost 50¢.)

Relief Socity Lesson Plans for 1974–75. Salt Lake City: The General Board of Relief Society, 1974–75.

A kit of materials that supplements the *Relief Society Courses of Study* and gives detailed descriptions of design, approach, and materials needed to implement each lesson. (Cost 25¢.)

Make It a Good Home. Salt Lake City: Paragon Press, 1972.

Descriptive materials designed to enhance family solidarity, to build closeness among groups of married couples in a ward and to strengthen, stabilize, and enrich marriages in all age groups. (Cost $1.00.)

Pamphlets

Why Families? Salt Lake City: McLean Associates, 1974.

A pamphlet describing in detail a Family Home Evening program suggested by the Church of Jesus Chirst of Latter-day Saints. (Cost 2¢.)

How Can I Encourage a Family to Pray Vocally? Salt Lake City: Corporation of the Church of Jesus Christ of Latter-day Saints, 1974.

A pamphlet giving specific suggestions to home teachers on how to develop shared family prayer. (Cost 2¢.)

How Can I Help My Companion? Salt Lake City: Corporation of the Church of Jesus Christ of Latter-day Saints, 1974.

A pamphlet giving specific suggestions to home teachers on how to enhance family relationships by developing more effective home teaching procedures. (Cost 2¢.)

When We Get Together as Companions, How Can We Prepare to Help Our Families? Salt Lake City: Corporation of the Church of Jesus Christ of Latter-day Saints, 1974.

A pamphlet designed to assist home teachers in being more effective in implementing programs to enrich family life. (Cost 2¢.)

How Can We Show by Actions That We Have a Special Interest in

Our Families? Salt Lake City: Corporation of the Church of Jesus Christ of Latter-day Saints, 1974.

A pamphlet designed to give a detailed description of specific activities that one can do to reinforce how much one cares about the family group. (Cost 2¢.)

Strengthening the Home. Salt Lake City: Corporation of the President of the Church of Jesus Christ of Latter-day Saints, 1973.

This pamphlet contains the text of a speech made by Harold B. Lee, past president of the Church of Jesus Christ of Latter-day Saints, in which he focuses on ways to enrich family home living. [Cost 10¢.]

Thirty Minutes for Your Family. Salt Lake City: Corporation of the President of the Church of Jesus Christ of Latter-day Saints, 1973.

A pamphlet reinforcing the value of Family Home Evening programs. (Cost 2¢.)

Essentials of Effective Priesthood: Home Teaching Evaluations. Salt Lake City: Corporation of the Church of Jesus Christ of Latter-day Saints, 1974.

A pamphlet designed to instruct home teachers on how to be most effective in enriching family life programs. (Cost 5¢.)

How Can I Encourage Families to Hold Home Evenings? Salt Lake City: Corporation of the Church of Jesus Christ of Latter-day Saints, 1974.

A pamphlet suggesting ways a teacher can encourage a family to hold special family programs. (Cost 2¢.)

Helping Families Understand What a Family Home Evening Is. Salt Lake City: Corporation of the Church of Jesus Christ of Latter-day Saints, 1974.

A pamphlet stressing the value of family home evenings and seeking to suggest ways a family group can be encouraged to adopt such a program. (Cost 2¢.)

How Do I Encourage Families to Improve Home Evenings? Salt Lake City: Corporation of the Church of Jesus Christ of Latter-day Saints, 1974.

A pamphlet giving suggestions on how Family Home Evening programs can be improved.

How to Encourage Those Without Children to Have Family Home Evenings. Salt Lake City: Corporation of the Church of Jesus Christ of Latter-day Saints 1974.

A pamphlet supporting the position that all families, regardless of size or family makeup, should hold family home evenings.

All of the above materials can be obtained by writing to the following address: The Distribution Center, Church of Jesus Christ of Latter-day Saints, 1999 West 17th South, Salt Lake City, Utah 84104.

Chapter 7

A Christian Marriage Enrichment Retreat
Herman Green, Jr.

THE CHRISTIAN MARRIAGE ENRICHMENT RETREAT ATTEMPTS to integrate universal Christian values into the understanding and experience of the marriage relationship. However, the retreat I will describe does reflect my own particular religious heritage (Baptist). This tends to be true of retreats sponsored by other denominations also. For instance, the first retreat my wife and I participated in, sponsored by the Methodist Board of Evangelism[1] was highly structured. The Marriage Encounter retreats of the Catholic Church emphasize the use of silence and contemplation. The Quaker Marriage Enrichment Retreats have very little planned structure. As a Baptist, I accept full responsibility for the way I interpret my faith in this Christian Marriage Enrichment Retreat.

As a family ministry consultant for the Baptist Sunday School Board, I started leading retreats in 1972. My wife goes with me whenever possible. She has chosen not to be a co-leader; but she enjoys being with me, sharing of herself and our marriage, and using her administrative talents to see that meals, assignment of rooms, and necessary clean-up run smoothly.

I prefer working with about six couples because I can stay personally involved with them during all the sessions and activities. However, I have served as a participant-observer in a facilitating role with up to seventeen couples. Such large retreats are beneficial to the couples, but they lack some depth and personal warmth. I have recently become the minister of pastoral care in a local church. In setting up a continuing program of marriage enrichment retreats, I have found that ten couples seem to provide the balance between the maximum of effectiveness and the minimum of expense.

The place for the retreat should provide comfortable conveniences, privacy, and the beauty of nature. Meals prepared by the retreat center or in a restaurant can save time and energy. However, preplanned meals prepared by the couples usually offset the limitations of strictly scheduled mealtimes and the high prices of restaurant food.

The retreat is usually held over a weekend. It begins Friday night after supper and ends Sunday afternoon.

The Purposes

A Christian Marriage Enrichment Retreat serves several purposes. First, it helps the couple focus upon their personal relationship rather than upon schedules and things. In commanding us to "love one another" (I John 4:11-12) the Bible emphasizes that people are more important than the things of our affluent society. Second, the retreat provides a time to integrate religious values into the whole of life. Too often our religious faith is segregated from the ongoing experiences of loving, understanding, forgiving, and being reconciled to each other. Third, a retreat setting away from home helps provide a genuine sense of restoration, balance, and a new awareness of the presence of God in our lives. The normal routines which become boring and inhibit relationships to God and people are broken. Fourth, the retreat's emphasis on growth rather than on therapy activates the co-creative power we have with God to "give a blessing." [2] In any significant relationship such as marriage, there are ambivalent feelings. The enrichment retreat helps a couple take a stand on the positive side of their relationship rather than being double-minded (James 1:6-8). The revealed Word "God is love" (I John 4:8) is put into concrete words and actions. Fifth, the retreat can enhance an authentic witness of enduring marriage and family relationships in Christ. This is needed in a world becoming increasingly disillusioned and cynical about marriage and family life.

The Retreat

The couples are asked at the beginning to make a covenant with me and before God. The covenant includes an agreement to (1) focus upon their relationship to each other in the marriage, (2) stay for the whole retreat, (3) try to be honest in their thoughts and feelings, and (4) say and do only what each person wants to say and do.

The following description is the basic retreat organization I designed. Variations, adaptations, and changes are made to meet the unique needs and interests of the couples. New ideas, insights, and techniques are incorporated as they are learned.

Session I

The first principle of a faithful Christian relationship is "known-ness."[3] It is only as we get to "know" people that we understand and accept them. Therefore, rapport is established through enjoyable games in which each individual is introduced to the group by another. One game involves sharing a memory from age six, a religious experience of the teen-age years, and when one feels one became a man or a woman. This eases the tension while providing a balance between wholesome humor and empathetic hurt.

Following this the participants each write (1) why they came to the retreat, and (2) how they would like their marriages to be in three years. Writing exercises are used for two reasons. First, they help people clarify their thinking. Second, Americans tend to take their written word as a more binding commitment than the spoken word.

The couples are divided into small groups of four or five couples to share these goals they have written. Each person shares his or her goals, and the rest listen. Discussion begins after everyone has shared.

The first session is ended in various ways. One principle used throughout all the sessions is balancing the verbal and nonverbal activities. This helps the couples to be alive in the present.[4] I enjoy closing with J. B. Phillips' paraphase of the Beatitudes from *Your God Is Too Small*.[5] The last verse is "Happy are those who help others to live together: they will be known to be doing God's work." This is what the retreat is all about.

The first night ends with the playing of recreational games (cards, etc.), eating, and talking, until everyone goes to bed.

Session II

Breakfast is eaten around nine o'clock the next morning. By 10:30 the couples are usually ready to begin. The session is introduced with a short didactic interpretation of Matthew 12:43-45 as it relates to marriage.[6] Wallace Denton's description of the sweet potato dry rot[7] makes a vivid analogy of the temptations that modern marriages face.

The participants are then asked to write down who they think should be loved first, second, third, and fourth among the significant persons in their lives. Another variation is to ask people to make a

priority list of importance from these items: other people, posses-
sions, self, work, children, God, and mate. This usually leads to a
lively discussion involving how we put God first, the dynamic need
to change priorities, the temptation of becoming a workaholic, the
problem of putting children before our mates, neglecting our families
for things and other people (I Timothy 5:8), and the importance of
self-love. Erich Fromm[8] and Clark Vincent[9] have excellent material
on the difference between selfishness and authentic self-love.

Agape love can be understood from the viewpoint of congruence.
First, it is a decision, involving the will, attitude, or spirit, to see
every person as being of worth and value. Second, love is a desire to
feel warm and close to a person. Third, it is behavior that is more
constructive, healthy, and redemptive than destructive, sick, and
sinful. Real love is "a relationship in which persons experience
themselves as unconditionally valued by others."[10]

Western culture has taught a false and simplistic dichotomy
known as "either/or." Life is either black or white, people are either
good or evil, and decisions are either right or wrong. The richest
teachings of Hebrew-Christian thought involve a "both/and" concept. Jesus was asked what the greatest commandment was (Mark
12:28-30). One of the best ways a person can follow Jesus' teaching
and put God first is by loving the self enough that he or she is free to
give love to other significant people. In marriage, this means one has
such a sense of self-worth from God that first-rate energy expresses
love for both self and mate in word and deed.

The discussion about love is followed by each person writing, "I
like myself because . . ." The participants describe themselves in
terms of what they do, how they look, and who they are. Most people
can wirte a much longer list of things they dislike about themselves.
Balancing these lists helps them accept the unacceptable side of
themselves. Then the men are separated into one group and the
women into another to share what each person likes about himself or
herself. The discussion leads to a reaffirmation of each person's
manhood or womanhood.

Before we break for lunch, each couple is requested to take a "trust
walk" sometime during the free period from lunch to about five
o'clock. On the trust walk one person shuts his/her eyes and, as
he/she is led on the walk by the other, listens to the impression of the
world his/her mate is seeing. Then the roles are reversed. This serves
two purposes. First, it helps each person to appreciate his/her mate as
a unique person rather than as an extension of him- or herself.
Second, it enhances the understanding and experience of the second
principle of a faithful Christian relationship, which is "trust." Our
ability to trust our whole body to the control of another loving person
has a lot to say about our ability to trust the God who made us, other

people, and the world we live in.[11] Dr. Wayne Oates suggests that it is more important for a couple to trust each other than to say "I love you" to each other.[12]

Session III

The third session begins before the evening meal. A dramatization of Virginia Satir's family sculpture called "We Face the World Together"[13] can be used. Many people marry mates they see as extensions of themselves or as being like their parents of the opposite sex rather than as unique persons to learn to know, trust, and love. There is nearly always something new and different about the insights the couples gain in role-playing and discussing this exercise. The personality of each retreat is as different as the uniqueness of the couples who participate.

Another exercise is to use chairs that are back to back, side by side, and face to face.[14] The couples quickly put themselves into these chairs as they recall the times they normally talk to one another. From these exercises, we all learn to laugh at ourselves and not take life too seriously.

Hopefully, the participants are now ready to focus attention on the positive relationships to their mates. David Mace thinks there is a taboo against spelling out in concrete detail what we mean by the words "I love you."[15] Each person is asked to write down what he/she loves about his/her mate in terms of behavior, looks, and being. A communication model is then taught and illustrated. One model is called "revolving dialogue." The first person makes a statement. The second person responds with his impression of what he heard. The first person either agrees with the impression or clarifies his statement. The second person expresses his feeling about the statement. Most of us try to short cut this process and then wonder why we are misunderstood.

The couples break into their small groups. Each couple in turn sits in sharing seats arranged in the center of the group. This eye-to-eye, knee-to-knee, and hand-to-hand approach helps each person to communicate with the whole body. Husband and wife use the revolving dialogue to share what they love about each other. Tears, joy, laughter, and spontaneity of expression result. Yet it is also the religious experience Rudolf Otto calls a *mysterium tremendum*.[16] It is the burning-bush experience of talking on holy ground. I still stand in awe of the power of such a holy spirit of love.

This whole session emphasizes the principle of a faithful Christian relationship known as "caring" rather than using people. As you can imagine, the evening meal is a delightful, warm, and filling experience.

Session IV

After the meal and a short period of relaxation, the couples are usually ready to begin again. This fourth session is built around the mutual need for intimacy and individuality in marriage. The emphasis is upon the principle of a faithful Christian relationship which is "responsibility" rather than irresponsibility or unresponsiveness. A variety of exercises are used, such as territorial games,[17] and exercises that illustrate William Schutz's three basic need areas of inclusion, control, and affection.[18]

These exercises are amusing, but three serious areas usually come up in the discussions. The first is the sexual relationship in marriage, the second relates to the handling of negative feelings in a marriage relationship, and the third revolves around the roles of a man and woman in marriage.

It is amazing how little adult-taught sex education men have received in growing up. Equally disturbing are the negative teachings that women received from adults. No wonder many men are irresponsible and many women are unresponsive in their sexual behavior. The idea that God created our sexuality, thought it was good, and intended it as a gift to be enjoyed in expressions of love between a husband and wife, has really never been heard by many Christian couples. One myth unfortunately reinforced in some Christian tradition is that it is better to give then to recieve. The truly graceful person knows equally how to give and how to receive a gift with unconditional love and joy. There is no better place to experience this than in the sexual relationship between a husband and wife. A work theology calls for us to perform in order to meet the unreal expectations of others. A pleasure theology calls for us to selfishly meet our own hedonistic needs. A grace theology integrates our love and sexual needs into the whole of life as a unique couple. Thank God for sex!

Further, many Christian people think it is wrong to get angry. They deny that their anger exists and hold it in, until it turns into depression, resentment, hostility, destructive behavior, or the opposite of love, apathy. Paul teaches two valid principles about anger in Ephesians 4:26. First, Christians are told, "Be ye angry, and sin not." This means it is all right to be angry, but we should not allow the anger to create a broken relationship. The withholding of anger usually leads to internalized barriers that hinder a loving relationship with the person at whom we are angry. The second principle is "Let not the sun go down upon your wrath." This means the time to deal with our anger is when we feel it. However, finding a constructive and redemptive way to express anger is easier to learn than to practice.

The roles of man and woman in a Christian marriage are a controversial area. Yet three biblical teachings have to be considered when a person is tempted to hold that the wife is subject to male domination in Christian thought. First, both men and women are created in the image of God (Genesis 1:27). Second, Jesus seems to have had a very high respect for the women he met. Third, even Paul, who was a child of the first-century culture where women were second-class citizens, admitted that in Christ there is no difference between men and women (Galatians 3:28). God calls Christian couples to make a commitment of unconditional and enduring love with the determination that the marriage shall last. This means the roles of men and women in our society have to be flexible in order for each couple to complement the unique persons they are rather than compete with one another. Part of the controversy is generated by threatened men with eggshell masculine egos who have never loved themselves, or established an adequate identity apart from putting someone down.

When the Saturday night session ends, the couples enjoy the rest of the evening as they did on Friday night. Sometimes cards or dominoes are played until three in the morning.

Session V

After breakfast on Sunday morning the couples write down what they wish their mates would do and would not do. They are told that the open and trusting marriage allows the sharing of wishes and fantasies with the mate. This does not mean a person is bound to do as the mate wishes. It is amazing the number of wishes mates really hear for the first time: "I wish you would stay at the table until I finish eating." "I wish you would not pick the pimples on my back." "I wish you would rest and relax sometime before we go to bed." "I wish you would not pout, but let it all hang out." "I wish you would do more just for yourself." "I wish you would spend more time with the children."

The wishes vary in depth and seriousness. The couples communicate some of these to each other in their small groups and the rest when they are alone. After the small group sharing, the couples are asked to walk together and to talk about where they would be willing to compromise on their wishes, where they would be willing to change, and where they would just respect each other's wishes.

Session VI

The final session is a worship service. This is usually mimeographed to be used with recorded music. However, the couples can create their own worship service to express to God what they are experiencing. The Lord's Supper, confessions, poems said in unison, testimonies, scriptures, the renewing of wedding voes, and new and old hymns can be incorporated into a meaningful worship of God.

I end the service with a nonverbal prayer. Each couple in turn stands in the center of the circle of couples. Then one at a time all the couples nonverbally express their appreciation before God for having experienced the retreat with the couple in the center. This is probably getting back much closer to the affirmation in the original meaning of the Christian "laying on of hands."

The retreat ends after the noon meal on Sunday. This leaves the afternoon free for the couples to enjoy. One couple usually give a testimony in church that night about what the retreat meant to them. Friendships are made on each retreat that continue to have a depth seldom experienced in our society. More important, foundations are laid or building blocks are added to each marriage that enhance the fifth principle of a faithful Christian relationship. That is the principle of durability. For as surely as the Resurrection proclaims that nothing can separate us from the love of God (Romans 8:38), so couples are raised to touch souls in an internal commitment that has an eternal quality.

Notes

1. I credit part of my structure to Dr. Carl Clarke, Florida State University, who designed the retreat for the Methodist Board of Evangelism.
2. Myron C. Madden, *The Power to Bless* (Nashville: Abingdon Press, 1970).
3. Wayne E. Oates, *Pastoral Counseling in Social Problems* (Philadelphia: The Westminster Press, 1966), pp. 97-102.
4. William C. Schutz, *Here Comes Everybody* (New York: Harper & Row, 1971), p. 137.
5. J. B. Phillips, *Your God Is Too Small* (New York: The Macmillian Co., 1972), pp. 92-93.
6. Herman Green, "Enrich Your Marriage," *Home Life*, December, 1973, p. 4.
7. Wallace Denton, *Family Problems and What to Do About Them* (Philadelphia: The Westminster Press, 1971), pp. 98-115.
8. Erich Fromm, *The Art of Loving* (New York: Bantam Books [1956], 1963), pp. 48-53.
9. Clark E. Vincent, *Sexual and Marital Health* (New York: McGraw-Hill Book Co., 1973), pp. 31-58.
10. Thomas C. Oden, *The Intensive Group Experience* (Philadelphia: The Westminster Press, 1972), p. 109.
11. *Ibid.*, pp. 89-117.
12. Wayne E. Oates, *The Psychology of Religion* (Waco, Texas: Word Books, 1973), p. 281.

13. Howard R. Lewis and Harold Streitfeld, *Growth Games* (New York: Bantam Books [1971], 1972), pp. 250-53.
14. William G. Hollister, *The Sermon of the Chairs* (Boston: Unitarian Universalist Association, 1963).
15. David and Vera Mace, *Marriage Enrichment Retreat* (Philadelphia: Friends General Conference, 1973), p. 19.
16. Rudolf Otto, "The Numinous," in John Hick, ed., *Classical and Contemporary Readings in the Philosophy of Religion* (Englewood Cliffs, N. J.: Prentice-Hall, 1964), pp. 243-67.
17. Wayne E. Oates, *When Religion Gets Sick* (Philadelphia: The Westminster Press, 1970), pp. 101-21.
18. Schutz, *Here Comes Everybody*, pp. 99-111, 131-48.

Chapter 8

Marriage Encounter: An Ecumenical Enrichment Program
Antoinette Bosco

MARRIAGE ENCOUNTER COMBINES SOUND PSYCHOLOGY, spiritual values, and a practical technique for reviving the relationship between husband and wife. It is a movement which is facing the root problem of what it means to be married in the modern, fast-changing world. It is answering that question in terms of the *personal relationship* between husband and wife, instead of obligation, responsibility, bonds, and the needs of society.

Speak to most couples who have made a Marriage Encounter and you become enveloped in their enthusiasm. They come back from the weekend holding hands, calling marriage wonderful, and almost levitating from what they say is a fantastic experience of renewal on both human and spiritual levels.

The Marriage Encounter is an international movement with a religious base, designed to make good marriages better. A group of couples meet on a Friday evening, usually at a retreat house, and spend the hours from then until late Sunday afternoon learning and applying a series to techniques which have proved to be effective in deepening the communication between husband and wife. God's role in their marriage is emphasized, but not in a churchy or denominational way.

Though it began among Spanish Catholics, as an outgrowth of the Catholic Christian Family Movement, Marriage Encounter in the United States is strongly supported by Protestant and Jewish couples too, and is growing rapidly from coast to coast.

Unlike a T-group or sensitivity session, The Marriage Encounter takes place between the husband and wife only, in privacy. As one couple put it, the weekend is "a crash program in experiencing what it means to be loved and valued by your spouse."

Whatever it is that takes place on that weekend, the couples come back giving testimony to a change within them, that is totally unexpected and absolutely accepted by them.

Exactly what produces such a dramatic effect on a couple after they have participated in an Encounter weekend is difficult for them to pinpoint in words. Some have called the experience a "rebirth"; some say their "real marriage" began not with their wedding day but at the Encounter. Some have even bought new wedding rings after the weekend to emphasize that they are beginning a deeper marriage relationship.

"What happens, in one word, is communication," said Jack and Edna B., parents of five, married twenty-five years. "But we're not talking about talking. The communication reaches the level of feelings, and you experience this vividly. This is what the weekend is all about—a crash program in experiencing what it means to be loved and valued by your spouse, feeling the bond between you, and actually seeing the loose ends that are a part of life, The searching, dissatisfactions, and frustrations, all fall into place."

They added that lack of communication is a symptom of society, "but we never thought it was in our marriage. A husband and wife never really take a hard look at the fact that they don't really understand what the other one is feeling. And if you don't reach that deeper level of communication in a marriage, you can settle into boredom—which is so destructive, they emphasized.

"We went not knowing what to expect," said Bob and Paula, "but found the effect it has is really and truly an encounter. You face up to each other and go beyond openness and frankness. Even what is buried is stripped part. The Encounter scraped off all the dust from the years, so that we were aware again of the richness we have in our marriage."

Couples come back saying that the Marriage Encounter unlocks hidden and unspoken feelings between husband and wife, releasing a realization of how much each means to the other. The effect of this new realization of love is limitless and explains some of the impact the Marriage Encounter has on couples.

"We all have such a desire to get some kind of meaning out of our lives. I wanted to be the loving guy to save the world," said Jim. "But I never thought of looking to achieve this through our marriage. Yet here's where you learn to be a loving person. The more I love Joan, the more I'll relate with love to every other person. All my relationships will be improved because they'll all now begin with loving. And how far can you go in loving?" he asked, deliberately leaving the question open-ended.

While Encounters do not follow an identical plan everywhere, the steps and tone of the weekends are basically alike. The one I attended began on a Friday night with an individual welcome given by the "team." The team—a priest and a couple trained to lead the other couples through the various steps and techniques which open up dialogue—is the essential and only "structure" to a Marriage

Encounter weekend. On this weekend, the team was extraordinary—
Jaime and Arline Whelan of Englewood, New Jersey, and Father
Frank Heinen, an assistant at St. Joseph of the Palisades parish in
West New York, New Jersey.

The place was Graymoor Monastery in Garrison, New York.
Introductions to the other eight couples were made as all had
refreshments—a glass of wine, cheese and crackers, sandwiches, and
cookies. The age groups varied from couples in their twenties to
some married nearly twenty-five years.

The couples began to talk with each other nervously. It generally
developed that the men were here to please their wives, and the
wives were here to get a weekend alone with their husbands, away
from the children for a change. Some of the little crusts which had
hardened between them over the years were exposed subtly in such
remarks as these:

"I told her if I'm going to spend the money to go away for a
weekend, I'd rather go to a resort than to a retreat house."

"I'm very well loved for eight months of the year—till the baseball
season starts!"

"She complains that I'm not home enough, but she's got to
understand that if she wants to stay in that nice house of ours in the
suburbs, I've got to be out working."

Except for mealtimes, a break on Saturday night, and a few shared
prayer sessions, this was the first and only time the couples had any
group conversation. The reason for this was explained by the
Whelans at the first conference: "Marriage Encounter is a personal
thing between husband and wife. It's a chance to get to know
yourself a little better than you did a few hours ago, and the
opportunity to grow in understanding your spouse and accepting the
other *as he is,* not as you wish he would be, or expect him to be."

They explained that the program of the weekend would be simple:
a number of conferences, followed by times alone, and times together
with your spouse.

These "times" were the heart of the Encounter, spent with a blank
notebook and a pen, first writing down by yourself the most honest
feelings you were able to express, followed by a sharing session with
your spouse during which you exchanged notebooks, read what the
other had written, and then talked about the feelings brought into the
open this way.

The team helped us to see, perhaps for the first time, that our way
of life inclines us to be people who too often communicate only on
the surface, unwilling or unable to express any deep feelings and
emotions to one another. The writing technique is a powerful way to
begin to break out of these crusts and defenses which hide the
honesty deep within us. As the Whelans explained:

When you communicate verbally, your freedom for total expression is limited, because the communication gets blocked. While one is talking, the other is half-listening, and half-planning his response.

Writing gives you the chance to express yourself freely, without interruption. It can be a process of self-discovery, though hard at first. We're not taught to be feeling people, and so we don't even have a vocabulary to express our feelings.

Usually we say, "I feel that . . ." and what follows? "I feel that *you should* . . ." We don't express our own feelings. Instead, we start off saying "I feel," and then proceed not to "feel" at all, but to make judgments about our spouses.

This weekend, don't do that. Every time you say "I feel," follow it with an *adjective.* I feel happy about . . . I feel sad that . . . I feel glad. I feel angry. Get to what's really happening inside you.

At the end of each conference, the Whelans gave the couples a few questions to write in their books—keys to help each person begin the unlocking-self process. For example:

Why have I come here?

What have been the happiest moments in our relationship?

What three times have I felt most united with you?

What are my reasons for wanting to go on living?

By the end of the weekend, couples had had the time to focus on:

—themselves, their strengths and weaknesses, their feelings about themselves

—the state of marriage in the world

—the illusion-disillusion aspect of all relationships

—the symptoms of "spiritual divorce" in their marriage, such as habitual sadness; boredom; dissatisfaction; lack of tenderness; ridicule of one another; and other such disruptive symptoms

—subjects which need much understanding in marriage, such as death, sexual relations, time, money, children, rest, relatives, etc.

—how to gain confidence in one another through dialogue

—the communicating sign—or sacrament—that is marriage.

Father Heinen's role was integral. But, as he put it, he was "not the leader." "Leadership should come from the couple." he explained. "The priest is a great influence during the team couple's training and preparation time, because of his knowledge of Scripture and theology. But during the weekend his role is to be supportive, be a good listener, add a sense of humor, and be available if anyone wants to talk to him privately."

By Saturday afternoon, it was evident that something had started to happen between the couples. They were holding hands, smiling, and commenting, "This is better than we expected."

"I didn't realize it would be just between the two of us," said one husband, noticeably at ease because the weekend had not turned out to be "group sensitivity sessions." And, just before dinner on Saturday, Friday night's outspoken husband proclaimed, "Just for the record, I'm glad we didn't go to a resort!"

The closing liturgy on Sunday afternoon was a magnificent experience of unity—of people bound in a curious way because, while they had shared something deep, personal, and crucial exclusively with their spouses, their joy of discovery spilled over to the other couples who had been likewise affected. The liturgy was an experience of sharing Christian life and love on a new level.

Logically, so deep an experience demands that the communication and relationships begun be continued, and so the follow-up aspects of the Marriage Encounter are important. How couples remain in contact with the movement varies according to the locality. Some methods used are one-day area renewal meetings held periodically in some central place for large numbers of couples; monthly renewal meetings for couples who made the weekend together, held in one another's home on a rotating basis; newsletters; and annual picnics.

The Marriage Encounter was introduced in this country at the summer, 1967, Christian Family Movement Convention in Notre Dame, Indiana. It had begun in Spain, in 1965, as an outgrowth of CFM there. A few Spanish couples came to the Notre Dame convention, mainly to interest Spanish CFM couples in this new idea for better marriages. During the convention the Spanish couples led an Encounter for eight English-speaking couples and six priests, with an interpreter "translating as it went along." The Whelans were one of the couples who made that original Encounter.

They, the other couples, and the priests brought the Encounter back to their home areas, eventually sparking the start of the movement in this country.

Marriage Encounter began to take firm root in the United States by late 1968, with the formation of a National Marriage Encounter Board. The fastest growth was in the New York City–Long Island area, under the leadership of Jesuit Father Charles Gallagher who organized the effort as Marriage Encounter Incorporated. National estimates to date place the number of U.S. couples coast to coast who have been "encountered" at about forty-thousand. Numerous couples have been trained to be team leaders, sharing personal experiences with couples on a weekend and guiding them toward the openness needed to begin the process of disclosing inner feelings to one's spouse through the written word. Priests who work for Marriage Encounter also undergo training to be better able to share with couples theological insights on the interplay of the two sacraments of Holy Orders and Matrimony.

Since the development of Marriage Encounter by Father Gabriel Calvo and the Christian Family Movement couples in Barcelona, Spain, in the 1960s, Marriage Encounter has become established in Canada, the Philippines, Taiwan, South America, New Zealand, India, and seventeen other countries, in addition to Spain and the United States.

Why is Marriage Encounter spreading so rapidly and with such enthusiasm among couples?

Ed Garzero, who participated in the first Marriage Encounter weekend in the New York area back in November, 1968, says "because it is an apostolate born out of need." He pointed out that in a world which is characterized by so much spiritual desolation— isolation of people from one another (even married couples), pressures of daily work, and distorted values—marriage is in a crisis environment. "Though marriage has a tremendous richness, most people never achieve this—not because of bad will, but because of so many distractions." Another couple said that their experience after two years with Encounter verifies this. "We've seen couples in good marriages finally become aware of the ways in which they are still 'married singles' during the Encounter weekend."

Timing may be a factor in the movement's success, according to a psychologist who is a Catholic and has made the Encounter. Dr. John Nolan of Long Island said, "Husband and wife are so straitjacketed into occupational roles and the need to be productive in these roles. The emphasis is on the marriage *partnership*, rather than on the love relationship." Thus, he went on, the human pulse of the marriage is diminished. Where is the time for reflection together, that walk in the woods, the touches which build up to exciting lovemaking? "Then Marriage Encounter comes along and tells you—and this really affects the men—that it's all right to give your emotions a roller coaster ride. All the masks between a couple, all the hiding places, start to go. Writing their feelings is a catharsis—like confession. They learn to tune into the other's feelings, probably for the first time." As a result, you get out of the occupational role you're supposed to play—to meet a person. And who is this person? The one you pledged to love forever, who has created children with you, who has shared your sorrows, joys, boredoms, and so much, with you. As the walls come tearing down, and you meet each other again, it's all this love released that's encircling you, transporting you, so that it's no wonder you land on "cloud nine."

Couples testify to another discovery during the weekend—in a word, God. It is as though they were speaking of conversion, using the expression "before and after" in referring to the impact of Marriage Encounter on their lives. It is not unusual to hear couples speak as Tony and Virginia F. do: "We can only explain our weekend by saying our love experienced the awareness of three hearts touching. We touched the reality of the Living God in our marriage for the first time, because we touched the reality of each other in our love as never before."

The wondrous effect of the Marriage Encounter on a couple spills over into the family, and the children quickly sense the heightened atmosphere of love in their home. "My parents came back so anxious to be patient with the five of us, really trying to be understanding and never to raise their voices at us," said Katie B., recently graduated from high school. Katie attended the annual Marriage Encounter family picnic held in her locale, and upon her return stated, "There were forty-six hundred people all together on the grass and on the hills—all happy, all sharing, all loving. I couldn't help but feel that it was the Bible scene of Christ and the loaves and the fishes, all taking place again here."

Katie's comment underscores the dramatic element in the Marriage Encounter movement, generated by couple-power—unity. Harriet Garzera had earlier expressed this as a personal experience: "What most impressed me was that the big thing in marriage is unity. This is what characterizes the sacrament and the vocation, not love alone."

Whenever a movement takes on with force and speed, it usually has some validity, rooted in need. The validity of the Marriage Encounter is that it has unlocked and given notice to a strength too long ignored but urgently needed by the world—the power of loving and communicating couples who see and utilize the goodness of their marriages for the building of a better world.

Don L. expressed this beautifully. "I became aware of the impact of love, and that the deep, personal love you share as a couple should be reflected out to others. This is an ongoing love, given through us to the world. I could see from that weekend what loving your neighbor means in a way I never saw before."

Resources

Any couples or groups interested in more information about Marriage Encounter are invited to contact the national team: Barbara and Armando Carlo, Father Jake Buettner, Marriage Encounter, 5305 West Foster Ave., Chicago, Ill. 60630.

See also:

Antoinette Bosco, *Marriage Encounter, A Rediscovery of Love,* (St. Meinrad, Ind.: Abbey Press, 1973). may be ordered for $4.95 from Abbey Press, St. Meinrad, Ind. 47577.

Chapter 9

The More Joy in Your Marriage Program

Herbert and Roberta Otto

MARRIAGE ENRICHMENT PROGRAMS ARE A MEANS FOR extending the vision of possibilities inherent in every marriage. Since so few models exist in our contemporary society of what a "good" marriage is, marriage enrichment provides a way of exploring and expanding our concepts. The marriage enrichment experience is a time of pooling resources, sharing experiences, and growing together and separately as couples and individuals. The effect on the couple is not only to enrich their relationship, but also to enlarge their own concept of themselves and their relationship to other members of the family. We therefore see marriage enrichment as family enrichment and, in a much broader sense, "society enrichment" as well.

We feel that, after a period of time, every relationship is in need of some enrichment and rejuvenation, for relationships sooner or later become bogged down in routines, habits, and daily pressures. The need to step aside and take a look at the relationship together then becomes a valuable and strengthening experience that usually leads to better communication, better understanding, and greater love, respect, and appreciation of the other. In addition to helping the relationship to be a source of growth and joy, such programs also have a strong preventive thrust in strengthening the union, before major difficulties arise.

The More Joy in Your Marriage program has gone through many changes and evolutions since its beginnings in 1961.[1] The very first program focused on helping participants to enlarge their awareness of family, marriage, and individual strengths. At that time the program was known as the Family Resource Development Program: The Key to Family Enrichment. This focus has been maintained today, although the means and methods used are different. In the mid-sixties a number of additional group methods designed to actualize human potential[2] were incorporated in the program. New methods, techniques, and approaches specifically designed to strengthen marriage and family life were in the field-testing stage of development throughout this time. The book *More Joy in Your Marriage*[3] resulted from this work. In 1968 the first ongoing class, the

Downers Grove Couples Group, was conducted in Illinois with a colleague, Dr. Lacey Hall, as co-leader.

By the time *More Joy in Your Marriage* was published in 1969, the program had gone through further changes as new and more effective approaches were incorporated. This has continued until the present. The writers have also been engaged in conducting leadership training programs for couples interested in leading marriage and family enrichment programs. Over the years we have received many requests for a Phase II or follow-up program. This is now in the process of being developed.

The More Joy in Your Marriage Weekend Program: Rationale and Theoretical Considerations

Our program is fairly structured in the sense that a sequence of specific experiences is adhered to. It should be made clear, however, that there is much freedom within the structure, and as group needs become evident, shifts in the sequence are made. This schedule usually begins Saturday morning at 9:00 and closes at 10:15 that evening. On Sunday the group meets from 9:00 A.M. to 5:00 P.M.

Schedule
The More Joy in Your Marriage Program

Saturday

9:00	Registration and orientation
9:30	List: "What I See as Our Marriage Strengths" "What Do I Want to Gain From This Workshop?"
9:50	Nonverbal 3 x 3
10:15	The Depth Unfoldment Experience (D.U.E.)
11:00	Break
11:20	Continue D.U.E.
12:00	Lunch break (together)
1:15	Relaxation and Sensory Awareness Experience
2:30	The Sex Stereotype Removal Experience (stranger groups of five or six)
3:45	Break
4:15	Working with marriage habits (individual work, couple work, total group feedback)
6:00	Dinner break (together)
7:30	Mini-lecture on accepting feelings plus recognizing and accepting feelings—a couple experience

8:30   Feedback on preceding experience and group brainstorming on Personality Strengths and Your Strengths Experience

9:15   Break

9:30   The Death in Life Experience
        Alternative: The Positive Feelings Experience

10:15   Close

Sunday

9:00   Feedback in total group and mini-lecture on holistic approach to life

9:15   Marriage strength sharing (group brainstorming on marriage strengths, plus individual work, couple sharing)

10:00   A model for dealing with interpersonal conflict (individual work, couple sharing, group feedback)

11:00   Break

11:30   Primal Sensory Experience

12:30   The Communal Meal Celebration

1:30   The Love Life Development Test (individual work, couple sharing, group feedback)

3:00   Break

3:30   The Marital Minerva Experience (individual work, couple sharing, group feedback)

4:15   Action programs—commitments (couples)

4:45   Evaluation of workshop, farewell

Orientation begins with housekeepings details. At this time we also point out to couples that during the weekend they will be doing some writing. We tell them that we have found that by writing out certain things people are able to "center" more, to become more aware of feelings and issues, and to focus more quickly on what is important to them. As a consequence, the subsequent interaction between people is more dynamic and deeper and less likely to deal with extraneous issues.

During the orientation we also introduce the Fantasy Mural,[4] which we use throughout the workshop. This is a device to enable participants to expand and use their imaginations and creativity. Since messages, poems, and other written material can be included in the mural, it also functions as a communication device. Often a participant will express something by utilizing the mural which he or she is not ready to express verbally in the group at that time. We also use such posters as "Loving Is the Best Way to Celebrate Living" throughout the workshop.[5] During the breaks we play music. The selections are for the most part highly rhythmic, and each piece has a positive message (e.g., Three Dog Night's "Joy to the World," the Beatles' "Things Are Getting Better") We invite participants to dance or to express their feelings by moving to music during the breaks.

At 9:30 A.M. we begin with a written exercise. We distribute pencils and paper and ask participants to write the heading "What I See as Our Marriage Strengths" (or ". . . Strengths in Our Marriage"). Couples are asked to write separate lists, but not to share their lists with their spouses, as to do this would greatly detract from and make less effective an experience using these lists which we will have later in the workshop. We usually give participants five to ten minutes to complete their lists, then ask them to turn over paper and write out the answer to the question "What do I want to gain from this workshop?" Again we urge couples not to share, at this time, what they have written out.

Next we have the Nonverbal 3 x 3 Experience.[6] This serves as an icebreaker, and following the experience, during feedback, we have a natural opportunity to initiate group discussion around two subjects: the function of nonverbal communication in marriage and the role of touching in marriage. We then begin the Depth Unfoldment Experience, or D.U.E.,[7] which, with break, lasts until noon. We have found the D.U.E. to be the most effective experience designed to create a group climate characterized by deep caring, empathy, and open communication.

After lunch we have a session on relaxation and sensory awareness.[8] We will often include the Dynamic Breathing Together Experience.[9] Another possibility is the Baby and Growing Game.[10] This is followed by feedback. We find that participants usually welcome such activities as they help people to tune in on and become more aware of their bodies. At the same time this sensory work effectively deals with the after-lunch sluggishness which sometimes sets in.

Next is the Sex Stereotype Removal Experience, short version.[11] This offers participants a chance to come to grips with stereotypes, biases, and prejudices about the opposite sex, that many do not realize they have. During the feedback period we also have an opportunity to share some of our feelings and concerns about role-functions and sex-roles in marriage. Following the afternoon break, the group works on marriage habits. The Marriage Habit Analysis Chart[12] is put on the blackboard without the "Change Designed to Tap Marriage Potential" heading. Participants are told that they have about fifteen minutes to fill in their charts. They are urged to do this by themselves and not to share what they have written with their spouses at this time. After about fifteen minutes, couples are asked to share their lists with each other and to discuss any change they feel is indicated in relation to marriage habits. The heading "Change Designed to Tap Marriage Potential" is put on the blackboard at this time. Finally there is feedback in the total group from each couple.

Following dinner, the "Mini-Lecture on Accepting Feelings"[13] by the Rev. Paul and LaDonna Hopkins is presented. This is a one-page typewritten sheet which couples are asked to read in preparation for the next couple experience. The couple experience entitled Recognizing and Accepting Feelings[14] is for individual couples. It is triggered by the instruction sheet and takes about thirty minutes. The aim is to help couples become more aware of the role feelings play in their lives and to encourage them to communicate their feelings. After feedback there is a brainstorming session (using the blackboard) on personality strengths.[15] Couples are then asked to sit facing each other for the Your Strength Experience.[16] They write what they perceive to be each other's strengths and then share what they have written. This is perceived as a highly ego-supportive experience by participants.

After the evening break, everyone has an opportunity to participate in the Death in Life Experience.[17] This experience in many instances triggers deep couple sharing about values, the meaning of existence, the role of spiritual values, etc. An alternative last experience of the evening is the Positive Feelings Experience,[18] which is designed to help each of the spouses to become aware of and identify what particular actions or behaviors result in positive feelings. If the workshop is not held in a retreat setting where food is furnished, the Sunday communal meal instructions are given as the last announcement Saturday evening. They are: "Let's make our Sunday noon meal a communal celebration of ourselves and each other. Let's all bring food—any real goodies that you would enjoy, such as fruits, cheeses, salads, breads, meats, and so on. And each couple bring enough for one other person in the event someone forgets. Then we will all have a communal meal together and share the food we bring, family style."

Sometime during the weekend, either before the evening experience or after feedback on Sunday morning, we discuss the holistic approach to life, how everything that surrounds us and everything we do effects us in some way. This understanding, we feel, is basic in determining direction and selection of activity for each person.[19]

On Sunday morning we begin with feedback in the total group. Issues and agendas which need further attention are handled at this time. The blackboard is next used and the group brainstorms marriage strengths.[20] After the material on the blackboard is erased (so that it does not become a copying exercise), participants are asked to look at the papers they filled out Saturday morning, listing marriage strengths, and to write down any additional strengths they feel may be present in their marriages. Following this, couples are asked to share their lists with each other, and feedback from the total group is elicited.

Next, couples work in the area of conflict resolution. A one-page leaflet on "Constructive and Destructive Patterns of Conflict"[21] is given out in preparation for the Rev. Terry Foland's "Model for Dealing With Interpersonal Conflict Experience."[22] This experience takes about an hour and is designed to help the couples acquire some practice in different means of dealing with marital conflict.

After a break, couples are divided into quadrats (two couples per quadrat) and then have the Primal Sensory Experience.[23] This method is designed to give participants an opportunity to explore wider dimensions of caring, and stroking, and to experience trust and dependence/interdependence. It is a deeply nourishing, ego-supportive experience.

Following the communal meal celebration each participant individually fills out the Love Life Development Test.[24] This is an instrument designed to help couples improve communication and to help them achieve greater fulfillment in the area of sexual functioning. Then the couples share their tests. There has been consistent feedback that this sharing is one of the highlights of the weekend for many couples.

Following the midafternoon break we have the Marital Minerva Experience.[25] Participants individually write out "what I consider to be the happiest moments in our marriage" (other than childbirth). Couples share their lists and then begin to plan how they can have more such Minerva experiences. At about 4:00 P.M. we put the following definition of Action Programs on the blackboard: "Action Programs are anything you do individually or as a couple that you feel would strengthen your marriage or actualize marriage potential." Action programs have four characteristics:

1. They are concrete and involve designed action or specific behavior (not generalization like "I will listen more").
2. They can be completed within a week.
3. The first three or four Action Programs must have strong elements of joy and pleasure and be fun to do.
4. You make a commitment to complete them in a week.

Couples are encouraged to develop Action Programs, which are then shared with the total group during feedback. We feel this is a very vital aspect of the More Joy in Your Marriage program, as Action Programs build a bridge to the back-home environment and continue the thrust of marriage enrichment after the couple leaves the group.

Finally we have a written evaluation of the workshop around the following or similar questions:

1. What did you gain from this weekend experience?
2. What was most helpful/least helpful?
3. Any other comments.

We also make this comment during the concluding phase of the workshop: "If you feel this workshop has been of value to you, please tell other couples and spread the word. We will send you announcements of the next workshop to pass out to anyone you feel might be interested."

Some Observations and Conclusions

We strongly believe that it is important to bridge the gap between the weekend experience and back home. To do this we place special emphasis on Action Program commitment, which ensures that the work begun during the weekend will continue. We also encourage exchange of addresses, and, on request, will mail out an address list to all participants. This seems to foster the formation of new friendships and relationships. Whenever possible we will have some books and materials related to marriage enrichment on display or for sale. We have also suggested to couples that they may wish to repeat the marriage enrichment weekend after a year has passed. We share with the group that it is clear from the feedback from couples who have done so that the second experience is like a new experience for most people, since growth and change has usually taken place in the interim. With the organization of ACME, we have literature available and encourage couples to consider formation of a chapter of the Association of Couples for Marriage Enrichment.

All experiences covered during a weekend can also be presented in a series of ongoing classes. Such classes usually meet once a week for two hours. We use the Action Program concept throughout and urge couples to become involved in Action Programs during the time between classes. Refreshments are served, and we encourage couples to set additional time aside following the class so that they will have an opportunity to meet informally and socially with other class members if they so desire. We have found that these informal get-togethers are often extremely valuable.

Occasionally a couple will enroll whose marriage is in serious trouble. In such instances we avoid spending a great deal of time working with them on their problem area, as we believe this is unfair to the rest of the group. We will, however, work intensively with the couple (in or outside the group) in order to effect a satisfactory referral to other sources of professional help.

The More Joy in Your Marriage program has been an ongoing

evolving program over the years. Our philosophy has been to continue to search out, devise, and try new methods and approaches designed to improve the effectiveness of the program. Throughout this time the focus has consistently been on the strength and resources present in the union and on helping couples to develop the potentials in their marriages. It is our hope that this chapter will both serve as a model and stimulate creativity and innovation in the development of marriage and family enrichment programs.

Notes

1. Herbert A. Otto, "The Personal and Family Resource Development Programs—A Preliminary Report," *International Journal of Social Psychiatry*, vol. 8, no. 3 (Summer, 1962), pp. 185-95.
2. Herbert A. Otto, *Group Methods to Actualize Human Potential: A Handbook* (Beverly Hills, Calif.: The Holistic Press, 1970; 3d rev. ed., 1973), pp. 40-44. May be ordered from the publisher, 8909 Olympic Blvd., Beverly Hills, Calif. 90211, $13.50.
3. Herbert A. Otto, *More Joy in Your Marriage* (New York: Hawthorn Books, 1969). Now available only from The Holistic Press (see n. 2 above), $4.50, including postage.
4. Otto, *Group Methods to Actualize Human Potential*, pp. 18-19.
5. *Ibid.*, pp. 40-44.
6. *Ibid.*, pp. 309-12.
7. *Ibid.*, pp. 25-37.
8. *Ibid.*, pp. 315-18.
9. Otto, *More Joy in Your Marriage*, p. 43.
10. Otto, *Group Methods to Actualize Human Potential*, pp. 329-30.
11. *Ibid.*
12. Otto, *More Joy in Your Marriage*, pp. 152-53.
13. This is part of the Leadership Materials Packet composed of all materials described in this article and not found in *Group Methods to Actualize Human Potential* or *More Joy in Your Marriage* or *Total Sex*. Available from The Holistic Press (see n. 2 above), $1.50, including postage.
14. Leadership Materials Packet.
15. Otto, *Group Methods to Actualize Human Potential*, pp. 60-63.
16. *Ibid.*, pp. 274-77.
17. *Ibid.*, pp. 99-106.
18. Leadership Materials Packet.
19. Herbert A. Otto and Roberta Otto, *Total Sex* (New York: Peter H. Wyden, 1972), pp. 349-58.
20. Otto, *More Joy in Your Marriage*, pp. 71-73.
21. Taken from George Bach and Peter Wyden, *The Intimate Enemy* (New York: William Morrow & Co., 1969). Leadership Materials Packet.

22. Leadership Materials Packet. The model is by Terry Foland, Associate Minister, Christian Churches in Illinois/ Wisconsin.
23. Otto, *Group Methods to Actualize Human Potential*, pp. 360-62.
24. *Ibid.*, pp. 228-43.
25. Otto, *More Joy in Your Marriage*, pp. 145-48.

Chapter 10

Marriage Renewal Retreats
Abraham and
Dorothy Schmitt

A SINGLE WEEKEND GROUP EXPERIENCE CAN RENEW A marriage relationship. This is the major lesson we have learned during the past three years conducting twenty-five marriage retreats. The responses of couples have been so positive that we have changed our title from Marriage Enrichment Retreats to Marriage Renewal Retreats.

Much more occurs in the retreats than simply a better adjustment to each other, or just another phase in the ongoing growth process. Very often there is a major breakthrough of insight, a new commitment, or an in-depth experience of each other. To some the weekend means a new marriage, including a new vow. The final moments are often experienced as a mass marriage commitment, which we now call a "Unity of Destiny" ceremony. In the future we may go one step further and call the weekends Marriage Rebirth Retreats—which would in fact fit the personality theory upon which these retreats are built.

Theoretical Base:
Experiential Psychotherapy

The theoretical model for helping in this weekend retreat, as well as the model for marriage and marriage therapy, is built on our interpretation of the philosophy of the founder of experiential psychotherapy, Otto Rank—the third disciple of Sigmund Freud to leave the inner circle. The model also incorporates selected parts of the humanistic psychology of Maslow, May, Moustakas, and Rogers.

The single basic premise of Rankian therapy is that it is the experience itself that heals, not the rationalizing about the experience. This is defined as emotional insight in contrast to cognitive insight. The entire weekend is viewed as a group experience as well as a marriage experience for each couple. The group is directed so as to enable every person to get intensely involved at both of these levels. To facilitate this group process very specific phases are delineated, namely, the beginning, middle, and ending phases. These will be described later.

All of life, according to Rank, is lived in relationship to people. Movement into relationship is an act of union when one discovers his likeness to the other and his likeness to humanity and hence his self-worth. Movement out of relationship is experienced as separation when one affirms his difference from another person or mankind and thereby discovers his identity.

Union and separation are viewed in dialectic relationship to each other, which simply means that each of the two opposites is needed to experience the other. One needs to have discovered his self-worth in belonging to another in order to dare to move out in self-affirmation to discover his difference; and he needs to be sure of his separate individuality to risk a union with another. Personal growth is an act of the will and occurs as one chooses to move in and out of relationship according to his internal need. Marital growth is no exception.

The unique part of this model of personality is the concept of rebirth of the self. With each union a person has to abandon his own will to another's strange will in order to enjoy the brief happiness of belonging to another person. He is then unaware of his own individuality. Such experiences must be short-lived because of the risk of annihilation of the self in the other. The union must be abandoned as the powerful will to grow moves the self on to a new self-affirmation, and a new height of self-discovery. Rank defines each of these later movements as the rebirth of the personality. Since these later experiences form the central core of his personality theory, as well as his therapeutic technique, his whole psychology is most accurately defined as the Rebirth Theory of Psychology.[1]

It is our view that we go one step beyond rebirth psychology by viewing the union that follows each of these experiences as a peak experience. After a person has affirmed his own individuality appropriately for a particular state in the developmental process, he returns to a new connection with a person or persons, only to find a new capacity for deeper encounter and a greater joy in such relationship. Maslow describes one aspect of the peak experience as a union following separation.

> As he gets to be more purely and singly himself he is more able to fuse with the world, with what was formerly not-self, e.g., the lovers come closer to forming a unit rather than two people, the I-Thou monism becomes more possible, the creator becomes one with his work being created, the mother feels one with her child, the appreciator becomes the music (and it becomes him) or the painting, or the dance, the astronomer is "out there" with the stars (rather than a separateness peering across an abyss at another separateness through a telescopic-keyhole).[2]

Conflict-Ecstasy:
A Model for a Maturing Marriage

We have taken the basic premises of the experiential model of personality and applied them to marriage, and have come up with a different model for marriage. We conclude that marital happiness comes as a result of the personal maturation that is possible for two people in a relationship. This is in contrast to the commonly held American notion that "they lived happily ever after" is an automatic gift of one long, endless, total, uninterrupted union received along with the marriage vows. Growth toward fulfillment for two people is the goal of marriage.

To equate intimacy, closeness, and blissfulness with love and marital happiness is only half of the truth of the process of marriage.

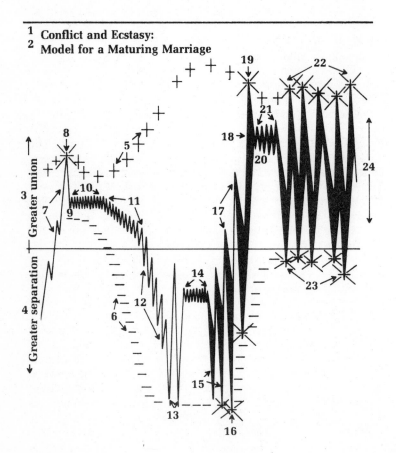

1 **Conflict and Ecstasy:**
2 **Model for a Maturing Marriage**

This first part is essentially the union which is a necessary aspect of the marital relationship.

The other half of the process is usually classified as a marriage problem. We prefer to interpret this aspect as a necessary movement of one or two people who must affirm individuality and separateness within that unique relationship. The marital crisis is nothing other than two human beings screaming to be rescued from a smothering encounter; begging to be helped to discover their own distinctive separation without destroying the partner in the process of declaring their freedom; rather hoping it will be understood as a necessary phase in the development. The more mature couple can pass through union and separation phases without being smothered by the union or devastated by the separation.

The American marriage generally moves through four phases: ecstasy; conflict; ecstasy; freedom. The first ecstasy is the natural part of the romantic model for mate selection. At the peak moment of closeness two people commit themselves in marriage for life. This is a time experienced as intense union, when a couple's total needs for intimacy are met. The main reason for experiencing this phase with

---

Key
1. Conflict-Ecstasy: a dialectic design
2. Maturing: the growth process
3. Union—likeness—self-worth celebrated
4. Separation-difference-identity discovered
5. Deepest unmet intimacy needs
6. Deepest unmet identity needs
7. Courtship: search for a complementary mate
8. Proposal: complementation previewed in ecstasy
9. Wedding: the ritual union
10. Honeymoon phase: an intimate union
11. The emerging differences denied
12. Change mate "into my image"
13. First conflict: resisting the mate's intrusion
14. Temporary truce: conflict unresolved
15. Conflict: deepest differences confronted
16. The final scream for acceptance
17. Yielding to each other's different needs
18. Conflict resolved: each other's uniqueness discovered
19. Second ecstatic union: complementarity realized
20. "Unity of Destiny" ritual: a renewed marriage
21. The second honeymoon
22. Glorious union experienced
23. Separate identity actualized
24. Two people free to be: near and far

such a high ecstasy is that a person really selects his mate unconsciously and chooses his complementary match—the mate who is most likely to eventually bring wholeness to both members.

A gradual process toward conflict begins soon after marriage, as two people attempt to communicate to each other that they are two different human beings whose identities are not to be lost in that relationship. Thus the identity needs become more and more intense and unmet. For most couples these needs can be communicated in no other way than the so-called American Marriage Conflict. If a husband and wife are capable of decoding the identity message that each is trying to communicate, and can then fully accept that message as right for the both of them, they will affirm each other's individuality and open the way for a new union which is experienced as a second ecstasy. A new marriage is now being born.

The immediate aftereffects of such a triple birth (two persons individually, and a marital identity) are beautiful to witness. Many couples then go into a mutual peak experience. This is followed by a sense of freedom—freedom to be close and freedom to separate as each needs it for his or her psychological welfare.

The Renewal Weekend

The retreat model evolves rather naturally out of the theoretical position defined earlier. Ten couples comprise an ideal number for the group experience. Each of the couples is helped to experience the phases of the marriage. The group as a whole also experiences these phases.

We begin the group by telling them that we will stay within the guidelines of marriage as defined in the article that they received by mail at the time of registration. It is a simple four-page printed statement defining our position: *Conflict and Ecstasy: A Model for a Maturing Marriage.*[3] We also distribute a chart (see pp. 112-13) and briefly review the basic premises of the entire model.

After an overview of the marriage model, we have a period of open discussion about the model as a whole, its validity, and its limitations. The general idea we wish to communicate is that this is a model of marriage, not the final answer. It is from the viewpoint of this model that they will experience their marriages in this group.

Each functioning group goes through a distinct beginning, middle, and ending phase. The beginning phase is similar to the courtship, marriage ceremony, and honeymoon. The pleasant coming-together, sharing of primarily positive feelings, and the general atmosphere of congeniality that is experienced together, help overcome the hesitancy and perhaps fear that the couples may have brought with them. Since this is where a group needs to begin, an appropriate task is to re-create what this phase of each couple's marriage was really like. By talking about courtship we experience the courtship period of the group. This has proved to be an excellent group technique to prepare each person in the group to share deeply. What could be less threatening than to share with a group of strangers how and why they chose to get married to each other?

The task is simply and explicitly stated. This method then becomes a model for all later tasks. We instruct each person to recall the specific moment and the exact reason that made each absolutely certain that he or she wished to be married to this spouse. We sometimes phrase the statement this way: "When we were courting, I knew we were meant for each other when . . ." Husband and wife process this information with each other as the group listens. One mate begins by completing the statement, the partner responds to this, and then the process is repeated with the other partner. They may wish to have free dialogue with each other about their mate selection as they now view it. Following each couple's interaction the group is invited to participate with the couple in this experience. This process is continued until all couples have completed the task.

This phase of the group occupies the three-hour Friday evening session. It becomes very apparent that each couple is beginning to emerge as a very distinct pair and that the group as a whole is accepting this difference. An atmosphere of joy and anticipation pervades the room. The pure enjoyment of each other is expressed by repeated outbursts of laughter. This is certainly a period of ecstasy!

The evening ends with the couples being informed that on Saturday we will move into the conflict phase, and that each person should begin to think how he or she would respond to the statement "There is something about our marriage that has bothered me for a long time; I have been meaning to tell you about this, and I am going to do it now." They are requested *not* to share the material that they will use in the group with their mates prior to the group session.

In checking out the group atmosphere on Saturday morning we always find two extremes. Some have continued the celebration of their courtship together after leaving the group and may have spent much of the night talking. Others are very apprehensive about the upcoming task; the conflict phase is preoccupying them.

We very cautiously introduce this Saturday task by returning to the model and clearly telling the couples that the conflict phase is a necessary phase in the growth process. Although they may have never thought of it in this way before, our task today is to prove to them that this can in fact be true. According to this model the struggle in marriage is essentially an effort by two people to affirm their individuality and their hope that this will not be obliterated, but rather will be accepted within that relationship. Conflict is but the agony of a marriage being born, not a symptom of sickness. Just as in all birth processes, there are labor pains.

The middle phase continues throughout two sessions, each lasting from two to three hours on Saturday. The intensity of the group now increases very markedly. Most couples will present to each other the deepest pain and agony of their marriage—to a level that they never dared touch before. Invariably after they complete their individual tasks the healing potential of the group will fold around them and they emerge more whole. They now for the first time understand, through experiencing it, that what may have felt like a "marriage problem" can in fact be a meaningful crisis that can be resolved and actually become a stepping-stone to growth. Then the really positive growth potential of an intense group process is unleashed as some group members spontaneously share similar experiences or discover their own potential to reach out to others who are in pain. As couples trust the group and share their deepest agonies the total group experiences an equal depth of suffering and the subsequent relief as healing ensues. That growth occurs through pain is frequently echoed in these sessions.

To illustrate what has happened during this phase of the group experience we cite this example. A middle-aged couple exhibited extreme bitterness and years of painful and apparently destructive fighting. They told the group very little about these events. They only alluded to the fact that it was horrible, even to the extent that their children has been damaged by the marital conflict. They passed off quickly and without any depth the initial task related to their courtship. Obviously the pain of the marriage made it almost impossible to recall that they had once deeply believed they were meant for each other. They said very little as the seven couples before them processed the "conflict task." However, Mrs. S. would periodically wipe away a tear. I became apprehensive when their turn arrived. To the amazement of the entire group Mrs. S. turned to her husband, took his hands, held them close to her, looked directly into his eyes, and said, "Honey, darling (and that I haven't said to you in twenty-five years), the thing that is wrong with our marriage is that I have been such a bulldozer that I have almost wiped you out. I know I did this in part because I really wanted you to stop me and be a man. I also now know that it all goes back to my childhood home, where everybody was always mowing everybody else down and only bulldozers survived. This has been totally wrong in our marriage, and it is going to stop, so help me God. I want you to be a man, stand up for your rights, but destroying you is not the way to help you."

As she finished her statement of commitment, the tears welled up in his eyes, and then trickled down his cheeks, but he said nothing.

She waited a moment, then threw her arms around his neck, as she gushed out, "Oh, honey, I didn't know you had tears in your head. If I could have seen them before, life would have been so different." The group responded by repeated affirmations such as "Oh, that's beautiful!" When I realized that they had no intention of coming out of the embrace, I asked if we could leave them and return later for the other half of the exercise. They could only signal me to go on without them. For about fifteen minutes they remained cheek to cheek as they silently whispered to each other. When we finally returned to him to pick up the "conflict task," he said he could not do it, since in no way was he going to spoil what had happened between them. Instead he took the occasion to tell the group how terribly traumatic a marriage they had, and that the scene we had all viewed was totally out of keeping with anything that had ever happened during their twenty-five years of marriage.

The following morning one of the other group members teasingly reported having seen this couple go hand in hand into the heavy woods that surrounded the camp, and asked what a couple their age would do in the woods so late at night. Mr. S. responded, "After twenty-five years of marriage of the kind we have had, we had the right to go into the woods and do anything we wanted to do."

For inclusion in this writing I contacted them for a statement of the effect of this weekend upon their marriage during the subsequent year. Their response was simply, "That weekend was the breakthrough of an impossible deadlock. We are now at least working on our marriage, which we could never do before."

For some couples the immediate response to the resolution of their individual conflict sends them into their own private ecstasy, even though the group as a whole remains in the conflict phase. For the Saturday evening and Sunday morning sessions we switch to a very rewarding task. The exercise posed to each couple is: "I have been meaning to tell you that I love you in a very special way because . . ." The mood of the group now turns sharply to mutual sharing of joy as each husband and wife affirm the deepest meaning they have to each other.

An appropriate illustration was one particular couple who caused a lot of agony in a group as they shared phase two. They recalled an endless amount of alienation, and as they spoke even more bitterness emerged. The group was deeply frustrated by their refusal to resolve anything. One group member even attacked the couple. The husband began the final task by resolutely embracing his wife, cuddling her in a way we all knew he had not done in years, and announcing, "We are going to make it!" The group responded with spontaneous screams and clapping. He then told us that the previous day's experience was the beginning of a very meaningful journey which ended in a deep resolution sometime during the night. Many members of the group wept for joy with this couple.

In order to better understand our Marriage Renewal Retreat some background information needs to be included.

We always conduct our retreats as a husband-wife team. To role-model a marriage is in itself valuable. Wives especially express gratitude for the female leader. We are also training couples for leading retreats. They first experience the retreat as participants, then later they join us as co-leaders. All these couples have prior professional training.

Our very different professional development means that we function very differently in the group. I (Abraham) come to this retreat after years of training, clinical practice in psychiatric centers, and private practice in individual, marital, and family therapy. I am a fully accredited marriage and family counselor and an approved supervisor with the American Association of Marriage and Family Counselors. Dorothy has a nursing and college degree with past experience teaching in a college school of nursing. More recently she is mothering four children and constantly participates intimately in my professional journey. Her most valuable assets in the group are an immediate awareness of every aspect of the marriage model, an intuitive sense of group process, and an avid belief in marriage renewal. She brings an insightful feminine view to all the relationships, which many couples accept and rely upon.

Abraham's qualifications need to be elaborated upon, since they have a very decided effect upon the group. He is very definitely trained in and is a believer in humanistic psychology, with an implicit commitment to the potential for change and growth, in contrast to other orientations that focus on the past and on pathology. He received his master's degree, doctorate, and marriage counseling training at the University of Pennsylvania, with emphasis on the theory of growth and change, and a special focus on Otto Rank—the great founder of humanistic psychology. Upon receiving his latest degree he was invited to a joint professorship at the same university, to teach experiential and humanistic psychology in the School of Social Work, the Department of Psychiatry, and the Marriage Council. Since the teachings of Otto Rank were his specialty he soon became a leading authority on Rank at the university and authored several articles on Rank. It is out of this background that he created the model for marriage, a style for marriage counseling, and eventually the renewal retreat. The paper *Conflict and Ecstasy: A Model for a Maturing Marriage* has been reprinted and thousands of copies distributed.

Because of this background and experience, couples tend to respond with an absolute trust that they will be guided through what may arise, since worse situations have been dealt with in the past. Groups tend to move in the direction of group therapy rather than a simple growth group experience.

The fact that we have heard of such positive and lasting results from group members may be largely attributed to the unique qualifications of the leadership team. We have literally been inundated with affirmations by couples, even years later, that one weekend was in fact the birth of their marriage. On several occasions, after participating in a weekend, ministers have declared to their congregations that they did not know the joy of marriage until they experienced a "renewal" weekend.

All of our retreats thus far have been conducted under the auspices of sponsors who provide the facilities and the group members. These have included seminaries, colleges, churches, church conferences and commissions, and retreat centers. Our favorite location is our church center at Spruce Lake Retreat, Canadensis, Pennsylvania, in the Pocono Mountains.

Our most recent contract is with Kirkridge in Bangor, Pennsylvania, a long-established retreat center under the direction of husband-wife Presbyterian ministers Dr. J. Oliver and Jane Bone Nelson.

For the future we envision establishing a more permanent Marriage Renewal Center.

In conclusion it seems appropriate to evaluate the advantages and limitations of this particular style of marriage retreat model.

Although very deeply troubled couples invariably emerge in these groups, the retreat is meant for people who want help in getting into a marriage relationship rather than out of it. As a result this type of group fails to have dialogue with couples who may need help in terminating the marriage. The literature mailed to inquiring couples makes this point very clear in advance. This is a model for renewal retreats, not the final answer to marriages.

The most striking contribution of these marriage retreats is that there is hope for joy in marriage. The fact that the crisis in marriage is interpreted as a necessary phase, and that the style of the group actually enables each couple to "walk through that valley" and emerge on a "mountaintop," communicates overwhelming belief in the future of marriage. The interpretation of marriage as a continuously growing experience, with meaningful high points of intimacy and low points of individuation, is a real asset. This too is built into the group experience.

When Almitra asked about marriage the Prophet responded: "You were born together, and together you shall be forevermore. . . . But let there be spaces in your togetherness."[4]

Union and separation—two really profound psychological concepts that open new possibilities for human relationships—were already familiar to the Prophet.

Notes

1. For further study see Abraham Schmitt, "Otto Rank," in Alfred M. Freedman, Harold I. Kaplan, Benjamin J. Sadock, eds., *Comprehensive Textbook of Psychiatry*, 2d ed. (Baltimore: The Williams and Wilkins Co., 1975).
2. Abraham Maslow, *Toward a Psychology of Being* (New York: Van Nostrand Reinhold Co., 1968), p. 105.
3. A reprint of the article *Conflict and Ecstasy: A Model for a Maturing Marriage* can be obtained at nominal cost from the author at 165 S. Fourth St., Souderton, Pa. 18964.
4. Kahlil Gibran, *The Prophet* (New York: Alfred A. Knopf, 1923), p. 15.

Copies of this article can be obtained from the author (see n. 3 above). Order in the following quantities: 8 @ 25¢ = $2.00; 18 @ 22¢ = $4.00; 50 @ 16¢ = $8.00; 100 @ 12¢ = $12.00.

Chapter 11

Positive Partners:
A Marriage Enrichment
Communication Course
Don Hayward

IT WAS HALFWAY THROUGH THE LAST OF FOUR GROUP sessions. Jack and Lisa—seated on the floor in the hallway—were five minutes over time on a twenty-minute assignment. Their task: to share with each other their individual ratings of their level of satisfaction with seventeen kinds of intimacy listed on an assignment sheet. The other five couples, who had completed the assignment and were waiting for the group to resume, kept poking fun at the slow couple. There was real pleasure in the banter because they all remembered that in the first session Jack and Lisa were able to spend less than two minutes together on a ten-minute assignment. As Jack said later, "We've talked together more in the last four weeks than in the last four years." The scene is typical in Positive Partners.

Some other things we hear frequently in one form or another:

—"After fifteen years of marriage, this is the first time we've ever talked about our sex relationship."
—"The limitation of dealing only with my husband in this group made it more threatening but also forced communication between us."
—"I am just beginning to realize I *can* make changes."
—"For the first time I can fully accept my sexuality."
—"I came the first night prepared to leave if it was an encounter group."
—"I've always known the *theory* of communication. The tools and exercises bring it into workable reality."
—"I thought everyone else's marriage was all sweetness and light."
—"It's really tough—and very helpful—to try to tell her exactly how I wish she would act differently."

A Marriage Enrichment Course
for the Average Couple

There is a certain limited number of individuals and couples who will join almost any group which promises to stimulate personal improvement. There are others who resist such experiences, but who are in such pain that, in desperation, they will enroll in a marriage group to save themselves or their marriages. The vast majority of couples either drift or struggle along in marriages that are from 30 percent to 70 percent as satisfying as they might be—with no realistic vision of what is possible for them in an improved marriage, or any notion of how to go about improving it. Their low motivation is insufficient to overcome the blocks which keep most from joining a marriage enrichment group.

Positive Partners was designed to reduce or eliminate those blocks for the ordinary couple—making their initial experience less threatening, less intense, and less costly, but very effective in improving their relationship. It has these characteristics:

—It focuses on improving communication between husband and wife.

—It deals effectively with real and unreal expectations of marriage.

—It requires a relatively limited time commitment.

—It can be taught by nonprofessionals, possibly volunteers, and is therefore inexpensive.

—It provides a supportive group experience for learning while preserving the privacy of each couple.

—It is presented in such a way as to reduce the resistance of those who fear "encounter groups" or feel that the act of enrolling in a marriage group is an admission of dissatisfaction or failure.

—It is effective in bringing about the positive changes desired by marriage partners.

Our experience and the ratings of participants say conclusively that Positive Partners does these things very well. A Positive Partners group

—has from three to six couples, length of marriage not important;

—has a nonprofessional individual or couple as group leader(s);

—meets from four to six times for two and one-half hours, preferably in homes;

—participates in a series of discussions and communication exercises, with each couple spending about half of each session working privately.

Goals for Positive Partners Groups

These goals are stated clearly at the beginning of the course, then form the bases for measuring changes in the participants' marriages at the end:

—Partners will talk with each other more openly on more topics in and as a result of the series.

—Partners will have some understanding of and practice in using simple tools that will help them to communicate more clearly and forcefully their attitudes and feelings—and solve whatever problems they are aware of.

—Partners will have some tools for evaluating what went wrong when they have had difficulty in communicating.

—Partners will have challenged their realistic expectations of the degree to which a marriage relationship can be continuously satisfying, completely harmonious, and togetherness.

—Partners will have some understanding of the nature of intimacy and how it may be achieved.

—Partners will have had some experience in evaluating their marriage together, setting goals for improving it.

Two Basic Principles of a "Good" Marriage

Positive Partners groups are built on just two basic principles: (1) The marriage is for the partners—for their individual fulfillment—to make life more meaningful and satisfying. It is not for marriage itself, or for society, or even for the children. As part of this, each partner has the responsibility for seeing that the relationship meets his or her needs. (2) Because each individual is unique, each marriage relationship should be unique. Open communication provides the means for this unique relationship to develop.

It follows, then, that *there are no acceptable checklists of a "good" marriage*—and such lists may even impede the development of a couple's own most satisfying way. Even suggestions from other couples on how they solved specific problems may be a distraction.

Course Outline
First Session
—Group building—trust building.
—Goals for the group (Handout Sheet: list of the stated goals for the series):*

- Marriage is for the partners—their growth, satisfaction, fulfillment as individual persons.
- No two marriages are alike—no checklist of a "good" marriage. Each couple must develop their own unique relationship.

—Participants' expectations of the course:
- List—discuss.

*Participants receive a folder in which to collect the twenty-three "Handout Sheets" as they are introduced by the leader.

—Leader's statement of his methods in this group—experiences he expects to provide—which of their expectations he will try to meet:
  • No group encounter—no group-solving of a private problem.
  • Guidelines and ground rules (Handout Sheet: suggestions for participants to make the experience productive).
—Expectations of marriage:
  • Marriage is to meet the needs of individuals.
  • Marriage expectations—hopes (Handout Sheet—couples work alone—asks them to list five expectations of marriage, rate the degree of satisfaction—ten ideals of spouse).
  • As a surprise, ask each to rate himself/herself 1–10 on the ten ideals he/she would like to have in his/her partner.
  • Share in group.
  • What *is* a good marriage?
  • What is realistic?
  • Discuss how much of what we expect of our partners is based upon our ideas about male and female roles. (Refer to their lists of expectations.)
  • Ideas:
    *where do we get our ideals about marriage—what a wife/husband should be like;
    *difficulty of trying to act like our ideals—or act out spouse's ideals.
—Each person write "What I hope our marriage will be like in five years." Share with partner.
—Assign homework (Handout Sheet: tell spouse three things you did today that made you feel good. Describe all emotions you felt today).

Second Session
—Group building—trust building.
—Couples share experiences with out-of-class assignments and other insights or experiences as a result of last week's session.
—Couples alone. Each makes a list of "five to ten ways I tell you I love you" and "five to ten ways I think you tell me you love me." Share with each other.
—It is important in communication to identify your feelings—and to use one or two words to describe them.
  • Each person state his/her feeling right now. (This is repeated occasionally throughout the series.)
  • Make a list of all feelings felt that day.
  • Feelings change rapidly—what this means in relationships with loved ones.

—Active Listening (Handout Sheet: describes Active Listening process, suggests topics):
  - The idea—to fully hear and let partner know you understand.
  - Practice with two couples observing each other.
  - Share experiences with whole group.
  - Ideas:
      *Listening for and seeking things not expressed in words.
      *Experience talking to partner back-to-back, far away, while he/she is reading, touching hands, eyes never meeting, standing and sitting, etc.
      *Discuss: "When do we make time to talk alone?"

—Checking out assumptions:
  - No way to know what another thinks or feels unless he/she tells you in some way. Must be checked out.
  - Each person, with partner, identify (1) some assumption I make about you, that I'm not quite sure of; or (2) some assumption I think you make about me that is not quite true. Share with partner.
  - Demonstrate "Do You Mean" technique (Handout Sheet: describes technique and suggests subjects for practicing).
  - Couples practice "Do You Mean" technique.
  - Share with group; discuss.

—Fill out sex questionnaire (Handout Sheet—to be filled out by each person—questions about past and present sex practices).
  - Assure complete anonymity.

—Out-of-class suggested experiences (Handout Sheet: make a date for one hour of uninterrupted time; discuss one area of marriage you would like to see grow).

Third Session

—Group building—trust building.
—Couples share out-of-class experiences and problems with applying communication methods.
—Purpose of communication skills—to get information to your partner about your feelings, thoughts, desires to bring about more satisfying, fun, fulfilling relations. If these are presented adequately there is a chance for a positive change.
—When there are differences—when needs are not satisfied—what are the alternatives? (Handout Sheet: the inevitability of conflict; seven ways we all deal with it.)
  - Couples sit together and give examples of how they have used each, as leader explains them.
—Resolving differences—to bring about a change:
  - The right time and place to ask for a change.

- Can people change?
- The inevitability of conflict, and the better relationship resulting when there is good will plus some skill in communication.
- Present "Eight Ways to Get More Information to Your Partner" (Handout Sheet describes the eight ways).
- Participants give examples to group as leader explains each.
- Couples practice alone, each partner taking a turn.
- Group discussion.
- Ideas:
  - *Importance of I-Messages.
  - *When is a third party helpful? When a professional counselor?
  - *Win-lose idea not useful (Handout Sheet: chart of win-win, win-lose, lose-lose situations).
  - *To what extent can one partner be responsible for the other's happiness? How much of all one's needs can be fulfilled with one's partner?

—Communication about sex:
  - Present questionnaire results.
  - Discuss reactions.
  - The problem of using any other individual's or couple's standards or actions to judge your own.
  - Danger in idea of performance.
  - Problems of impotence, frigidity, no orgasm, premature orgasm, can usually be solved with minimum professional help.
  - Couples alone (each tells the other):
    - *When I become aware of a desire for sex:
      - *a.* How I feel, become aware.
      - *b.* How I try to make you aware.
      - *c.* Ask: how do you react to that approach?
      - *d.* Ask: what could I do that would make sex better for you?

—Out-of-class experiences (Handout Sheet: the thoughts I have while we are having sex—exploring and pleasuring without having sex).

Fourth Session
—Couples share experiences of the week.
—Opportunity for feedback on unmet expectations of the group.
—Intimacy:
  - Definition: sharing of self and experiences with another.
  - Degree desired and areas to be shared vary. Purpose here to make aware of possibilities and to try some of them.

- Discuss.
- Couple use checklist (Handout Sheet: lists seventeen kinds of intimacy; couples agree on areas of satisfaction and dissatisfaction).
- Barriers to intimacy—list them. Discuss.
- The importance of spaces in togetherness (Handout Sheet: *The Prophet*—Almitra's statement).

—Nonverbal intimacy:
- Experiences (in pairs—touching, being aware, playing, catching, etc.).

—Sharing views on values and important questions (Handout Sheets: suggested exercises).
- Additional Handout Sheets: suggest use during following weeks.

—General discussion: questions, concerns.

—Fill out evaluation form (Handout Sheet: identifies individual changes in goals and practices during the eight weeks).

The course is very flexible; it has never been repeated in exactly the same way. More material is available than could possibly be used effectively, so leaders make choices. A six-session outline is available.

Group Leadership

Positive Partners groups were designed to be led by nonprofessionals with no specialized training in marriage education or counseling. If they accept the philosophy and methods outlined in the *Leader's Manual*, there is little danger of getting into "sticky" marital problems—no more than in the average social situation.

The leader should feel good about his own marriage.

A couple seems to be better than one person, though we have had effective groups either way. The couple, talking openly of their own communication difficulties, along with their positive feelings about their relationship, sometimes reassure and motivate less experienced couples.

Experience in group work and being comfortable in the group leader role, being accepting and nonjudgmental—these are the basics. The rest can be learned by participating in a Positive Partners group. (Special weekend groups to train leaders have been arranged frequently.)

Promoting the Groups

The most effective way of enrolling people in Positive Partners has been through existing church and Y groups. Couples clubs and couples classes seem to produce easily the four to six couples needed for the first group. It works best if one couple invite the group to meet at their home.

The original concept was that Positive Partners would be for couples in their first year of marriage. The plan was to ask ministers as they did premarriage counseling to get commitments for the new couples to participate in a group from six to twelve months after they were married. We have never really tried that, but we are convinced that it will work. We have formed groups from recently married couples referred by ministers.

Acknowledgments

The important contribution of the Rev. Richmond Johnson in the early stages of the development of Positive Partners and the assistance of my wife, Nancy Hayward, and Bob and Lou Prock in testing and revising several models with many groups, are gratefully acknowledged.

Resources

Positive Partners materials may be ordered from the National YMCA Family Communications Skills Center, 350 Sharon Park Dr., Menlo Park, Calif. 94025. Participants' packets costs $3.00 per set; *Leader's Manual* for group leaders, $3.50 per set.

Chapter 12

The Jewish Marriage Encounter

Bernard Kligfeld

THE MARRIAGE ENCOUNTER MOVEMENT WAS BEGUN ABOUT ten years ago in Spain by a Jesuit. Father Gabriel Calvo has become a powerful force in strengthening Catholic marriages. Perhaps hundreds of thousands of couples in the United States and in other parts of the world have been affected. Shortly after the Encounter became established, "encountered" couples began to invite their Jewish friends to attend these weekend sessions. About four years ago, a group of Jewish couples on Long Island started looking for a rabbi and rebbitzin (rabbi's wife) who would serve them in their ongoing Encounter activities as encountered Catholic priests serve the Catholic encountered couples.

I was at that time chairman of the Family Life Committee of the Central Conference of American Rabbis. I had heard about the Encounter, and decided to investigate to see if its techniques and methods could be used for strengthening Jewish family life. My wife and I attended an Encounter weekend, intending to be simply observers. Unexpectedly, we found ourselves caught up in the process. When the weekend ended, we felt that our lives had been profoundly changed. That feeling has persisted for more than three years. Together with the Jewish couples mentioned earlier, and with the help of other rabbinic couples who subsequently "made the Encounter," as well as with the support of the Catholic Encounter movement, we developed what we called Marriage Encounter—The Jewish Expression. In August, 1974, it became a separate entity, no longer structurally affiliated with the Catholic Marriage Encounter. It is now known as the Jewish Marriage Encounter, and maintains fraternal relationships with the expressions of Marriage Encounter of other faiths.

The Encounter is a weekend during which thirty couples gather in a setting where each couple can have a private room and where there is a public room large enough for all to meet together. Talks on a series of topics dealing with what marriage is and what marriage can and should be are presented to the group. Each presentation is made by a "team couple" and a rabbinic couple. The team couple are a husband and wife who, having previously made the Encounter, have continued to use Encounter methods of communication and have completed a special program in which they are trained in the techniques of making public presentations. The rabbinic couple has had a similar experience.

After each presentation, each individual writes a reflection on a question that has been given to all. The question is related to the topic of the preceding presentation. The spouses then meet, in the privacy of their own room, to exchange reflections and to share their feelings with each other. The sharing of feelings follows a special dialogue pattern which is taught during the presentation. After the dialogue, couples return to the central meeting room for the next presentation.

Marriage Encounter, its name notwithstanding, is neither sensitivity training nor group therapy. It is an educational experience concerning the meaning and purpose of marriage and the technique of "dialogue" which can help a couple pursue a new goal. The Encounter is not a group communication. It takes place solely between husband and wife. At only two points during the weekend are participants given the opportunity to share publicly their feelings or experiences.

The Encounter has proven to be very powerful, and its power probably lies in the emphasis on the positive in the individual as well as in the relationship between husband and wife. Generally, most couples come away from the weekend with a sense of emotional and spiritual upliftment, convinced that their commitment to each other has been deepened as well as renewed. In addition, therapists and marriage counselors, as well as rabbis, have reported that the Marriage Encounter has added insight and warmth to their work.

Since the beginning of the Jewish Marriage Encounter we calculate that about ten thousand Jewish couples have participated in the program, and a very large proportion continue their involvement. At the time of this writing no follow-up study has been made from which some "hard" facts may be derived. However, the development of such a study is in progress, and the results will be published as soon as they are available.

What are the goals of Marriage Encounter? The goals of the Catholic Encounter have been expressed by Father Gallagher, leader of the New York Encounter, as follows: "To bring couples closer to the Church and to revive the Church." He sees the Encounter as a means of spreading God's love to all mankind. He envisions encountered couples spreading the message of Encounter to their friends and acquaintances so that the Encounter can grow by geometric progression and in a limited number of years cover the entire globe.

It is not clear whether many of the encountered couples share this view of the goals of the Encounter, but many of the lay leaders of the Catholic Encounter apparently see it as part of their involvement in the church. That is to say, the growing ability of the couple to actively express love to each other, as part of a growing matrimonial unity, enables them to sense the presence of God more positively than it would otherwise be possible for them to do. In living their love as a couple they see themselves as expressing God's love for others and helping to create the loving community which the church should be. Thus, from this point of view, the spiritual aspects of Encounter are absolutely essential. It is the "God" aspect of the Encounter which gives the special concept of marriage built on a religious foundation its power. On the basis of this concept one can be motivated to "give one's all" to the marriage as a foundation platform from which all life with other persons proceeds.

Most couples are originally motivated to make an Encounter by the surpassing experience glowingly reported by newly encountered couples. They want the feeling of euphoria, of "flying high," of renewal of the excitement first felt in marriage. They also want to believe that love, when properly understood, does not grow cold but grows stronger with the years. Others hope to repair the damage they feel their marriages have sustained. Any experience that effects their friends so deeply is probably powerful enough to help them also. Yet others go out of simple curiosity.

The entire program is administered by volunteers who organize the local, regional, and national boards. The volunteers usually have as their goal a high-level maintenance of the interaction which they learned at the Encounter. For this purpose they participate in "renewals" (at which one or another part of the Encounter weekend is repeated), "rap sessions," "image groups" (a small number of couples who meet regularly in homes to experience a deepening of their Encounter), and, uniquely in the Jewish Marriage Encounter, "Havurot" (groups of encountered couples who meet regularly to confront their Jewish identity from the vantage point of the Encounter experience).

The team couples and rabbinic couples who give the presentations on the weekends seek not only to share their experience with other couples and in so doing to strengthen their own sense of the value of the Encounter experience, but also to spread the impact of Encounter as a force to strengthen Jewish marriage and family life. They also seek to achieve the satisfaction of having worked together as a couple in a meaningful activity. They wish to gain from their preparation for the weekends and from participation in them, and from the fellowship of other couples, the strengthening of their own relationship. This latter, it seems to me, is the major goal of the team couples and rabbinic couples who participate in the weekends.

In summary, I would say that the overall goal of the Jewish Marriage Encounter is to strengthen Jewish family life through the strengthening of marriage.

It is important to indicate that the Encounter experience is not aimed at couples who feel they need marriage or individual therapy, but rather at couples who feel they have good marriages, which they can make even better. The general goal is to improve the community through the improvement of the family, and the relationship between family members and those outside the family, and to bring to the community the kind of warmth and openness which a husband and wife develop as they participate in the ongoing Encounter experience.

The Encounter developed out of the family movement in the Catholic Church, which was based on the theory that marriage is a sacrament ordained by God and that functions as a sacrament to the extent that husband and wife become as one. Father Calvo, the Spanish priest who first developed Marriage Encounter, consulted with social scientists and workers in the helping professions, as well as with theologians and church teachers, to develop the original plan for the Encounter. Buber's notion of the dialogic relationship between the "I" and the "Thou" obviously played a most important role in Father Calvo's thinking. If the purpose of the marriage is "communion," then what the husband and wife have to share with each other most profoundly is not thoughts, or concepts, but rather feelings. Feelings are the most intimate part of a person. They represent an innermost core, which is not controlled by an act of will. Actions are controlled by will; feelings just *are*. Therefore, feelings are not to be judged, but are to be accepted, and the process of becoming "one" with my spouse involves being open to her feelings, sharing them, and "feeling" her feelings, reaching out to "taste" and "savor" them.

In turn, her openness to me involves her positive decision to open her innermost self to me, which is her innermost feelings. What prevents these feelings from being shared in ordinary discourse is not only the training we receive in the course of our development to suppress and negate our feelings, but also our tendency to put on "masks," patterns of behavior, thought, and attitude that we unconsciously use to protect the vulnerable inner self, our innermost feelings, from our own and others' awareness. We have learned to devalue our own persons. This devaluation is behind the "masks." As we probe deeper into our feelings we discover that the devaluation also is a "mask." Behind it is a genuine sense of our worthiness, which we dare not face. It would demand too much of us, it seems. In religious terms, this sense of worthiness represents our sense of being "in the image of God."

The philosophic underpinnings of the program are primarily theological and assume the primacy of the family in human life, and, within the family, the overarching significance of the marital relationship. Marriage is not simply a bond between two individuals which happens to have a social function, but it is of cosmic significance in that it enables man to relate to his fellow in the deepest and most profound sense, and to find in such a relationship the echo of what is meant by man's having been created "in the image of God." Man is basically worthy, and has the capacity to behave in a "worthwhile" way. The determination of what is "worthwhile" is made by himself, but religious "sancta" provide man with the best direction for his life. Thus, the Scriptures provide a source of what marriage *should* be, regardless of current moods and modes.

The purpose of marriage is only very incidentally to find happiness and individual fulfillment. More basic is the establishment of a relationship between two individuals, each of whom is a supreme value, such that the relationship itself will become for them a supreme value. This relationship, both theoretically and practically soluble, is ideally permanent and primary in its totality. This kind of relationship can be devastating to the individuals involved if they do not actively work to ensure that the bonds between them are continually strengthened. Persons are often afraid of losing their individuality in "too close" a relationship. However, in a marriage in which each partner has a clear notion of self-worth, it is possible to create a complex unity in which the individual is strengthened rather than lost. The term "love" is very important in this system.

In the Encounter, love is taken to be an action rather than a feeling—an act of will and decision. It is analogous to the action of the pious Jew who daily practices his rituals of worship, regardless of how he happens to feel, because he accepts the commitment to act "in love of God." Thus, one makes the decision to act lovingly or to act in love toward one's spouse regardless of the state of one's fluctuating feelings toward the spouse. The scriptural command "Thou shalt love thy neighbour as thyself" is thus understood, not as a command to *feel* loving, but as a command to act out of a commitment toward the neighbour, who is valued as a person just as one values oneself. "Thou shalt love the Lord thy God . . ." means, therefore, making a decision to act (however one understands the details of what is required) with positive commitment to the relationship toward God. The daily decision to love one's spouse, to act so as to express positive commitment to the marriage relationship, is the method for achieving matrimonial unity.

If one assumes the God-image in man, marriage is a unique circumstance in which one can relate so deeply and profoundly to another individual as to have experience of this "God-image" unreachable in any other way. The growing matrimonial unity of husband and wife, in which their individual distinctiveness is essential, remains, as it were, an adumbration of that "Oneness" which is referred to in "God is One." The unity of God, which is so central to Judaism, is not merely a numerical unity, but is a "Oneness" or unification of the complexity of existence.

It is assumed, in Marriage Encounter, that marriage-matrimony is the human activity par excellence, since the achievement of matrimony, in the sense spoken of above, is a result of decision and exercise of will by persons who have a remote goal in mind, and who are willing to defer present gratification for the sake of achieving that remote goal. It so happens that, in the process, the present, the today, becomes more and more gratifying to the partners.

When husband and wife set their relationship in love as the prime value of their lives, they open avenues of communication with children, co-workers, friends, and even casual acquaintances, which lead to greater warmth and personal involvement. This takes place, not on an absolute scale, but relative to whatever the couple has achieved at any point before entering upon Marriage Encounter.

Outline of the Weekend

The Encounter weekend has what is called a "sweep." It moves from "Encounter with the self" through "Encounter with the spouse," "Encounter with God," and "Encounter with the world." There are ten "presentations," each lasting about an hour. Each is followed by reflection, during which individuals write, in great detail, answers to a question which is posed at the end of the presentation. Afterward the couples meet in their individual rooms for a dialogue, during which time all notebooks are exchanged so that each will read the other's reflection, and then they explore each other's feelings so that each can "taste" the other's feelings. A typical time schedule would be:

> **First night**
> Worship service, Havdala—separating Sabbath from the weekday
> Introduction and first dialogue
> Orientation into the weekend
>
> **First morning**
> Prayers, meal
> Encounter with the self

How marriage is viewed in the modern world
Meal
Areas in which we can reach out to each other
Openness toward each other
What marriage really is
Meal
The importance of confidence and trust
Open-ended dialogue

Second morning
Prayers, meal
Sanctification and the couple
Marital evaluation
Meal
Matrimonial spirituality
The open couple
Information about the community Encounter
Closing service
Departure

Outline of the Presentations

Introduction

The mood is set for a weekend of work and, at the same time, the couples are put at their ease. Their cooperation is solicited in observing "the discipline," which requires attendance at all sessions, and "the gift of silence" during reflection and dialogue periods so that others who are concentrating at the Encounter will not be disturbed. The couples have found notebooks and pens on their chairs for the purpose of taking notes during the presentations and for writing reflections. To begin immediately with the focus on the spouse, and to indicate the positive emphasis of the weekend, we begin introductions by naming an endearing quality of our spouse. It is explained that spouses separate during reflection period so that the writing will be the result of pure reflection and concentration on communication with the other, without interference by the kinds of reactions and responses that are elicited in ordinary conversation. Such responses tend to lead us to censor our production in the light of them. The couples are asked to write on "Why did I come?" and "What do I hope to gain?" At the conclusion of the reflection time they are asked to go back to their rooms, exchange notebooks, read each other's reflection twice, and then share their feelings about these reflections.

Focus on Feelings

Many of the couples come to the Encounter weekend with prejudgments and misconceptions. This presentation seeks to clarify more precisely what Marriage Encounter is, as well as to explain in greater detail the external technique of the Encounter. To understand what a feeling is, is essential to the success of this weekend. The presenting couples explain how to recognize a feeling, and how to avoid confusing feelings with judgments and thoughts. The notebooks are to be used, not for taking ordinary notes, but to write the feelings that the presentations arouse so that these can serve as take-up points for reflection. Feelings are to be written openly and honestly in the notebook during the presentation and personal reflection, and in both the writing and the conjugal dialogue each spouse is to reach out to the other with openness.

The questions given for reflection and dialogue at the end of each talk deal with the feelings each spouse has about the quality in the other, and the quality in both of them together, which he or she likes best. Some typical mistakes in the reflection are pointed out. There is a temptation to solve problems rather than to share feelings; to get rid of unpleasant feelings and dump them on the other instead of trying to share oneself with the other; to change the other person rather than to simply reveal oneself to the other; to write in order to please the other instead of to tell the other one's true feelings; to judge one's feelings and edit them instead of being open and honest.

Some of the barriers to making a good weekend include the following:

—"We have a good marriage; why should we try." (If it is good why not make it better?)
—Intellectualizing—one is afraid of involvement.
—"To show one's feelings is considered wrong." (Without sharing feelings we cannot get close to one another.)

Encounter with the Self

The purpose of this presentation is to lay the groundwork for the matrimonial encounter. First must come an encounter with self, which involves learning how to get behind the "masks" with which we hide from our inner selves.

In Encounter terminology, the "mask" is not simply a facade which we seek to remove, but rather an element of the personality which we justifiably respect and admire in ourselves, but which nevertheless covers an inner aspect of the self from our own view as well as from the view of others. Thus, my "core mask" is usually my best quality. It may be kindness and consideration, or power and strength, or efficiency, or helpfulness. Looking behind these masks, we find them to be devices which "protect" us from confronting our sense of personal inadequacy. To clarify what is meant in the presentation by the teams an incident is chosen from childhood, adolescence, and a most recent time to show how one was made to feel "put down." The listeners are thus enabled to identify and to recall their own feelings of inadequacy. "It is because I consider myself so unworthy," one may say, or "it is important for me to be a good provider," or a ". . . gracious lady," or ". . . controlled in my emotions."

One sign of our own sense of worthlessness is the almost universal inability to accept compliments graciously as though we were worthy to receive them. When we are asked to list our virtues and defects in two columns, we almost always find the list of defects to be much longer than the other. We apply a double standard to ourselves. Virtues must be absolutely perfect. Any imperfection in ourselves we tend to generalize into a defect—a fault. The truth is that the sense of inadequacy is also a "mask," which obscures the fact of our being "in the image of God." No man is "junk." Every human being is an incommensurable value. This value does not depend on his talents, on what he can and cannot do, on his "contribution" to society, but on the very fact that he is human, that he has the qualities of personhood, that he has the capacity to love and be loved, that he can feel.

In the Hebrew prayerbook we address God saying, "The soul which Thou hast given me came pure from Thee." Our "masks" are, then, our shield against our feelings of worthlessness, which in turn hide from us the fact of our supreme worth and value. The question for reflection and dialogue deals with discovering our masks, and how we really look at ourselves.

Marriage in the Modern World

Every one of us is carefully trained for marriage by the impact of his environment, of friends, books, movies, television, etc. We are trained to seek self-fulfillment and to regard love as a kind of possession of the loved one. We think of marriage as a fifty-fifty proposition in which we take out in proportion to what we put in. Our privacy must be respected. Men and women are different. Each must "do his own thing." Marriage must not destroy our pursuit of our personal goals. In this kind of marriage husband and wife are more "married singles" than a conjugal couple. One sign of this kind of relationship is the "nuts and bolts" content of our communication. More often than not it involves the business of the marriage—what to do, how to do, when to do, how to manage. Rarely, if ever, do we share ourselves as persons with each other. We are happiest when the men are doing men's activities, and the women women's activities. We judge ourselves by the marriages we see around us. In the "happiest" marriages the husband is successful and the wife takes care of the house whether or not she works outside the home. The partners do not cross each other too often. They do not quarrel, and present a united front to the world.

In most "good" marriages that follow this plan disillusionment has set in. The marriage originally began with romance. Partners found in each other admirable qualities. Later, these admirable qualities became the source of disillusionment. True joy is rare—true joy being that state in which the couple feels deeply and closely united.

We are disillusioned because the romantic notion of love has not been sustained. We have not replaced it with a more mature and more correct version. The clue of the true nature of love is found in the commandment in Leviticus 19:18, "Thou shalt love thy neighbour as thyself," and also in Deuteronomy 6:5, "Thou shalt love the Lord thy God with all thine heart, and with all thy soul, and with all thy might." Love is commanded here, not as though it were a feeling over which we have no control, but as though it were an act of will, a decision. What is involved is not a decision to be pleasant, but a decision to have a total relationship, a decision to belong, to be total with the beloved.

In the Encounter, the decision to love is acted out in writing a love letter. This includes terms of endearment. What distinguishes a love letter, however, is not the outer form but its inner purpose and the way it is written in order to fulfill that inner purpose. A love letter is written with the beloved in mind, so that whatever is conveyed is conveyed in such a way as to be a reaching out toward the beloved—to the sharing of the self with the beloved. In such a letter even tough and unpleasant feelings can be conveyed with gentleness and love. One strives to share oneself totally with the beloved in such a letter, and one's honest, deep feelings are conveyed—conveyed not to punish, judge, or manipulate, but to share one's feelings with acceptance of oneself and with trust in the other.

Each individual checks a list of symptoms of spiritual divorce and writes to the partner concerning those symptoms about which feelings are strongest. The reflection is written as a description not of what is wrong but of one's feelings about that symptom. The writing is in the form of a love letter written not in criticism, not in judgment, but in openness and honesty, with love and with gentleness.

Some Symptoms of Spiritual Divorce

1. Moods of sadness in the marriage.
2. Feelings of disillusionment, boredom, and emptiness, loneliness in the relationship.

3. Indifference to each other's problems, interests.
4. Occasions of coolness toward one another.
5. Lessening of gentleness and small courtesies.
6. Feelings of insecurity, jealousy.
7. Some feelings of being better understood by others than by one's spouse.
8. Nagging or persistent "bugging."
9. Little planning of things together.
10. Not enough personal conversation—most communication mechanical, routine, and on the surface.

Areas for Reaching Out

In this presentation we concentrate on those goals in our lives which are most private, such as sex and death. In these areas it is most difficult for us to be in touch with our own feelings, much less to share our feelings with others. Different levels of toleration are discussed. First of all, beyond rejection, is the stage of toleration where we are ready to put up with whatever annoys or irritates us in our spouses. The next stage of toleration is when we manage not to be affected by each other and become like "ships that pass in the night." At a still higher stage we have such understanding of our partners' feelings that we agree that we would feel the same way if we were in the same position. The next highest stage is one where we feel ready to make all sorts of sacrifices so that "our partners may continue to feel that way. A still higher stage of toleration is one where we make a positive judgment of our partners' feelings. These are worthy in our eyes. We value them and would not want to change them. On an even higher level we are ready to make all sorts of sacrifices to help our partners feel that way. The highest level which we strive for is acceptance. On this level, without judgments, we can reach out and take into ourselves something of the very feelings which our partners have and are offering to us.

The presenting team describes a series of dialogues on sex and on death which show how in these crucial areas one can reach out and accept the feelings of the other. It is made clear that the reflection and the dialogue have as their purpose not simply to put feelings down on paper but to build a relationship that would flow out of a reaching toward a total awareness of each other. The purpose of the dialogue is not to achieve decisions, not to solve problems, but solely to reach out to each other to feel each other's feelings so that there may be movement toward total mutual awareness.

The couples are given a list of "areas for reaching out," among which are included, in addition to sex and death, money, time, work, children, and relatives. The couples dialogue on those areas in which they have the strongest feelings.

Openness

The purpose of this presentation is to develop the concept of being completely open toward one another. How does one recognize privacy? How does one go about avoiding privacy? In the dialogue, privacy consists in withholding feelings because one fears the reaction of the spouse. The teams describe a series of dialogues which led to the greatest experience of closeness they can remember. Questions that are given for reflection and dialogue include "Where am I being private in not being open to you?" and "Where am I being private in not listening to you?" Also involved in this presentation is the concept of openness as developed in the Jewish religious tradition. So, in Hasidism, the question was once asked: Where does God live? and the answer was given: God lives where man lets him in. When we are open to each other we are also open to God.

Martin Buber taught that in a true dialogue, a true "I-Thou" relationship, the "Eternal Thou" is always present. He tells a story about a student who once came to see him. Buber considered that he was giving the student the best advice he could give him as he tried to listen carefully. Subsequently he discovered that the student had committed suicide. In thinking about the incident, Buber concluded that he had not been totally present to the student. He had not been aware of the totality of what the student was bringing to him. He was convinced that, had he been aware of the student in his totality as a person, as a human being, he could have given him what he most desperately needed at that moment and the suicide could have been prevented.

Openness grows. It is not achieved once and for all. It is sought for, and striven for, in every dialogue, and in the day-to-day relationship with one's spouse.

Marriage and God's Plan

In contrast to the world's plan for marriage, in contrast to the training for marriage which we receive from the world in which we live, there is a plan for marriage that is implicit in our religious tradition. It is expressed in Genesis 2:24, where the man and his wife are to become "one flesh." This has more than sexual meaning. It expresses a spiritual oneness. The goal of marriage in this light is not happiness. The goal is unity. Unity is not just togetherness; it consists of totally and absolutely feeling the beloved. The world's plan for marriage is to be "married singles." What we call "God's Plan" is for a couple to become as one. The progress of such a marriage is expressed in the story of Isaac and Rebecca (Genesis 24:67). When he saw Rebecca, Isaac took her into his mother's tent. She became his wife. He loved her. This is taken to be a reflection of the process of unity. Love is the process of building a unity, not the occasion for marriage. The verse concludes with "He was comforted for the loss of his mother." The comfort we understand to be experienced as a healing which came from the love which they acted out toward each other.

The couples are asked to reflect and dialogue on instances in which they felt closest to each other. These do not need to be the big moments in life. They are to describe not the instances but the feelings of closeness: "Try to re-create those feelings so that the spouse can experience them now."

Confidence and Dialogue

In Judaism the Jew is asked to have *Bitachon*—confidence in God as the lover of man. Confidence is the key to dialogue. Confidence is also not a feeling but a decision—the decision not to be private with the beloved. It is the decision to be open so that the "toughest" feelings can be revealed. The teams describe how they struggle to reveal their toughest feelings to each other. The couples are told that the dialogue is something which is practiced by the teams in their daily lives. It is a struggle, but the struggle is worthwhile. They are asked to dialogue on "What feelings do I have that I find most difficult to share with you?"

Sanctification

The purpose of this presentation is to convey the Jewish concept of marriage which is expressed in the word *Kiddushin*, meaning "sanctification." *Kiddushin* is a technical term which refers to the ritual of marriage, but it implies much more—the raising of the quality of the relationship to a level of supreme value. The quality of the relationship is not an artifact of the ceremony. It is not something imposed on the couple from without, but it is that which grows out of the nature of the relationship—out of the manner in which they live it. So, the story of Isaac and Rebecca, and the order in which the words occur, convey the kind of relationship in marriage which is an ongoing sanctification.

The religious basis for marriage is found in the scriptures "For it is not good for man to be alone" and "They should be as one flesh." The relationship is therefore one ordained by God, and the ongoing sanctification of that relationship is a *mitzvah*, a commandment, which the spouses fulfill to the degree that their marriage is sanctified. The presentation emphasizes the importance of each couple; the relationship of the two human beings is a sacred value, a sanctification. The relationship is not merely one that concerns husband and wife. It is of cosmic significance and is an expression of the basic holiness of life, the awesomeness and beauty of the matrimonial relationship. Every day the decision to love is made. It is not easy. Nevertheless, it is made because there is a goal which can be achieved no other way.

The home is known in Judaism as a *Mikdash M'at*—a small sanctuary, a place where God is sought and his presence can be felt. In marriage we create the Mikdash M'at through the sanctification of our marriages, raising the relationship between husband and wife to the highest value in our lives, from which other values flow. If we are to sanctify this relationship, if we are to build a Mikdash M'at in our homes, we must reevaluate our relationship to all things and focus on the supreme importance and value of our marriages.

This presentation leads to what is called in Marriage Encounter the "matrimonial evaluation." The couples are asked to write extensively on questions which probe very deeply into their conceptions of the meaning of their lives and their feelings about the future. This evaluation comes after the extensive reflections and dialogues that have taken place thus far. The matrimonial evaluation, a three-hour-long reflection and dialogue, is the heart of the Encounter. For most couples it is a profoundly moving "peak" experience which offers the beginning of a new life.

Matrimonial Spirituality

The purpose of this talk is to convey to the couples, following their matrimonial evaluation, how the relationship changes in the day-to-day practice of the dialogue technique after one has accepted the implications of the reevaluation of the relationship of husband and wife which came after the last talk.

Marriage Encounter offers a way of life which is to be practiced every day so that the new attitudes toward marriage can remain alive and find daily expression. The instrument we use is the daily dialogue, including ten minutes of reflection and questions such as those that were presented during the Encounter weekend. To continue the daily dialogue is a struggle, but the daily dialogue is an expression of the decision to love. It is analogous to the practice of *mitzvah*, of the commandment, by the observant Jew, who, out of love for God, practices the rituals that have been given to him, regardless of whether he "feels like it" at the moment or not. Suggestions are given to the couples for ways in which they can pursue the practice of daily dialogue and also how the Scriptures can be used for dialogue. It is emphasized that the dialogue is not an end in itself but is simply a means toward the freeing of ourselves for being total with each other. Matrimonial spirituality implies a new way of life together.

Using "Couple Power"

In this talk the teams share how they have come to spend their couple love and to apply "couple power." Wherever possible they have resigned from non-couple activities and have become involved in the Encounter community as well as in the Jewish community. As loving couples they reach out to their rabbi, their temple, their community to make a loving temple and a loving community. The commandment to love is expressed in "Love thy neighbour as thyself," which requires us to spend our love in the community. A description is given of activities in the Encounter community in which the couple should become involved, and also appropriate activities in temples and local communities.

It should be noted that the above are but brief summaries of the contents of the various talks. It should also be understood that only a complete transcription of a talk would give the reader some indication of its possible effect on the hearer. The only way to "taste" the flavor of the Encounter, at this time, is to experience it personally.

Chapter 13

The Gestalt Perspective: A Marriage Enrichment Program

Joseph C. Zinker and
Julian P. Leon

AS GESTALT THERAPISTS WE VIEW A MARRIAGE AS TWO individuals who have chosen to share the same environments on a frequent and ongoing basis. Their interactions are first and foremost present, with a history of experiences together, and the decision to have future experiences together. Each individual has his/her own individual needs, wants, and expectations which are ever-changing and which may or may not be met by what the other "is," has, or does. If one person wants to get his/her needs, wants, or expectations met by the other, he/she must be aware of what he/she wants and must send a clear message; the other must be aware of that message, and must decide to respond in some way which satisfies the first person. Otherwise the first person can try to rely on coincidence, believe in the efficiency of mind reading, or continue blowing in the wind (because blowing in the wind has its own merit at heart, not necessarily his/hers). The other individual's response depends on his/her awareness, the excitation which that awareness generated, the decision to act on the excitation in some way which is uniquely his/hers, and the contact that results from his/her movement toward or away from the first person.

This paper presents some major theoretical and practical concepts which guide our work with couples. After each conceptual presentation we offer some examples of exercises which we use to facilitate the couple's movement with each other. The examples are meant to underscore the concepts and in and of themselves may be useful to others. We are experimental clinicians and very rarely use "canned" exercises, but rather tailor exercises to fit the emerging picture of the couple's progress. We see couples for varying lengths of time. Consequently, we may use these kinds of exercises in a one-hour individual session, a twenty-hour weekend workshop, or a six-hour diagnostic clinic session. We wish to keep our clients and ourselves alive by being present, fresh, and creatively experimental.

These are some of the values we hope the marriage can have, and therefore we care enough to model those values in our interactions.

Marriage as a System

We view marriage as a system which is a combination of the ever-changing qualities of the individuals involved. Just as the individuals are unique, so is the system they create. When they are each flexible, enlivened, sexual, and oriented, they will produce a system which includes those qualities plus interesting additional qualities which are the products of each individual's own style of asserting those qualities. Their marriage is a creation of their own, open or closed to modifications from themselves and others. They may feel that they are stuck with it, or moving away from it, that it is becoming something as yet unknown, they may feel scared of it, or bored with it. The system is theirs to have and to hold from this day forth, or to change and let go of from this day forth, or any combination of the above. The couple can alter the system as they see fit, agree to, decide jointly or individually, dare to. They can agree (directly or indirectly—the effect is the same) to try to keep their relationship immovable despite the ever-changing quality of the rest of the real world.

Human beings need more than good meals, clean homes, economic security, and a general feeling of stability. For once those things are acquired, people are left with the work and the pleasure of sharing their very beings. People need to stimulate each other's feelings and reach for aesthetic, spiritual, emotional, and physical renewal. Two people can do that for each other if they keep on confronting each other, sharing ideas, and maintaining real contact.

We work with each partner and with their interactions. We try to project their system onto a screen so that they may clearly view their own creation. If they do not like what they see, we become available as resources to help introduce ways for them to experiment with changing their system.

Exercises

1. Each partner lists five distinctive characteristics of himself or herself. The couple are then asked to collaborate in describing their relationship by combining the two sets of characteristics. This gives them a sense of how they function as an integrated system.
2. Ask the couple to view themselves from the perspective of two new friends coming to visit them. As these friends, how would they describe these people?

Marriage as a Dialogue

We view marriage as a dialogue between two individuals. The dialogue is first with oneself, then with the other. One's self-concept is a combination of these two kinds of dialogues.

All of us have a concept of ourselves, an intellectual notion of what we are. Fritz Perls was fond of saying that we try to actualize an image of the self, rather than the authentic self. Our self-concept is often unipolar. Generally we do not conceptualize ourselves as being on a continuum of changing selves. For example, we may see ourselves as honest, certainly not dishonest, and usually not less than honest. We may see ourselves as generous, certainly not stingy, and usually not less than generous. If we envision the full spectrum of polarities in the structure of self as a wagon wheel, the unipolar view of the self takes recognition of only some of the spokes of the wagon wheel and not others. This means that we are limited in our view of the inner self, and because of the limitation we are susceptible to other people's conflicting view of the self.

One may not seek out another who might help one expand one's self-concept. One may instead seek out a spouse who is nonthreatening, approving, and supportive of one's view of oneself, and who therefore thwarts any potential conflict, loss, and even annihilation of one's self-concept. Such fear of loss and annihilation prevents constructive dialogues and creates the kind of environment where nothing seems to be happening. What is happening is a seemingly endless agreement. It is agreement at the cost of real contact. It is lack of differentiation of two ego boundaries. The couple live in the same "psychological body." It is the avoidance of conflict, the spoken "yes" which stifles the felt "no." It is the teetering accumulation of little angers clothed in false smiles. It is confluence which results in silent, deep hatreds.

In a real dialogue there is conflict, the butting up of your edges to my edges. In this relationship we see, and hear, and feel our differences. We touch each other. Living with the other means being in touch with the other. Being in touch, contacting, is not an automatic outcome of loving. It is work. It takes conscious intention.

Conflict is a natural concomitant of living with the other. It is the recognition that two differentiated egos differ from each other and have the possibility of learning from each other. Avoidance of conflict results in a slow, malignant, pernicious undermining of a relationship. Conflict leads to the restructuring of a relationship and, when handled nondefensively and creatively, further leads to growth rather than annihilation. The fear of annihilation prevents constructive dialogues. In the creative dialogue one can abandon one's need to preserve one's status quo, one's esteem, and enter into the world of the other. This kind of exchange usually leads to mutual feeling and mutual regard. Contact, conflictual or not, makes for real-life, gut-level relationships.

Exercise

To husband: Tell your wife ten things you are sure she knows about because you have already shared them with her in the past. For example, "You know that I think you are a generous person because I have told you that a number of times," or, "You know that I feel excited when I am with you because I have shared that feeling with you in the past."

This exercise helps discriminate dialogues which are intrapersonal from those which are interpersonal. What we say in our heads is different from what we say to each other. Being concise, saying it seriously, saying it because it matters are important coaching factors. Reverse the exercise.

Working with the Emerging Situation

Our program conforms with the Gestalt notion of working with an emerging situation. During the first session we may take some traditional kinds of case histories. Later we are interested in history only as it supports that which is going on in the present. We are concerned with what happens in the present as it takes place in the consulting room. So, as an example, if a couple come in and say they wish to work on their financial budget arrangements and, while making that request, seem to be ignoring each other, we will tend to pay attention to their ignoring behavior since it is happening in the present. Our rationale for this approach states simply that what is happening right now is a good indication of what has happened in the past and may happen in the future unless awareness is brought to it. We don't believe that the whole picture can ever be presented. We believe that the picture is never complete but is constantly expanding. This attitude on our part attempts to support the individuals' awareness of their responsibility in dealing with their daily expanding lives, and their awareness that new behaviors are always necessary.

Contact which is disturbed in the present must be improved before we will allow new content to be introduced. We will stay focused on the money management issues for the content if present contact is not disturbed, but we will continually be aware of the process by which they discuss these issues. "Process" communication is of primary importance in our view of work with a couple. "Process" is *how* people say their piece. The content is *what* they say. *What* the individuals are saying may indeed be of secondary importance to *how* they are saying it. We encourage the couples to be constantly aware of their process of communication.

I can convey the same content in a multiplicity of ways. I can say that I disagree with you in such a way as to convey our differences without placing a judgment on your integrity, intelligence, or experience, or I can say it in a way which implies that you are naïve, dishonest, immature, or stupid. I can spout words which indicate interest in you and at the very same moment convey my nonverbal disinterest. I can ask for your opinion and interrupt you each time you begin, by looking away, changing the topic, looking as if you will never have an impact on me, or by hearing you out and talking as if you hadn't said anything relevent. In working, we actively respond to the entire communication, process and content. We respond to the whole spectrum in order to clarify what the communication is *all* about. Since we are interested in enriching the contact that can take place between two people, we explore all the processes and contents that may be interfering with maximum contactfulness. We encourage the couple to use each other's name, instead of "the wife," "she," "her," "you," whether they are talking to each other or to us as the third party. We support eye contact, instead of carpet-, ceiling-, fingers-, cigarette-contact. We will ask the couple to exaggerate their process, e.g., "Turn your back and do not attempt to look at your wife as you talk about the money problems." This will heighten the husband's awareness of his almost absent eye contact. Or, the polarity of heightening his awareness will be the instruction "Sit in front of your wife, touch her hands, and look in her eyes while you tell her about the money difficulties." With the process in mind we therefore concentrate on the sound of the voices (whining, loudness), abruptness or fluidity of language, and relevence of response. We encourage getting to the point and discourage rambling, circuity, lectures, or indirect allusions. We ask each: "Do you like to be screamed at, whined to, seduced by your spouse? What effect does his/her haranguing mode of statement have on you? Do you like to be interrogated as a prosecuting attorney interrogates the guilty party? How does his/her silence affect you?" We intervene in a couple's dialogue in order to pick up and make overt the part of the process which appears to be overlooked, or not overtly responded to.

Exercises

    1. The therapist asks each partner (in turn) to speak in basic Gestalt awareness language intended to bring attention to the ongoing process:

        "Now I am aware of . . . (the expression on your face)."

> "Now I see you . . . (trying to make yourself comfort-
> able in the chair)."
> "Now I think you . . . (are not hearing what I am
> saying)."

2. Therapist: As he (she) is talking to you, pay attention to your
husband's (wife's) voice, and to the way he (she) is
looking at you. How is what he (she) is saying different
from the way he (she) *looks* when he addresses you? (The
therapist may imitate the voice to exaggerate a contradic-
tion between content and expression.)

Criticism, Support, and Confrontation

We are interested in three ways of being with another person in the
present that are necessary for the growth of the relationship:

1. Criticism of past efforts. Each partner needs to feel open to
criticize his or her spouse's behaviors from the past in order for that
spouse to know "how I'm doing with you in our relationship." We
assume that one person's behavior has an effect on another person,
and sometimes the effects are negative. That other person needs to
know about his effect in order to be able to keep up-to-date with the
relationship. He needs to enlarge his nondefensive, self-examining
system, and to hear, re-create, and process such criticism. No system
can grow without feedback and the ability to process that feedback.

2. Support in the present. We need to know how to verbalize
support for behaviors which we enjoy. Some form of communication
is necessary to demonstrate that the spouse likes what is happening.
Just because you tell somebody you love him once, it does not mean
that is sufficient for the rest of his life. We tend to have very short
memories for verbal and nonverbal behaviors which recognize and
respect us for what we do, that love us for who we are. Couples tend
to take each other for granted, and to act as if what has been done for
them is not as important as it really has been. Being critical about the
past without any support in the present is a fine trip to lay on a
masochist. It is also a fine way to play out our sadistic qualities.
However, it doesn't do very much for a nourishing relationship.

3. Confrontation for the future. Confronting has two parts,
criticism and a bridge to the future. Confronting is facing the person
with his own behavior, what it does to you, and, more important,
providing a bridge to the future of the relationship. It's not sufficient
to tell somebody you don't like him for something that he did unless
you wish to create distance between you. Subsequently to criticizing
somebody, you need to tell him you care enough to create new ways
of being in the future. This is the bridge that enables the other
individual to see that even though what is present is not palatable,

new food is being presented which will enhance the relationship later on. With confrontation a relationship can grow. In order to grow, people must continually move beyond the status quo of their relationship. We all tend to stay with the environment that is comfortable, and familiar. Oftentimes we confuse familiarity with comfort. That which is familiar is frequently not comfortable, so we try to have individuals learn to differentiate between comfort and familiarity.

It is important to teach individuals these three basic relating habits before encouraging the use of criticism in the present, and support of past behaviors. Most couples know these last two quite well.

Exercise

Therapist: Tell each other three things that have annoyed you about the other in the past.

Now, share three things which you appreciate and enjoy most about the other.

Now, share three ways you wish the other to remain the same and three ways you want him (her) to change in the future.

(The therapist may introduce the notion of a contract here and ask if they wish to make some firm agreements about changing concrete behaviors in the near future.)

Unresolved Conflict

Conflict often occurs between a husband and a wife when one accuses the other of a polarity which he or she cannot face in himself/herself, and the other, having accepted the unattractiveness of the polarity, counterattacks. Unresolved conflicts between husband and wife usually have the following characteristics:

a. They are stereotyped. Each chooses a role to play out, such as the accused and the accuser, the maligned and the maligner, the winner and the loser.

b. They have a win-lose quality in which one person's victory occurs at the cost of a loss for both.

c. They are usually unimaginative, in spite of the fact that the individuals may be very bright.

d. They are circular. That is, the couple continue to repeat their mutual accusations without being able to get out of the vicious cycle. Instead of trying to stay focused on the impasse, they retrace their steps and start over again.

e. They are often "dirty" and deflective. Each partner hits the other below the belt. An example of a below-the-belt action may be when we are talking about my stinginess and my wife supports her argument by bringing my cousin Charlie into the picture because he is stingy also. Charlie is an irrelevant sore point which cannot be resolved, especially since Charlie is not present.

f. They are generally self-centered rather than problem-centered. By this we mean that each spouse is too busy protecting his/her own self-concept to use his/her creative power in the service of solving the problem that occurs between them.

Exercises

1. The couple are asked to tape-record their arguments at home. They are instructed to listen to the recordings with a specific question in mind: "What is it about the nature of your arguments together that doesn't get either one of you anywhere? What is counterproductive and useless in your conflicts? Please make a list of these characteristics together and bring the results to our next session."

2. We suggest that the couple try to agree on the "facts" that surround one of their disagreements. Thus we heighten the amount of counterproductive energy which gets used up in such an endeavor.

Self-Centeredness vs. Problem- or Other-Centeredness

In order for two individual selves to resolve a problem or conflict between them, they must move from protecting their self-concepts to hearing the other's concept of himself, then to stretching their own self-concepts. In order to do this each individual needs to have a working understanding of the concepts of projections and polarities. Herein lies the creative understanding of a conflictual situation which can make a marriage more exciting.

If we will not acknowledge our polarities and explore them so that we can be fuller human beings, we will act to disown them. Projection is one disowning mechanism. We will not see our own stinginess, but will say our spouses are stingy. We will try to disown those characteristics which we think are unattractive in ourselves. Our disowning attempts often go beyond some real needs to modify objectionable behavior. We are all stingy, or withholding, or sparse in some aspect of our lives, with some people, under certain conditions. Being this way is not necessarily objectionable, but indeed may be wise. It is when we fight so hard to seem generous that we lose perspective of the range of our existence and become less permeable to outside inputs.

Consider another example of the interplay between unassimilated polarities and projection. If we believe that we are always assertive, and cannot recognize or face our own need to withdraw, then we may project withdrawal and even depression on our spouses, and see it as an unattractive characteristic in them. Thus in an argument we may accuse our spouses of being listless and disinterested, and thus disown the varied aspects of ourselves which are related to these characteristics. So what originally started as an internal dialogue between our assertiveness and withdrawal becomes an externalized struggle between ourselves and our spouses.

Exercise

Therapist: You say he (she) is sloppy. Have you ever thought of addressing your own repressed sloppiness? Okay, put your sloppiness in the empty chair and talk with it (or, put your neatness in the empty chair and deal with it, etc.) Now that you understand something about your own neatness (sloppiness), how do you want to talk this over with your spouse?

Creative Conflict—The Necessary Work

A. Letting Off Steam:
Prerequisite of Good Fighting

Before a couple can begin to be problem-centered in their conflict (rather than self-concept-centered), they need to let off steam. In our Gestalt program we may encourage the couple to shout and scream at each other, to exaggerate their accusations, to beat pillows, to push each other, and to participate in any other physically safe activities. Such experimentation gives recognition to the couple's chronic, repressed anger and may not only help them to express their energy, but may also free them to move into a more verbally satisfying state of negotiating issues. Having allowed themselves to express their energy, they may now be able to hear each other's words, and to move beyond the notion of winning an argument. The couple has been launched into the creative conflict situation.

B. "Leaning Into" the Accusation:
Taking Ownership for Your Part

The object of the creative conflict model is to allow each person to see himself in the full range of his polar system. This can be achieved through the technique of "leaning into" the accusation, or experimenting by taking ownership of unwanted polarities. Each partner makes a list of the spouse's irritating characteristics, and they each take turns accusing the other, using these characteristics. The person who is accused is instructed to take ownership of the characteristic, rather than automatically rejecting it. (Far from being a childish introjection, this is a way of trying on for size a new characterization of oneself.) It is explained to him that if he can give his spouse an example of how he *has* been this way, then he may begin to develop a broader view of himself, and at the same time give recognition of the validity of his partner's resentment. Thus, if my wife thinks that I am stingy, because I haven't given her money this week or I've cut down on the amount of money I can give her to take care of the house, then instead of righteously accusing her of not being understanding, or of energetically explaining how generous I am, I would try to support her view of my stinginess in as many ways as I can. Here's a sample of such a conversation:

Wife: You are a stingy bastard. I am broke and you don't care.
Husband: I guess you could call me stingy this week because I simply haven't given you the money I usually do.
Wife: Yes, what the hell is the matter with you?
Husband: Well, I've had a very bad week this week, and I simply haven't got the money to give you; and I can see how badly you must feel, considering the bills that are coming in.
Wife: I hope you realize how insecure I feel when I don't have a few extra dollars in my pocketbook.
Husband   (here leaning into her experience of him): It must be really difficult for you to get into your car and go somewhere without having a few extra dollars.
Wife   (becoming more problem-centered): What can we do about not getting into this fix every few months?
Husband   (following the example of problem-centeredness): Well, I think that every week I should put money in the bank, so that when things get rough I can still give you the money you need.

Leaning into the accusation is not merely a gimmick to pacify your spouse. It is a way of validating his or her own experience of you, as well as a way for you to see yourself as a certain kind of person, even though you do not like to see yourself that way generally. Thus, in this example, the husband can conceive of himself as a stingy person, even though he may have various justifications for not seeing himself that way. In fact, the Gestalt therapist even encourages the husband in this case to give examples to his wife of situations and ways in which he is stingy with her. His stinginess may not be monetary. Stinginess may be expressed in a variety of ways, such as not sharing thoughts or elaborating the wealth of his inner experience with his spouse. It may be his lack of generosity with his language or his refusal to share his work situation with his wife. Thus, by leaning into his wife's accusation of him, he begins to practice seeing the ways in which he impoverishes her experience of him by holding back. In the process, he is able to complete a polarity and see a fuller range of himself, not only as a generous individual but also as a stingy one, not only as an indifferent person but also as a compassionate one, not only as a vain person but also as a modest one, and so on. The outcome is that what began as a bitter conflict between husband and wife slowly develops into an enriching learning situation in which each spouse begins to see him- or herself in a broader, more comprehensive way as a human being.

C. Facing Projections, Another Technique

Our system assumes that the accuser is rejecting in himself the very characteristic which he attributes to the other. Thus, when we ask him to pick another accusation, he must precede it with "As an expert in . . . " before he can continue the accusation. The program of creative conflict requires that the accuser share how he or she is this way himself. Thus, in the above dialogue, the wife would be asked to repeat the accusation by saying, "As an expert in stinginess, I can tell you, Charlie, that you are being very stingy with me." This is a method of taking ownership of the projection. Taking ownership does not mean that the accusation has no validity; it merely assumes that there are no pure projections, and that we see in others, often with clarity, the very characteristics which we are sensitive to and which we have difficulty facing in ourselves. We are allowing the individual, once again, to see the ways in which he has the same characteristic in himself, as well as to receive validation from his spouse. (If I can take ownership of a characteristic, I defuse my spouse's need to righteously defend and counterattack.)

The object of both leaning into the accusation and taking ownership of the accusation by the accuser is to expand the self-concept. If the person can learn to see himself on both extremes of numerous polarities, then his self-concept is "stretched": he has a fuller, broader, richer understanding of himself. He is no longer as threatened when accused by another. He can see himself more objectively. He can rise above the situation and have a better chance of being problem-centered rather than protecting his own esteem, his limited self-concept. Here is an example. The situation is that a person arrives late at a dinner.

Host: John, I'm really pissed off at you. You are very selfish to come so late.

John (leaning into the accusation): I see how you can be mad when I get here after the second course. And I can see how you experience my selfishness.

Host: You *are* selfish. You could have called and told me that you were going to be late.

John: I didn't realize that you had an unlisted number, and I was simply delayed and I couldn't do anything about it. Look, when I really get selfish I don't even give excuses. I hope you can accept mine.

Host   (calming down and seeing the situation more clearly): Well, I'm sorry that you're late, because you missed a damn good dinner.

John: Well, if you will stop punishing me, I will stop punishing you. How can I catch up with you?

In this vignette John could easily have become defensive and have counterattacked the host for not being understanding and for being selfish himself. Instead, the visitor leaned into the accusation and tried to take ownership of the way in which he was seen. This made it possible for the two to talk about the situation and solve the problem with greater clarity.

Exercises

The above sections imply their own experiments. They are built into the discussion. Here are two more. In each example the therapist speaks.

1. *Couple as polarized system*
   "Reverse roles, please—you play the stingy one and you play the generous one. See how that feels. Imitate the other's stinginess/generosity. What did you learn from that?"

2. *Projected, unassimilated polarities of spouse*
   "Imagine that her stinginess has some goodness in it—what might the goodnesses be? Now say that in the first person. Imagine that he is being sued for this characteristic and you are his lawyer. Now defend him—support his world view in the defense."

Conflict Results in Loss

With resolved conflict there is growth. Part of every growth is the experience of giving up and losing, as well as the experience of gaining and finding. We destroy precious preconceptions, and we create enlivening contactfulness. It may be loss of the precious concept that marriage and bliss are one and the same thing. It may be loss of any of one's concepts about oneself or the other. It may be loss of a privilege (getting all your meals prepared), loss of an image ("I am always powerful, I never cry"), loss of an idea ("I thought I was a perfect husband"). To give away means loss; to get means making room for it and changing something in the process. The loss we mention is not always evident, but we make the assumption of its presence.

As an example of loss, when I give up the notion of being a perfect husband, I gain the freedom to make mistakes. When I give up the control of the checking account, I gain the help of shared responsibility.

Exercise

Therapist: What will you lose if you allow yourself to be . . . (powerful, weak, imperfect, etc.).

Standing Alone

In the final analysis love is not eternal, for one of us may leave or die. A loving marriage is not two organisms feeding on each other for sustenance. It is two separate beings, developing in their own idiosyncratic ways, and at the same time touching each other's life profoundly. When the time comes to separate, we can't shrivel up and die. We must assert our individual dignity, power, vitality, and unique integrity.

Kahlil Gibran wrote:

> Give your hearts, but not into each other's keeping.
> For only the hand of Life can contain your hearts.
> And stand together yet not too near together:
> For the pillars of the temple stand apart,
> And the oak tree and the cypress grow not in each other's shadow.[1]

Notes

1. Kahlil Gibran, *The Prophet* (New York: Alfred A. Knopf [1923], 1964), p. 6.

Resources

Fagan, Joen, and Shepherd, Irma L., eds. *Gestalt Therapy Now*. Palo Alto, Calif.: Science and Behavior Books, 1970.

Frantz, Rainette. *Polarities: Differentiation and Integration*. Cleveland: Gestalt Institute of Cleveland, 1973.

Goldstein, Kurt. *The Organism*. Boston: Beacon Press, 1963.

Janov, Arthur. *The Primal Scream*. New York: Dell Books [1970], 1971.

Maslow, A. H. *The Further Reaches of Human Nature.* New York: Viking Press, 1971.

Perls, F. *Ego, Hunger and Aggression.* San Francisco: Orbit Graphic Arts, 1966.

———. *Gestalt Therapy Verbatim.* Moab, Utah: Real People Press, 1969.

Perls, F. *et al. Gestalt Therapy.* New York: Dell Books [1951], 1965.

Polster, Erving and Miriam. *Gestalt Therapy Integrated.* New York: Brunner/Mazel, 1973.

Pursglove, Paul David. *Recognitions in Gestalt Therapy.* Colophon; New York: Harper & Row [1968], 1970.

Reich, Wilhelm. *Character Analysis.* New York: Noonday Press, 1963.

———. *The Function of the Orgasm.* New York: Noonday Press, 1942.

Rogers, Carl. *On Becoming a Person.* Boston: Houghton Mifflin, 1961.

———. "A Process Conception of Psychotherapy." *American Psychologist,* vol. 13 (1958), pp. 142-49.

Zinker, Joseph C. "Dreamwork as Theatre." *Voices,* vol. 7, no. 2 (1971).

———. "Gestalt Therapy Is Permission to Be Creative: A Sermon in Praise of the Use of Experiment in Gestalt Therapy." *Voices,* vol. 9, no. 4 (February, 1974), p. 75.

———. "Marriage: Myth and Reality." Lecture delivered to the Miami Valley Unitarian Fellowship, Dayton, Ohio, 1969.

———. *On Loving Encounters: A Phenomenological View.* Cleveland: Gestalt Institute of Cleveland, June, 1971.

———. *The Phenomenological Here and Now.* Wellfleet, Mass., 1972.

Chapter 14

Transactional Analysis Tools for Use in Marriage Enrichment Programs

Hedges and Betty Capers

IN THE MARRIAGE ENRICHMENT PROGRAMS CONDUCTED BY the San Diego Institute for Transactional Analysis, a variety of techniques are used. These vary with the needs of the group, and there is no structured prior agenda or program which is invariably followed. As an introduction to this work some of the major transactional analysis concepts will be presented and related to specific exercises used in marriage enrichment programs.

Learning to Communicate with Each Other

Transactional Analysis provides a framework within which we can understand how and why we act the way we do. Briefly, Transactional Analysis says that we come on differently at different times. Sometimes we imitate our parents; sometimes we process information like a computer handling data; sometimes, regardless of our age, we come on like a five-year-old child. Each partner in a marriage has this repertoire of behavior patterns, called ego states, at his or her command. Each ego state—Parent, Adult (computer), or Child (when capitalized these words refer to ego states, otherwise to actual people)—has its own particular set of facial expressions, postures, words, voice tones, and attitudes. A person shifts from ego state to ego state, depending on the stimulus. A person in charge of his life chooses which ego state he wishes to be in, while most people allow the stimulus to determine their ego state for them.

The Parent Ego State

Our Parent ego state is made up of mental tape recordings of how we perceived our parents or other important people in our growing-up years. We can get in touch with the behaviors and attitudes we associate with our parents with the following exercise:

Exercise: Your Parents as People
  To get in touch with your Parent ego state, start by becoming more aware of your actual parents.

—Imagine yourself in a room. In the room is audio-visual equipment you can use to replay your Parent videotapes. Include tapes of mother, father, grandfather, step or foster parents, older siblings, housekeeper, or any other persons in authority over you in your childhood.

—Imagine the tapes are labeled according to subject matter. Read each set of questions, then turn on the videotapes to get the answers. . . .

Crisis

—What happened in family crisis such as death, illness, accident, unwanted pregnancy, divorce, or natural calamities?

—Did your parents respond differently to different types of crises?[1]

Discuss the behaviors and attitudes you "inherited" from your parents and which you may be using inappropriately in your own life and marriage.

Other subjects for questions in the above exercise are suggested by Muriel James and Dorothy Jongeward in *Born to Win*; topics covered include money, fun, family meals, and listening patterns.[2]

The Parent ego state has several aspects which can be distinguished from each other. It might be nurturing (taking care of), or it might be critical (sitting in judgment). It might be protecting and giving you permission, or it might be restricting and limiting. The Parent ego state has its own ideas on many topics; when you have reviewed your own Parent tapes on the subjects mentioned above, you might consider how your parents felt about sex, youth, or education. After looking at your parents from this perspective, ask yourself what you do. Do you copy them? Or do you do just the opposite? In either case, you are acting under the influence of your Parent ego state.

Some words and phrases which are clues to indicate when you are in your Parent ego state are as follows:

Critical Parent	Nurturing Parent
Should	Good!
Ought	Ahh!
Childish	Cute
Have to	If you want
Obviously	Splendid
Naughty	It's okay to
Ridiculous	That's all right

Some of these words and phrases may not hold true for you, while others may provide personal clues to your own Parent ego state. We all have the option of relating to people from the Parent ego state; sometimes it is appropriate to do so, but at other times it keeps us from getting what we want. The decision of when to use it can be yours.

The Child Ego State

We all carry in our brains and nervous systems information about how we experienced what we saw and felt as children—and the way we responded to it. Now we have grown-up muscles and vocabulary, but at times we will come on exactly as we did when we were five years old. This is the Child ego state. The part of the Child that is natural and uncensored and untrained still has an archaic residue in the grown-up person. It wants its own way—now! It is loving and spontaneous and fun to be with. Sometimes it is fearful and aggressive. Along with the Natural Child there is an Adapted Child that acts as if someone were watching it—telling it how to act and feel. It is under Parental influence. It uses automatic patterns of behavior to get attention from the important people in its life. If the Child ego state is repressed or blocked off, it may express itself in inappropriate ways and cause trouble for us. Couples can use the following exercises to get information about their own Child ego states. Remember that insight comes with the gathering of data and the experiencing of emotional awareness through self-discovery.

Exercise: The Child in You Now

Try to discover what currently activates your Child ego state. Begin by becoming aware of how you act:

—when under stress, sick, tired, disappointed, etc.

—when someone "comes on Parent" to you.

—when the Child in another person provokes or invites the Child in you.

—when you go to a party.

—when you want something from someone else.

Next, try to discover if you have a pattern of "coming on" Child inappropriately.

—Do you do or say things that elicit frowns or ridicule from others?

—Do you do or say things that turn people off or embarrass them?

—Are there certain people that you habitually respond to from your Child ego state? If so, why? When you transact with them, how do you feel and how do you act? What responsibility do you take for the nature of the transaction?

If you discover inappropriate Child behavior patterns, explore alternative ways you could act. . . .

Exercise: Your Childhood Adaptations

Think back to the methods—verbal and non-verbal—that were used to train you. Try to compare what you *wanted* to do (i.e., climb on Daddy's lap, stay up late, play outside with the kids) with what you *had* to do (i.e., act stoic, go to bed early, do your chores before playing).

—What words, looks, etc. were used to keep you in line?

—What words, looks, etc. were used to encourage you?

—What limitations were set on your activities? Were these rational and necessary, or were they unnecessarily inhibiting?[3]

Take turns talking to each other about how childhood experiences may be affecting your marriage relationship. Discuss alternative ways of responding to one another that will bring more satisfaction.

Exercise: Letting Your Free Child Out

The free Natural Child in you senses the world in its own unique way. Get back in touch with that Child by focusing on some of the things you liked to do when your only responsibility was to grow up.

Talk with each other about some of the fun things you can do today to free up your Natural Child. For example:

—Lie in the sun, soak it up, feel its good rays on your skin!

—Fly a kite!

—Revel in the water—blow bubbles, kick, splash!

—Eat a popsicle—or a banana split!

—Do anything that was child fun! Like a child, have fun!

As with the Parent ego state, there are some words which often indicate when one is in the Child ego state:

Adapted Child	Free or Natural Child
Wish	Wow!
Try	Fun
Can't	Want
Hope	Let's
Won't	Yippee!

Exercise: Nurturing and Being Nurtured[4]

This exercise helps couples to get in touch with what the Child inside each of them really wants and needs in the way of nurturing; at the same time, they can learn about their own Nurturing Parents.

—Give everyone a large piece of paper, at least 15" x 18", and have them sit on the floor. Toss a lot of bright colored crayons onto the floor and instruct the couples as follows:

—"Using your wrong hand; i.e., the hand you don't write with, describe in short phrases on one side of your paper what you think a perfect Nurturing Parent is like."

—Using the wrong hand will help people to get in touch with the time when they were learning to write and their own nurturing needs were very great. When everyone has finished, have people share out loud with the whole group what they've written on their papers. Ask for additional suggestions not already mentioned. This gives people permission and encourages them to use loving words without embarrassment. Then continue:

—"Turn your paper over and on the reverse side, still using your wrong hand, write the words *you* need to hear from your Nurturing Parent. Avoid any Critical Parent comments, and stay away from comparisons and negatives; e.g., 'You're not ugly' or 'You're the best (or better than) . . . '"

—When everyone has finished, ask spouses to exchange papers and, in a loving, caring, responsive way, to read to one another what each needs to hear.

Below is a copy of one person's nurturing exercise, written during the summer of 1974 at a workshop at the San Diego Institute for Transactional Analysis:

Nurturing Parent Description	Nurturing Parent Messages
Shares feelings with me	You're delightful
Loves me	You're fun to be with
Hugs me	Have fun
Accepts me as I am	You're beautiful
Listens, really listens, to me	You don't have to be perfect
Isn't always right	I love you
Practices with me	How do you feel?
Enjoys things . . . and me	Let's talk
Talks with me	Smile
Reads to me	You have a lovely laugh
Encourages me	I won't ever leave you
Protects me	You can do it
Takes care of me	I'm glad you're you

The Adult Ego State

The Adult ego state is used to test reality. Based on the information it gathers from internal sources (the Parent and Child ego states), as well as external sources, it estimates probabilities. It computes with logic and without feelings. If it has insufficient data, it does not make accurate computations. It must be constantly updated. It doesn't work automatically, but must be plugged in; a decision must be made to use it. *Elegant solutions to problems come from the Adult ego state when it listens to Parent tapes, is aware of Child feelings, and sees the outside reality.* The following are words and phrases which alert us to the Adult ego state:

> It computes
> It works
> Correct
> Who? What? Where?
> How? When? Why?
> Practical

Using Parent-Adult-Child Information in Husband and Wife Problem Solving

Exercise: Six-Chair Technique[5]

In this exercise each spouse has three chairs, one for each of his or her three ego states, with the Parent, Adult, and Child chairs of each partner facing one another. The facilitator is seated at the end, near the Child chairs. Ask for a couple to volunteer to demonstrate this exercise.

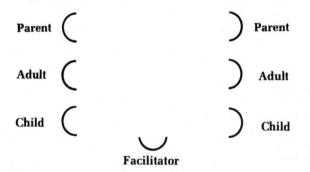

The couple begin by discussing a problem they wish work on; e.g., where to spend vacation, income tax, a mother-in-law who lives with them. As the discussion progresses, they move from chair to chair choosing their ego state in accordance with what they are saying, or feeling, or how they are acting. In this way, the exact nature of the transactions—non-verbal messages, ulterior motives, what's going on beneath the surface—is clarified. If one spouse moves into his or her Parent chair with an evaluation of the other, chances are that the partner will be hooked into the Child chair to respond. Elegant solutions are usually found when both partners are in their Adult chairs. The facilitator acts as monitor to point out ego state changes and suggest chair moves when those changes occur (see above diagram).

This is a practical way to confront husbands and wives with their actual behavior and the positions they are assuming. It is important to remember that with all our ego state options, there are naturally times when we do simply react instead of deliberately choosing our ego state. This doesn't mean we're a total zero or a big washout, but that we are a combination of and reflections of many past experiences, both good and bad. Using the six-chair technique helps people to acknowledge this about themselves without too much loss of self-esteem. It helps a person to strengthen his Adult for its function of examining the Parent and Child data. One can see how tapes "from olden times" can come on to ruin present transactions. Using this technique also enables a person to sort out which ego state he or she is operating from. If that ego state is not working to his satisfaction—not leading to good feelings about himself and others—the person can choose to transact from the ego state which will get him what he wants. Actual moving from chair to chair facilitates awareness of the ego states and their changes. It helps each spouse to own his or her own ego states and, at the same time, it decontaminates the Adult ego state—that is, rids it of Parent prejudice and Child delusion. The Parent often contributes prejudices, unexamined data, such as the following:

—"You always embarrass me in front of people."
—"You never listen to me."
—"No one ever does anything right around here."

The above statements may seem like factual material, but in reality they are Parent evaluations. The Child may also contaminate the Adult by passing off feelings as facts and creating delusions:

—"I can't do anything."
—"Nobody likes me."
—"I'll never make it."

The six-chair technique is also an effective means of negotiating or renegotiating marriage contracts. *We believe that it is important for a husband and wife to regularly examine their marriage contract and to update it when necessary.*

A person may operate from one ego state more often than from the other ego states, to his loss. Such a person has not taken charge of his life and is probably coming on Critical Parent or Adapted Child a good deal of the time. This not only leads to bad feelings about oneself, but also enhances the neurotic and locked-in relationship with one's spouse. There seems to be a correlation between Critical Parent behavior and Adapted Child behavior. If one spouse comes on

Critical Parent and sits in judgment of the other ("You're stupid . . ."), the injured spouse will probably respond from the Adapted Child position, feeling confused and inadequate. One invites the other into action. There is also a correlation between Nurturing Parent and Natural Child behaviors. Spouses can nurture each other and invite Natural Child responses. We do have the option to choose to respond from whichever ego state we want. I know a husband and wife who have worked out a system for nurturing. Both work at demanding jobs and get home from work each day about the same time. The one who feels more tired and in need of nurturing speaks up. The other then gives him or her ten minutes of undivided attention—cuddling, caressing, or "strokes" of whatever nature the spouse asks for.[6]

Collecting Good Feelings

Each person in a marriage must satisfy the basic need called stimulus hunger. In Transactional Analysis, a unit of recognition is called a stroke and it is a form of stimulation. Research indicates that babies need physical stimulation (stroking) in order to survive.[7] Later, strokes can be verbal, nonverbal, or physical, and, as a person grows older, he learns to substitute recognition strokes for some of the physical strokes he needs to survive. Words, smiles, any means of acknowledging that you are there, is a stroke. Couples can live together in the same house and yet be deprived of the strokes they need to live. Spouses are encouraged to *look at their stroking patterns*—how they get strokes and how they give them. If they were brought up on good, loving, positive strokes, these are the ones they will want as adults. If the strokes were conditional ones ("I love you if . . ." or ". . . for what you did" or ". . . if you got . . ."), or if they were negative ones (beatings, put-downs, "You're not worth loving"), then these are the kind they will go after as adults. These were the strokes which meant survival as a child, and they will continue to seek them until insight or example shows them a better way to live.

An important point is that *each partner in the marriage should assume the responsibility for getting what he wants and needs*, that he should not expect his spouse to read his mind; loving someone does not mean knowing just how he feels or exactly what he wants. It is believing in magic to think that someone can read another's mind and know what he wants. It is also important to ask for strokes in straight ways and to reject the idea that asking for something (a stroke) devalues it.

Exercise: Stroking Patterns

Have couples ask each other the following:

—What kind of strokes do you want?

—Do you want to be stroked for achievement?

—From whom do you most value strokes?

—What will you do to get the strokes you want?

—How will you have to change your behavior?

—What do you (will you) do with strokes once you get them?

—Where do you like to be touched? How?

Have couples contract with each other to give more positive strokes.

Exercise: Stroking Philosophies

Have the couples (as individuals, not together) put the following statements in the order which best describes their own beliefs.

1. I believe I can make you feel good.
2. I believe I can make you feel bad.
3. I believe you can make me feel good.
4. I believe you can make me feel bad.[8]

In a recent class we asked some husbands and wives to rank the above statements in order of their importance to them personally and to put their answers on the blackboard. What we discovered was that they usually dovetailed; e.g., those who believed that others could make them feel good had spouses who believed that they could make others feel good. The first statement, "I believe I can make you feel good," takes the position of a Rescuer looking for a Victim.[9] The first person is called a Rescuer because he says things like "I'm only trying to help you" and he feels as though his partner wouldn't make it without his help. When the Rescuer "helps" someone, he is meeting his own needs, not his spouse's; he conveys the message that the spouse is inadequate, while "proving" that he himself is capable and worthy. The Victim is someone who goes along with these attitudes, accepting the idea that he is helpless and inadequate. The second statement, "I believe I can make you feel bad," is made by a person who has critical thoughts of others; he thinks that if there is a problem, it's the other guy's fault. One of his favorite expressions is "If it weren't for you . . ." This is the position of a Persecutor looking for a Victim. A Persecutor is one who bolsters his own self-esteem at the expense of others. "I believe you can make me feel good," the third statement, flips the coin and represents the Victim, in this case looking for a Rescuer. His position in life is "Poor little me." The person who accepts the fourth statement, "I believe you can make me feel bad," is a Victim looking for a Persecutor. His favorite miserable feeling is sadness or confusion, and he expects his spouse to come on angry. Continue the above exercise as follows:

> Discuss with the couples how each of the four statements is an illusion. A person cannot be autonomous, in charge of his feelings and actions, as long as he believes any one of those statements. Have the couple contract with one another to stay out of all three positions—Rescuer, Persecutor, or Victim. This is a big undertaking; it means learning when and how one acts in each of the three roles; it means making a conscious decision to stay out of them; it takes a lot of practice to do so.

What Else Is There?

Intimacy

"The closer people get, the more independent and self-contained their relation becomes. Therefore, the closest relationships are the ones we know least about. . . . Intimacy is a candid Child-to-Child relationship with no games and no mutual exploitation." [10]

Intimacy is a close relationship without games. There is no exploitation. It is a candid Child-to-Child accepting and being accepted, holding and being held, relationship. It is arranged by the Adult ego state of both parties. Contracts, spoken and unspoken, are agreed upon, and commitment results. (This is most apt to happen if both Parent ego states also give permission to be close.) As trust develops, the Parent and Adult ego states gradually retire from the scene, and the Child in each person begins to relax and become free. Intimacy takes place between the two Natural Child ego states, with the Adult as protector in the background making sure that the contracts are being kept and that the Child is protected. Once a person is free from Adult caution and Parent threats, he can experience his Child ego state with elation and awareness and spontaneously respond with trust and without fear.

Exercise: Intimacy

> Spouses sit close to each other and keep eye contact while talking straight to each other for fifteen minutes. The contract is that they do not withdraw, do not engage in rituals or superficial pastiming, do not engage in extraneous mental activity (planning menus or solving other problems), do not play games with each other, do not get into Victim, Persecutor, or Rescuer roles with each other. They stay in present time, in the here and now, and are receptive to one another.

Our experience has been that two people who look at each other, and really see each other, and talk straight with each other, end up liking each other. Lovers spend a lot of time before marriage enjoying each other's face, looking at each other. Contract with yourself to look at your own spouse more often and get those most powerful of all strokes.

"But"

"The key word that prevents intimacy and all the well-being it can bring is B-U-T. 'But' prevents more loving than any other word in the English language, with 'if only' running second. Intimacy is very much a matter of experiencing and enjoying what is here and now. 'But' repudiates here and now, and 'if only' moves it somewhere else or puts it off till later. 'But' means apprehension for the future, and 'if only' means regret for the past. Good sex contributes to well-being because it is right now. Living right now is seeing the trees and hearing the birds sing, and it is necessary to see the trees and hear the birds and know that the sun is out, in order to see people's faces and hear their spirits sing and know that the sun of their warmth is there; and that is the way to attain intimacy. That bright here and now of the open universe out there is what should be before going indoors and living in the closed here and now of each other. For those things to happen, it is first necessary to have a clear mind and to forget for the time being all forms of tedious shuffle: shuffling papers and shuffling people and shuffling things in your head ... it isn't time that is passing, but you who are passing through time—non-stop."[11]

Notes

1. "Your Parents as People" up to this point is taken from Muriel James and Dorothy Jongeward, *Born to win* (Reading, Mass.: Addison-Wesley Publishing Co., 1971), pp. 118-19.
2. *Ibid.*, pp. 118-23.
3. "The Child in You Now" and "Your Childhood Adaptations" up to this point are taken from *ibid.*, pp. 152-53.
4. Adapted from Hogie Wyckoff, "Permission," *Radical Therapist*, vol. 2, no. 3 (October, 1971), pp. 8-10. This article includes several other permission exercises which can be used effectively in marriage enrichment groups.
5. Adapted from Edgar Stuntz, "Musical Chairs," *Transactional Analysis Journal*, vol. 3, no. 2 (April, 1973), pp. 29-32.
6. Muriel James, lecture at San Diego Institute for Transactional Analysis, July, 1972.
7. Rene Spitz, "Hospitalism: Genesis of Psychiatric Conditions in Early Childhood," *Psychoanalytic Study of the Child*, vol. 1 (1945), pp. 53-74.

8. "Stroking Philosophies" is taken from Taibi Kahler, lecture at International Transactional Analysis Association Conference, August, 1974.
9. Stephen Karpman, "Fairy Tales and Script Drama Analysis," *Transactional Analysis Bulletin*, vol. VII, no. 26 (April, 1968), pp. 39-43.
10. Eric Berne, *Sex in Human Loving* (New York: Simon & Schuster, 1970), p. 139.
11. *Ibid.*, p. 230.

Resources

Articles

Karpman, Stephen. "Fairy Tales and Script Drama Analysis." *Transactional Analysis Bulletin*, vol. VII, no. 26 (April, 1968), pp. 39-43.
Spitz, Rene. "Hospitalism: Genesis of Psychiatric Conditions in Early Childhood." *Psychoanalytic Study of the Child*, vol. 1 (1945), pp. 53-74.
Stuntz, Edgar. "Musical Chairs." *Transactional Analysis Journal*, vol. 3, no. 2 (April, 1973), pp. 29-32.
Wyckoff, Hogie. "Permission." *Radical Therapist*, vol. 2, no. 3 (October, 1971), pp. 8-10.

Books

Berne, Eric. *Games People Play*. New York: Grove Press, 1964.
———. *Principles of Group Treatment*. New York: Grove Press, 1968.
———. *Sex in Human Loving*. New York: Simon & Schuster, 1970.
———. *The Structure and Dynamics of Organizations and Groups*. Philadelphia: J. B. Lippincott Co., 1963.
———. *What Do You Say After You Say Hello?* New York: Grove Press, 1972.
Harris, Thomas A. *I'm OK—You're OK*. New York: Harper & Row, 1967.
James, Muriel, and Jongeward, Dorothy. *Born to Win*. Reading, Mass.: Addison-Wesley Publishing Co., 1971.
———. *Winning with People, Group Exercises in Transactional Analysis*. Reading, Mass.: Addison-Wesley Publishing Co., 1973.

Chapter 15

We Call It ACME*
David R. Mace

I ONCE BELIEVED THAT, IF ONLY WE COULD TRAIN ENOUGH
professional counselors, we could cut back marriage and family
failure rates to a level that our culture could comfortably tolerate.
Acting on that belief, I have devoted most of my life to the
development of marriage and family counseling, involving programs
and projects in some sixty countries.

It was only when a heart attack stopped me in my tracks, and gave
me time to think, that I saw at last the irrefutable logic of the old
adage that prevention is better than cure. It became painfully clear
that, as long as our interventions in marital and family dysfunction
were remedial only, we would make only a limited impact on the
state of family life in our culture as a whole. To wait until couples are
in serious trouble is to choose the worst possible strategic ground for
the application of our hard-won knowledge and skill. This seems
eloquently demonstrated by the fact that we now have tens of
thousands of highly skilled and dedicated professionals involved in
marriage and family counseling—and the family is sinking deeper
and deeper in a sea of trouble.

This is, of course, an oversimplification. Marriage and the family,
like all ancient and honorable institutions, are in violent transition in
contemporary society. Besides, not all marriages will work and some
families are best disbanded. Yet when all allowances have been

*Reprinted from *Small Group Behavior*, vol. 6, no. 1 (February, 1975), pp.
31-44, by permission of the publisher, Sage Publications, Inc.

made, the fact remains that large numbers of men and women still want, expect, and hope for a happy and fulfilling marriage. Even the failure of a first marriage finds most of them ready to try again. Enduring dyadic intimacy has been a basic human quest throughout the entire span of recorded history. In legend and the arts alike, romantic love is a recurring theme.

How then, the question presented itself, can we provide married couples with the kind of preparation, guidance, and support that will maximize their chances of attaining the goal they so fervently desire? The logical answer was: "Enable them to develop such good relationships that they will keep out of serious trouble." The next question followed: "But *can* we do this?" The answer to this one was not so clear; but at least I believed we could do very much better than we have been doing—and that was a good enough reason to make a start.

I figured we had now enough *knowledge* to offer real help to married couples. In recent years we have been gathering useful new data about communication, about conflict resolution, about sexual adjustment; but we have not yet achieved much in the direction of *making it dynamically available to couples.* The average American couple are no more able to make use of our present knowledge of marital interaction than is the Indian peasant farmer to draw on the resources of agricultural science. The result in both cases is the same—a miserable yield for much effort expended.

So, we had the resources. But how were we to make them available to couples? That was the toughest problem of all. The fact that finally emerged was so staggeringly illogical that at first I could hardly believe it. The sober truth is that *married couples desperately want to have loving relationships, but fanatically resist attempts to enable them to get what they want!* A more comprehensible way of saying this is that our culture exalts the concept of the happy marriage, and then builds in a series of roadblocks to make sure that very few couples achieve it!

The first roadblock is what Clark Vincent has called the "myth of naturalism." It says, Anyone can make marriage work. You have all the built-in equipment. Just follow your instincts. Only an incompetent fool, a really deficient person, could fail in such a simple task." That's what the culture tells us. It's an unexamined prejudice that persists in the face of all evidence to the contrary. To admit you're having difficulties in marriage ranks as a humiliating confession of failure in an elementary human task.

The second roadblock is privatism. It is obviously related to the first. It says, "Marriage is very private, very personal. Whatever you do, don't ever talk to anyone else about what goes on inside your marriage." To a reasonable degree, this makes sense. There are all sorts of good reasons for taboos. But when a taboo is retained at an appalling cost, it must be reexamined. And this "intermarital taboo," as I have called it, is today doing far more harm than good. It is shutting married couples up together in lonely little boxes where in their fumbling ignorance they destroy the very things they most desire. They are allowed to break out and seek help only when so much havoc has been wrought that the counselors to whom they turn can often do little to repair the ravaged relationship.

A third roadblock is cynicism. You have to sharpen your wits to become aware of the extent to which we are cynical about marriage. Listen carefully, however, to the boisterous jokes, the snide remarks, the subtle innuendoes, that pervade almost any discussion of marriage. Indeed, in ordinary social conversation, marriage hardly ever *is* seriously discussed. It is openly or covertly ridiculed.

So what our culture is saying, in effect, is, "Only a fool would need to *learn* to be married, or would ask for help. However, if you really *must* seek help, don't seek it till the situation is absolutely desperate. And it probably won't be any good anyway, because marriage is a grossly overrated institution."

The problem, therefore, is how to counteract these powerful cultural pressures. How can we get married couples to shed these gross misconceptions, and accept the true facts: that marriage is a deeply rewarding experience when you really make it work; that in order to do so we all need a great deal of training in very complex skills; and that most of us also need the help and support of other married couples in the process?

All this I came to see clearly. It presented a formidable task. Yet it was a task vitally important, because without good marriages you can't have good families, and without good families you can't produce the kinds of citizens who will shape good communities.

My wife and I, after about two years of thinking this through, and talking it over with professionals and married couples, came up with the best answer we could find. We call it ACME. Spelled out, it is the Association of Couples for Marriage Enrichment. But the word ACME has its own appropriate symbolism. In Greek it means the highest peak to which you can climb.

A National Organization for Married Couples

We decided to form a national organization of married couples, because we believed the only way to challenge the taboo was to meet it head on. Most people have not considered the startling fact that never in the world's history, so far as I am aware, have married couples organized themselves in support of good marriage. Yet human beings are incurably gregarious, and in all but the strict taboo areas their natural instinct is to band together round a common interest. Photographers organize to promote photography, astronomers to promote astronomy, artists to promote art, musicians to promote music. Blacks have united, women have united, retired persons have united, to foster their shared interests. Married couples have organized for social, recreational, and religious purposes. They have even united in the P.T.A. to promote their interests as parents. What they have never done is to unite to promote the cause most central to their welfare—the cause of good marriage. That is forbidden territory.

On that forbidden territory ACME has raised a small flag, and calls on married couples to gather round it. We invite couples to support four objectives:

1. To work for the enrichment of their own marriages. Our slogan is "To work for better marriages, beginning with our own."
2. To unite with other couples for mutual support, by planning programs together for marriage enrichment.
3. To initiate and support more adequate community services designed to help marriages.
4. To improve the public image of marriage as a relationship capable of promoting both individual development and mutual fulfillment.

At this writing, ACME has been in existence more than two years. What has happened?

We have established a North American organization with national officers (all couples) and a national headquarters. We have secured encouraging support from all the principal professional organizations in the field of marriage and the family, from many concerned religious groups, and from a number of enlightened public figures. We have appointed state representatives (again couples) in about half the states. We have completed plans for a National Conference on Marriage Enrichment co-sponsored by eight national organizations in the field. We have made contact with groups all over the continent which are developing marriage enrichment programs of one kind or another, and which seem to reflect a genuine grassroots movement to take marriage more seriously.

In two directions our progress has been slow. One is in the area of publicity. The mass media just aren't interested, so we are obviously not news. The *New York Times* put a small notice of ACME's formation on the obituary page one morning, and dropped it in a later edition to make room for the announcement of someone's death. Two leading free-lance writers have tried persistently, and failed, to secure any interest in an article for one of the national magazines. Two interviews written up for prominent daily papers never made it into print. A national newspaper called three times for information, and finally printed nothing. No radio or TV program has shown the slightest interest in the idea of couples uniting in the interests of good marriage.

One other area of slow progress has been the recruiting of ACME members. All our assumptions about the taboo have been abundantly confirmed. Couples generally are very interested in ACME, and curious about it. They often commend us for what we are doing. Some say we have a good idea. But when invited to join, they become evasive and make excuses. They say ACME appears to be an organization for perfect marriages. and they don't qualify. They say their marriages are all right, thank you, and they don't need our help. They say they'll think it over, they haven't the time to devote to it, they can't afford the twelve dollars annual dues. A few tell us honestly that they couldn't face their children, their neighbors, their relatives, colleagues, or friends, because they would be mercilessly ridiculed for joining an organization to improve their marriages.

Nevertheless, couples are joining ACME, in a steady trickle if not a swelling stream. Those who join tend to be unusually mature, purposeful couples who don't mind challenging the taboo. What is abundantly clear is that the whole idea of marital growth and enrichment is so new that most couples have as yet no frame of reference in which to see it in logical perspective. What we find, however, is that once they grasp the idea they become enthusiastic about it. Once an ACME chapter is established in a community, it grows steadily as member couples persuade their friends and neighbors that it is a sound idea.

We are therefore now convinced of two facts: that ACME will inevitably grow; and that it will inevitably grow slowly, through couple-to-couple advocacy. Our concern, therefore, is to develop what we already know to be the best means to promote that growth—couple group interaction.

Relaxing the Intermarital Taboo

The intermarital taboo has locked us into stereotyped patterns of thinking about marriage which are grossly inaccurate just as our taboo on sex allowed a farrago of foibles and fallacies about human sexuality to dominate our thinking. The accepted view of marriage is that it is static—a state, or estate, brought about by the legal contract, which it is the duty of those concerned to preserve in a condition of stability or permanence. Our culture recognizes only two kinds of marriage—good and bad. All marriages are judged to be good when they start, and to continue to be good unless or until they are in such serious trouble that the couple seek counseling help or resort to divorce.

Once a group of couples are able to relax the taboo, however, they soon begin to see marriage quite differently. They discover that the average marriage is neither good nor bad, but a mixture of desirable and undesirable components. They realize that "stability" is an almost meaningless term, because the relationship between marriage partners is dynamic, fluid, constantly changing as they themselves change and as their life situation changes. They begin to perceive that the really important question about a marriage is whether the processes of change taking place in it represent upward growth or downward degeneration. They realize that the guilty, problem-oriented attitude to the inevitable difficulties of dyadic adjustment is quite inappropriate, and that the concept of overcoming obstacles together in a process of mutual growth makes much better sense.

In other words, when groups of married couples, by breaking the taboo, are able for the first time to see the inside of one another's marriage, their whole perception of marriage undergoes significant change. It is for this reason that the marriage enrichment movement, with a few notable exceptions, has found couple group interaction to be its most valuable tool.

ACME, as a comprehensive national organization, recognizes all patterns of group interaction that demonstrably produce marriage enrichment. We are continually studying, comparing, and contrasting the available models to assess their value. Let me report a few of our findings to date.

Broadly speaking, marriage enrichment groups either meet for a continuous and intensive shared experience (usually over a weekend) or for a series of evening meetings once a week. Within one or other of these contexts, we have identified three models, which will be described in some detail in a future publication.

What are the distinctive characteristics of marriage enrichment groups, as compared with other forms of group process?

First, it must be clearly understood that a group of married couples is not a group of individuals, and that the group dynamics involved differ significantly. What we are considering here is a group of subgroups, each of which is a preexisting and continuing social unit. This means greater complexity, because it includes intracouple and intercouple interactions, neither of which play a significant part in groups of individuals.

Second, these are not therapy groups, for it is the general rule that the participation of couples with serious difficulties is strongly discouraged. This means that leadership of such groups can be successfully undertaken by carefully selected and trained nonprofessional persons. The evidence of their effectiveness is reassuring.

Third, the general consensus is that the best facilitators for such groups are married couples who play a fully participative role as members of the group rather than the separate, authoritative role as normally assumed by the therapist. There is much evidence that the leader couple serve as models for the couples in the group, and are "adopted" as surrogate parents.

Fourth, because the objective is not therapy, these groups are not normally problem-oriented. The emphasis is on the growth concept, and on the search for positive methods of moving ahead to new and more rewarding behavior patterns. Some clinicians who learn this are inclined to regard it as manifesting evasion of the real issues. Yet in fact, although therapy is not the goal, a surprising amount of effective therapy does take place incidentally.

Fifth, these are not encounter groups in the usual meaning of the term. They seldom employ confrontation tactics. Negative emotion is not deliberately evoked, though when it emerges, as it inevitably does, it is accepted with compassionate understanding. Care is usually taken, also, to make all active participation entirely voluntary. I can remember one retreat in which a particular couple, after the first introductions, chose to remain interested spectators throughout.

Marital Group Interaction

What processes occur in these group experiences? First, there is the relaxing of the taboo, which becomes possible through the building up of trust and the willingness of couples to make themselves vulnerable. This brings a state of relaxation and openness of the couples to each other. An immediate result is reassurance as couples realize that their supposedly unique difficulties are in fact shared by others. Cross-identifications then develop between couples with similar situations, who tend to get together for deeper sharing outside the group sessions. A great deal of modeling takes place as couples see how others have dealt with, and are dealing with, adjustments currently confronting them. All these processes build an atmosphere of strong mutual support among the couples, who often find themselves forming something like a loving family circle with the leader couple as parent figures. The bonds that unite a group are enduring. When members meet again later they immediately resume the close "family" relationship they experienced at the retreat, dropping the defense systems characteristic of normal social interaction patterns.

We find that these group experiences can bring about a remarkable degree of relational growth and change in a short period of time. The couple's perception of their interaction pattern rapidly gains accurate perspective. They are encouraged to formulate goals for mutual growth, and to take first steps in the direction of achieving them. They see the futility of self-defeating patterns and agree together to abandon them for more creative ways of interacting. This provides a powerful stimulus for continuing the process of change, and later contacts with couples who have really entered into the group experience almost invariably show that marriage enrichment has taken place. It seems that the retreat breaks logjams and gets couples moving again in the direction of marital growth.

Of course, some couples derive limited benefit. These are the ones who are resiting change and growth too stubbornly to be able to move. Or they are couples who have considerable pathology, and should never have come to a retreat. Such couples do get under the wire occasionally despite all our precautions. Sometimes one partner is ready for change but the other cannot cooperate. In some of these situations the leaders are able to refer the couples to professional help. Indeed, couples are often made aware of their need of marriage counseling through the group experience, and later seek it.

Although marriage enrichment groups undoubtedly are powerful agencies for initiating change and growth, it would be unreasonable to see them as a wonder-working panacea. Poor patterns of marital behavior cannot be radically altered in the course of a weekend retreat or a few weeks of participation in a growth group. One of our main reasons for launching ACME was our awareness that the group experience is for most couples a very promising new beginning, but that this alone is not enough. It is true that the fall-out rate following couple groups appears to be far lower than for groups of individuals, because a social unit in which change has been initiated manifests greater momentum for continuity. But it is a fact that most current programs for marriage enrichment function on a one-shot basis, and this I would consider to be unsatisfactory. Worse still are programs which offer so-called "marriage enrichment" experiences of such short duration, so superficial, or so poorly led, that participating couples gain very little and conclude there is nothing more to it.

ACME's goals are long-term, and offering retreats and growth groups is only part of the program. True, we want our couples to have these experiences. But we want them also to become associated, through their local chapter, with other couples who are committed to working toward substantial realization of their own marital potential, and also to providing similar help and encouragement to other couples in their community.

Developing marital potential covers many areas of relationship, and our idea is that the ACME chapter should provide for all of them, combining with professionals to develop comprehensive services. This would mean training courses in couple communication, help in developing successful patterns of decision-making, conflict resolution, sex adjustment, and the like. Some of these services would be organized by the chapter for groups of couples; others would involve referral to marriage counselors and other professionals whose competence had been checked out. The scope of services offered could be widened where necessary to include contraception, natural childbirth, financial planning, real estate purchase, household management, parent effectiveness, and the like.

One of our long-term hopes is that the role of the marriage counselor can be shifted to an increasing emphasis on preventive rather than remedial intervention. Some day every sensible married couple will have their own marriage counselor, just as every sensible family now has its own physician and dentist; and they will go routinely for an annual marital checkup. Why not? The dentists have persuaded us to have our teeth preventively cared for, and surely we value our marriages as much as our teeth? This will mean a radical change in public opinion; yet no more so than has already occurred in the widespread acceptance of family planning, which at one time was bitterly opposed. As ACME develops, we shall ask member couples to volunteer to commit themselves to the annual marital checkup by way of setting an example to others.

It is also our intention to use ACME couples, when they are ready and willing, to help other couples in need. Through marriage enrichment groups we have come to realize the vast untapped potential that lies in the power of married couples, once the taboo has been relaxed, to help each other. We think this can be very productively used.

For example, we are now experimenting with what we call extension growth groups. The concept is to enable two or three ACME couples to interact with perhaps three other couples who can benefit form close interaction with them. One form of this would be a marriage preparation group in which the other three were moving toward marriage. Because of the taboo, young people today have no opportunity to observe effectively working models of the new pattern of companionship marriage which is our emerging marital goal. In such an extension growth group, the engaging couples could observe how warm, loving relationships are achieved, and this could be a better learning experience for them than any other we are able to provide.

ACME couples could similarly be placed in groups with couples in difficulties before, during, or after marriage counseling, under appropriate professional supervision. There are other ways in which they could serve as counselors' aides. One possibility would be for ACME couples to man a "hot line" which a couple in a crisis situation could use to get immediate support, followed up by a meeting with an ACME couple and referral to appropriate professional help. Another possibility would be to move recently divorced persons into a group with several ACME couples, to support them in the post-divorce trauma and help them prepare for later remarriage. An experiment has already been carried out in organizing marriage enrichment groups for married men nearing the end of their prison terms and their wives, to prepare them for the difficult readjustments involved in their forthcoming reunion.

Conclusion

We call it ACME, and it beckons us to climb difficult peaks. Yet it is my conviction that the concept of marriage enrichment, with all its diverse implications, is one of the most hopeful grassroots movements we have seen in a long time. It is directed toward the rehabilitation of the nuclear human relationship that is the foundation of the family, which in turn is the foundation of human society. Father Gabriel Calvo, the Spanish Catholic priest who founded Marriage Encounter, summed it up when he said, "We believe that helping a married couple to form a true community of love, a community open to the love of their children, and to the love of the whole society around them, is really working at the root of things."

Resources

For further information about ACME, write to 403 S. Hawthorne Rd., Winston-Salem, N.C. 27103.

The only book about ACME is David and Vera Mace, *We Can Have Better Marriages, If We Really Want Them*—(Nashville: Abingdon Press, 1974). ACME members receive a bimonthly newsletter, and four supplements on particular topics, each about the length of this article, have been issued: *Provisional Guidelines for Local Chapters; Retreats for Married Couples—Provisional Guidelines; The Case for Marriage Enrichment; ACME and the Professionals*. Copies may be purchased for 50¢ each, including postage. These and other papers are to be published in an ACME Handbook now in preparation.

Chapter 16

The Minnesota Couples Communication Program*
Elam W. Nunnally,
Sherod Miller, and
Daniel B. Wackman

Introduction:
Distinctive Features of the MCCP Program

An excerpt from Session 2 highlights some distinctive features of the Minnesota Couples Communication Program:

Participant A: I heard you make a clear intention statement, Jim, when you told Carol that you would like some time for just yourself when you get home from work.

Participant B: Yeah, he did, and I heard Carol—

Instructor (interrupting): Will you speak directly to Carol?

Participant B: Okay, Carol, I heard you make a clear intention statement when you told Jim that you want some adult companionship after spending all day with the kids.

Participant C: I heard some "checking out" from both; for example, Jim, when you asked Carol whether she thought you were trying to avoid her when you buried your nose in the newspaper, and, Carol, when you asked Jim how he felt about your wanting more of his company in the evening.

Instructor: Did you note the absence of any skills that you would have liked to hear Carol and Jim use in their dialogue?

Participant C: I can't recall either of you saying how you *felt*—no "feeling statements." Carol, I was especially aware of this when you were talking about being alone all day with the kids and then Jim comes home and

---

*Reprinted from *Small Group Behavior*, vol. 6, no. 1 (February,1975), pp. 57-71, by permission of the publisher, Sage Publications, Inc.

starts reading the paper. I was thinking you might
be feeling deprived, or hurt, or angry, or—

Participant D   (interrupting): All of the above.

The excerpt above is from a feedback episode—group members providing feedback to Jim and Carol, one of the participant couples, immediately following a three-minute dialogue between them. The excerpt is from an exercise in which partners discuss a real issue for three minutes and then receive five to ten minutes of feedback from other group members. Feedback focuses on the skills used or missing in their exchange. The exercise occurs toward the end of Session 2, at a point when group members have been introduced to several of the skills and concepts taught in the program. Characteristics of the program illustrated in the excerpt include the following.

Equipping with Skills

The focus is on *skills*, on *process* rather than content. This is an educational program in which partners practice using effective communication skills in dialogue around meaningful issues and receive immediate feedback from other participants on skills demonstrated and skills missing from their dialogue. (If one of the group members begins to offer solutions, or begins to speculate about why a couple is having a particular problem, the instructor will interrupt and encourage the participant to limit his feedback to identifying skills used or skills lacking in the dialogue.)

In addition to skill practice in the group session, structure is provided for *transfer* of learning to situations outside the group, through practice assignments to be carried out at home between group sessions. For example, each participant chooses a particular skill to work on in his communication with his partner during the following week, and at the beginning of the next session the couples report back to the group on their progress.

Dyadic System Focus

In this program the focus is on the dyad rather than on the individual or on relationships among nonpartners in the group. Feedback is addressed to partners about the communication skills and patterns observable in the couple's interaction. This contrasts with an encounter group where the focus may be on a single individual, e.g., how he comes across to one or more other participants in the group.

MCCP groups are composed of "live systems." Each partnership has its own past, present, and anticipated future patterns of relating. Each participant learns with his partner within the context of the system for which his learning is intended—the couple. This feature distinguishes MCCP from programs which partners attend individually in hopes of bringing back something to the relationship. In MCCP they bring their relationship to the program.

Because of its live system characteristic, instructors must have considerable skill in order to effectively lead an MCCP group. The instructor must be able to accept and help partners deal with a range of possibilities which may be experienced within a three-minute dialogue without getting into counseling.

Group Context for Learning

One advantage of a group context for learning—as distinguished from a context in which a couple meets alone with an instructor—is that the partners have an opportunity to receive feedback from peers, from other couples like themselves who are there to improve communication skills. In a warmly supportive peer group, a couple receives encouragement to learn and permission to make mistakes in the process of learning. Another advantage of the group context is that each participant has many opportunities to identify skills used by other participants and to practice giving "useful" feedback. In the feedback episode at the start of the paper, there were several examples of useful feedback: specific skills were identified and descriptive behavioral data reported so that the recipients could know just what the observer saw and heard that led him to identify a particular skill. When a participant offers merely an impression (e.g., "I heard a putdown"), the instructor will ask the participant to report *what* he heard or saw, i.e., what was the impression based upon: "What did you hear Jim say that sounded to you like . . . ?" etc. The many opportunities provided in the group context for giving and for receiving quality feedback serve to heighten participants' awareness of interaction patterns and to integrate skills so necessary for successful relationship work.

Voluntarism

Another characteristic of MCCP is conveyed by the terms "voluntarism" and participant "choice." We assume that learning is most effective when the learning experience is voluntary, that is, when an individual takes initiative for his own learning. Before joining a group, each couple meets with an instructor to discover what the program is designed to teach and to clarify whether or not this is what *each* partner is seeking. If they elect to join the program, the "contract" is for active, conjoint participation of both partners. During the group sessions, participation remains voluntary: at any point during a group session, one or both members of a couple may choose whether or not to participate in a particular exercise or to receive group feedback on their interaction process. Each couple privately reaches a conjoint decision about what the partners are willing to discuss, prior to initiating a couple dialogue for the group to observe and provide feedback.

Objectives and Rationale

The immediate objectives of MCCP are to equip partners with (1) tools for heightening self-awareness, other-awareness, and interactional awareness, and (2) communication skills for creating more effective and mutually satisfying interaction patterns, if they choose to do so. The longer-run objectives are to increase the flexibility of the dyadic system in dealing with change and to enhance the autonomous functioning of the partners. With heightened awareness and with skills to express that awareness, graduates of the program can *choose* to play, to debate, to speculate and openly disclose themselves, utilizing modes of communication appropriate to their intentions at the moment. The program is aimed at equipping partners to become *active agents* in building their relationship, rather than mere responders to events that "happen" to them.

The emphasis on acquiring skills and concepts for building or remaking an intimate relationship results from our conception of couple relationships as ever-changing systems, influenced both by events occurring outside the system (changes of job, residence, financial and social opportunities) and by changes occurring within the system (aging, addition of a new member, changes in value priorities). Our view of the couple relationship as a dynamic, developmental process is reflected in a model of organizational development (see figure, p. 184).

Looking at the phases presented in the model, we view "disruption" as a fact of life, an ever-recurring phenomenon in intimate relationships. If a couple lacks skills for renegotiating, the partners will usually try to return to the way things used to be. They probably cannot return to the status quo, because the disruption introduces new contingencies and new awareness into the system, which, for better or worse, differentiates the system-in-the-present from the system-as-it-was-before. Failing to return to "the way things used to be," some couples resign themselves to a depleted relationship at the expense of personal growth and mutual relational satisfactions, a status which one family sociologist has termed "holy deadlock" (LeMasters, 1959). Another option is to terminate the relationship, an option chosen by an increasing proportion of married couples, usually after some years of alternating between resignation and unsuccessful attempts to create change.

Couples equipped with skills for monitoring interaction patterns, and effectively expressing their awareness, are better able to move

Preventive Maintenance Model for Couples[1]

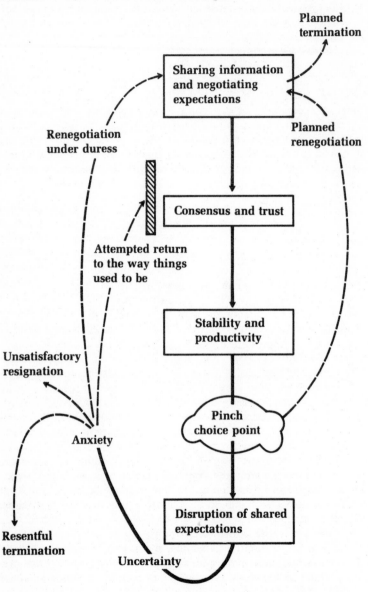

into a new phase of sharing information and negotiating expectations, reestablishing consensus and trust. Furthermore, these couples more often are able to head off a major disruption by initiating "planned renegotiation" when a "pinch" is first noted.

Examples of "pinch" messages:

—"I'm getting to feel more and more envious of all your outside interests, and more and more frustrated about not being able to do something with my college education. I want to do something about it. You up to talking about it now?"
—"I thought your going to work was a good idea, and I guess I still think so in a way; but, I'm feeling overloaded with doing my share of the housework in addition to the extra hours I'm having to put in at the office. I'd like to figure out some way to deal with this."

When a couple lacks ability to identify a "pinch," the partners may enter a period of acting out negative feelings—escalating toward a disruption—instead of disclosing their impressions, feelings, and intentions directly and dealing with the issue explicitly. A relatively simpel *personal* issue (e.g., one partner feeling overloaded with work) is less likely to evolve into a complex *relationship* issue (e.g., who counts most or who decides) when the partners are able to tune in to feelings and wants, disclose these directly, identify the issue involved, and openly discuss alternative solutions.

Origins and Theoretical Bases

Work on the program was initiated in 1968 by a small group of researchers, theorists, and therapists from the University of Minnesota Family Study Center and the Family and Children's Agency of Minneapolis. The project group was influenced by family development theorists (e.g., Hill and Rodgers, 1964; Rapaport, 1963), symbolic interactionism (e.g., Foote and Cottrell, 1955; Foote, 1963; Turner, 1962), and modern systems and communication theory, particularly as presented by theorists working in the areas of marriage, family, and group therapy (e.g., Watzlawick *et al.*, 1967; Satir, 1967; Hill, 1965, 1967; Bateson, 1942; Ruesch and Bateson, 1951).

The family development literature suggested that couples and families move through recognizable stages in their careers together, and that critical role transitions occur as they move from one stage to another, i.e., successful handling of certain developmental tasks facilitates satisfactory transition.

The study team focused on identifying skills and developing skill-training modalities in order to equip couples to meet the challenge of their developmental tasks, to accommodate to change, and even to create change in order to keep the relationship viable over time. Assuming effective communication to be basic to developmental processes, the team turned to systems and communication theory. The literature suggested that the social system which functions most effectively has rules which both define interaction patterns to ensure some degree of stability, and, at the same time, provide procedures for changing patterns to maintain flexibility and to deal with conflict (Speer, 1969; Sprey, 1970). Thus, to provide for both stability and change within the system, the team designed a program around two sets of skills: (1) skills to enable partners to understand their rules and interaction patterns (i.e., awareness skills), and (2) skills to enable them to change their rules and interaction patterns (i.e., communication skills).

MCCP Skills and Conceptual Frameworks

In the first session, participants are introduced to the Awareness Wheel, a framework for identifying dimensions of self-awareness to help them tune into their own self-information. They also learn specific skills for verbally expressing their awareness, congruently and self-responsibly.

Example:
> "I'd like to go out more often with you" (self-responsible—speaking for self).
> *not*
> "You never want to go anywhere!" (overresponsible—speaking for other).
> *or*
> "It would be nice to go out" (underresponsible—speaking for no one).

In the second session the focus shifts to listening skills, skills for facilitating the partner's self-disclosure, skills for assuring that each partner's messages are understood accurately. Three specific behavioral skills are introduced, along with the Shared Meaning conceptual framework for matching messages sent with messages received.

The third session is built around the Communication Styles Framework, which can be used effectively to "step outside" the system and talk about "what's happening." This is a form of verbal metacommunication essential to the process of "planned renegotiation." In the process of identifying the differential impact and utilities of alternative communication styles, couples become more aware of their choices: *what* they communicate and *how* they communicate.

In the fourth session, attention centers on the relation between skills and styles and one's intention to build or to diminish self- and other esteem. One additional framework is presented to help integrate all material presented in the program and to facilitate the creation of patterns for effective work on relationship issues.

Program Format

Groups are composed of five to seven couples who meet with one or two certified MCCP instructors for twelve hours, usually in three-hour sessions meeting weekly for four weeks. Some instructors like to schedule the first three sessions in a weekend retreat, with the fourth session following a week to ten days later. Each session builds upon lecturettes, exercises, feedback, and discussions from prior sessions. A book, *Alive and Aware: Improving Communication in Relationships,*[2] supplements the work carried on in the group sessions and provides a number of exercises to help couples practice at home, thereby transferring learning to their everyday relationship outside the group.

MCCP Instructors and Instructor Training

While instructors do not have to be married, or even teach the program with a partner, many MCCP instructors prefer to co-lead couples groups with their spouses. Leading groups as a couple increases credibility when participants see the instructor couple utilizing the frameworks and skills themselves. Working jointly can provide fun and work; it can also provide opportunities for both partners to join together in helping others to grow.

In MCCP the instructor reduces his own social and psychological distance from the group by doing all the things he asks participants to do. The instructor differs from participants primarily in the number and quality of the roles he is competent and prepared to carry out. As a *member* the instructor demonstrates his involvement by receiving as well as giving feedback. In doing this, he dispels doubts participants may have had about his own personal commitment to growth and development. As a *teacher,* the instructor tries creatively to include participants in understanding and mastering the materials presented. He articulates and demonstrates the goals, frameworks, and specific behavioral skills of the program. The instructor who has personally integrated the conceptual frameworks and the communication skills into his own life senses that he has something to teach and that he is prepared to do so. He shows his own convictions about the usefulness of what he has to teach through his own personal familiarity, comfort, and competence with the material he is teaching.

MCCP instructors represent a number of professional disciplines, including social work, clinical psychology, psychiatry, education, and the ministry. The prerequisite for enrolling in an instructor training workshop, however, is not a professional degree but rather experience and ability in group leadership. The first step toward certification is the completion of a three-day instructor training workshop.[3] Following the training workshop, the instructor trainee conducts three MCCP couples intern groups and secures written evaluations from group participants. Participant evaluations provide an important additional basis for approval or denial of certification. Instructor trainees and instructors are invited and encouraged to attend periodically scheduled review workshops.

Interpersonal Communication Programs, Inc. (the parent organization for instructor training and distribution of materials) does not enter into any franchise arrangements with instructors; hence, instructors are free to serve whom they wish, and they are also free to determine what fee will be charged to couples enrolling in an MCCP course. ICP, Inc., has certain expectations for instructors, but these expectations have to do only with professional competence and responsibility.

Evaluation of the Program

Effects of MCCP were tested in a field experiment. Descriptions of the experiment and the findings are available (Miller, 1971; Nunnally, 1971; Miller, Nunnally, and Wackman, 1974). In brief, the findings indicated that the program increases participants' awareness of dyadic interaction and leads to greater use of communication styles appropriate to work on relationship issues. The field experiment was not designed to assess the long-range impact of communication training on the couples' relationships, and research directed to this issue is needed.

At the present time, assessment of the impact of MCCP on couples' relationships is obtained informally through reports from instructors and from several hundred participants. (Approximately eight hundred MCCP groups have been conducted.) Typical of the positive comments offered by participants are the following:

—"A very effective way of bringing out one's awareness and how to use this awareness in everyday situations. We have learned it is possible to disagree without an all-out fight. The skills can be applied with anyone if I try, and I have had some success with the children, too."
—"This experience has really done wonders for me. I was always taught not to show feelings. I have now been able to

break that barrier and discuss real feelings without fear of being put down."

—"We have learned we don't have to be defensive with each other."

—"More awareness of myself as a separate person, different from my partner. More courage to share this difference. More confidence in myself."

—"Very, very positive changes in our couple relationship and also carry-over to my relations with others. 'Intention statements' were difficult for me, and since the course I can feel comfortable with them."

—"Prior to the program I valued open communication but lacked skills. The program presented me with a framework from which to operate. We now have a 'shared meaning' of what desirable communication is."

—"We are much more secure with each other now that we have a way to work out everyday problems."

—"Frankly, I have been amazed that such 'simple concepts' have been able to help our relationship so much."

Relatively few negative reactions to the program have been observed. Such criticism as has been received usually falls along one of the following lines: (1) concern that gains made during the program will not be maintained after the program ends; (2) belief that the program is too short (twelve hours) to permit integration of the material; (3) disappointment that the spouse did not learn as much as the participant had hoped. Consistent with the low rate of negative criticisms, dropping out appears to be a rare phenomenon. We believe that the practice of holding a ten- to fifteen-minute pre-session interview with each couple—to assess the commitment of each partner to the objectives of the program—is an important factor in the couples' satisfaction with the program and the low frequency of drop-outs. In response to criticisms 1 and 2 above, many instructors now regularly plan for one or more sessions following the termination of the twelve-hour series. Instructors report that these follow-up sessions appear to be very useful in helping couples to continue utilizing skills learned in the program.

At the present time, MCCP has proven attractive primarily to people with at least some college education. Some modifications may be required to make the program attractive to less educated couples. A limitation on the program is the necessity of restricting the size of the training group to not more than seven couples. The size limitation results in a cost to participants higher than would be the case if the group could include ten or twelve couples. The size limitation is necessary when working with "live systems," so that enough time and attention can be given to each couple to avoid incomplete training experiences, i.e., heightening awareness without skill and choice.

Experience with more than eight hundred groups has revealed several advantages of the program.

1. The program has been found to be beneficial to partners at any point in their career (pairing, living together, during marriage, or in anticipation of remarriage).

2. Groups have been conducted in a number of different settings—churches, university continuing education divisions, YMCAs, social agencies, etc.

3. Although the program is clearly educational and developmental rather than therapeutic in objectives and structure, marriage and family counselors report that the program can be extremely valuable complement to counseling and therapy. (In no way, however, does this imply that the program can or should be viewed as a substitute for counseling or therapy. In using the program as a complement to therapy, the therapist will need to give consideration to group composition and to the timing of the MCCP experience in relation to the stages of therapy.)

4. The program offers a meaningful supplement, or alternative, to more traditional methods of preparation for marriage.

5. Finally, the program can be offered as a module within a "functional" college or university course in marriage and family or interpersonal relations.

Summary

The Minnesota Couples Communication Program offers a structured educational experience directed toward equipping couples with skills for (1) heightening awareness of oneself and one's contributions to interaction, (2) effectively expressing this self-awareness, (3) accurately understanding the partner's communications, and (4) flexibly choosing to maintain or to change ways of relating to one another. The program is conducted by instructors who are certified after completion of an instructor training workshop and receiving favorable evaluations by participant couples.

Notes

1. Adapted from Sherwood and Scherer, 1975, by the authors of this paper.
2. Available from the publisher, Interpersonal Communication Programs, Inc., 2001 Riverside Ave., Minneapolis, Minn. 55404, $6.95.

3. Instructor training workshops are conducted in many localities in the United States and Canada. Information about dates, locations, costs, and other details can be obtained by writing to Interpersonal Communication Programs, Inc. (see n. 2 above).

Resources

Bateson, Gregory. "Social Planning and the Concept of Deutero-Learning." *Science, Philosophy and Religion.* Second Symposium, 1942, 2, 81-97.

Foote, Nelson N. "Matching of Husband and Wife in Phases of Development." In Marvin B. Sussman, ed., *Sourcebook in Marriage and the Family.* Boston: Houghton Mifflin, 1963, pp. 15-21.

Foote, Nelson N., and Cottrell, Leonard S., Jr. *Identity and Interpersonal Competence: A New Direction in Family Research.* Chicago: University of Chicago Press, 1955.

Hill, Reuben, and Rodgers, Roy. "The Developmental Approach." Chap. 5 in Harold T. Christensen, ed., *Handbook on Marriage and the Family.* Chicago: Rand McNally & Co., 1964, pp. 171-211.

Hill, William Fawcett. *Hill Interaction Matrix: A Method of Studying Interaction in Psychotherapy Groups.* Los Angeles: University of Southern California, Youth Studies Center, 1965.

————. *A Guide to Understanding the Structure and Function of the Hill Interaction Matrix.* Los Angeles: University of Southern California, Youth Studies Center, 1967.

LeMasters, E. E. "Holy Deadlock: A Study of Unsuccessful Marriages." *Sociological Quarterly,* 1959, 21, 86-91.

Miller, Sherod. "The Effects of Communication Training in Small Groups upon Self-disclosure and Openness in Engaged Couples' Systems of Interaction: A Field Experiment." Ph.D. thesis, University of Minnesota, 1971.

Miller, Sherod; Nunnally, Elam; and Wackman, Daniel. "A Communication Training Program for Couples." Submitted for publication, 1975.

Miller, Sherod; Nunnally, Elam; Wackman, Daniel B.; with Ron Brazman. *Alive and Aware: Improving Communication in Relationships.* Minneapolis: Interpersonal Communication Programs, Inc., 1974.

Nunnally, Elam W. "Effects of Communication Training upon Interaction Awareness and Empathic Accuracy of Engaged Couples: A Field Experiment." Ph.D. thesis, University of Minnesota, 1971.

Rapoport, Rhona. "Normal Crisis, Family Structure and Mental Health." *Family Process,* March 1963, 2, 3-11.

Ruesch, J., and Bateson, G. *Communication: The Social Matrix of Psychiatry.* New York: W. W. Norton & Co., 1951.

Sherwood, John J., and Scherer, John J. "A Model for Couples: How Two Can Grow Together." *Small Group Behavior*, February 1975, 6 (1).

Speer, David C. "Family Systems: Morphostasis and Morphogenesis or 'Is Homeostasis Enough?'" *Family Process*, 1970, 9 (3), 259-78.

Sprey, Jetse. "The Family as a System in Conflict." *Journal of Marriage and the Family*, November 1966, 31, 699-706.

Turner, Ralph H. "Role Taking: Process Versus Conformity." In Arnold M. Rose, ed., *Human Behavior and Social Processes*. Boston: Houghton Mifflin, 1962.

Watzlawick, Paul; Beavin, Janet H.; and Jackson, Don D. *Pragmatics of Human Communication: A Study of Interaction Patterns, Pathologies and Paradoxes*. New York: W. W. Norton & Co., 1967.

Chapter 17

The Marriage Enrichment Program —Phase I

Del and Trudy Vander Haar

"Bob and I have been able to express ideas meaningful to both of us for the first time in our marriage. It's as if we gained a certain amount of trust in each other and we can now relate to each other in more than just a superficial way."

"We're so glad we learned the Request for Change technique. It used to be so defeating to see Mary's eyes get that glazed look before I was halfway through a sentence and to realize that she was already thinking up defenses and that she wasn't hearing a thing I said."

"Instead of just taking each other for granted, we've learned to evaluate our positive traits and we have an appreciation of how God has created the two of us to complement each other."

"On Sunday morning when you asked us to look our partners in the eye and to say 'I forgive you,' I could not do it! However, that's when the wall came tumbling down and we communicated—the rest of the session, almost all night, and several days thereafter. As a result I seem to have forgiven him twenty-five years of problems and am happier than I've been for years. Thank you."

THESE ARE A FEW OF THE MANY RESPONSES THAT WE HAVE received from the marriage enrichment experiences. How often, too, we have heard people say, "Oh, how I wish we could have had this experience many years ago when we were first married," and, "Why wasn't the church involved in this type of thing long ago?"

Why wasn't the church actively involved in marriage enrichment? The church has always had a very lofty concept of marriage. We believe that from the very beginning God knew of man's loneliness, frustration, and estrangement and of his need for a deep, abiding relationship. We believe that because of this need God gave man a partner, one with whom there could be total trust, openness, and commitment for life. The church feels that this union of husband and wife is the closest, deepest relationship two people can experience in life. Our very model for marriage has been Christ's sacrificial and voluntary gift of himself for the church. But somehow, although this has been taught in the church for centuries, we lacked the ability to make it experiential.

Then, just when marriage seemed to be fighting for survival, and all the lofty teaching and myriads of words didn't seem to be reaching people where they had needs, the Spirit brought renewal to the church. This renewal brought new understanding of some basic old concepts.

1. There is a new understanding that God is primarily concerned, not with doctrines or dogma, but with people and their relationship to each other.

He wants people to discover who they are as persons and how they can interact in an acceptable way with others. God interacted with people in a very personal way when he sent his Son, Jesus, to live on earth. Jesus' total ministry was concerned with the forces, causes, and motives that divide people. His life story reveals his care and concern for people as persons, and how he sought to draw them together in a loving relationship with God and with each other.

The idea of a "relational theology" has many ramifications for the church. In particular it brings into focus God's concern for individual persons in the husband-wife relationship. God wants couples to live together in a relationship as intimate as Christ's love for the church. This gives the church a goal for marriage which is not based primarily on security, sexual fulfillment, or self-satisfaction, but rather on the discovery of a deep, abiding love which enables both partners to see each other's value, and to work together for the fulfillment of each other. This new emphasis on personhood enables the couple to respect the rights of each other in their marriage relationship and at the same time creates intimacy which brings out the best in both spouses. This makes life worth living.

2. There is a new awareness of man's need to be vulnerable. The church has learned that within its fellowship we can be helpful to each other only when we are willing to risk revealing an imperfect self. We must be willing to share with each other what our inward pains and anxieties are. We must be willing to confess that we have not attained the perfect love that God desires of us and that we are seeking to grow in our relationships. The apostle Paul refers to this concept when he says, "My power is made perfect in weakness" (II Corinthians 12:9 RSV).

This concept also applies in marriage. The ability for the husband and wife to share both strengths and weaknesses becomes the very foundation for growth in their relationship. Couples must remove their masks and learn to accept each other in weakness, providing mutual support so weaknesses may be overcome.

3. The church has discovered the value of small groups within the church community. These have proved to be the ideal setting in which a person can be vulnerable and can receive healing. The fresh wind of the Spirit has often made such small groups a place where love, concern, understanding, listening, forgiveness, and prayer may be experienced in a meaningful way. Such a supportive community has made the Marriage Enrichment Program a dynamic experience in the lives of so many couples.

Simultaneously with renewal in the church, the behavioral sciences have brought us new insights, especially regarding the way in which learning takes place. Growth comes when one's total self, including feeling, thought, and action, is involved. Thus, the Marriage Enrichment Program seeks to incorporate the total person in the process of marital intimacy.

Marriage enrichment doesn't mean that suddenly everything becomes beautiful and perfect in a relationship; rather it opens doors by which couples can grow together and deal with issues or problems in a much more creative way. It does give the church handles for enabling couples to begin to discover the warm, loving, caring, forgiving, trusting relationship which God intended for persons in marriage.

The Marriage Enrichment Model follows on pages 195-204. For further information on the time structure, the setting, the lead couples, and the role of facilitators, see Appendix A, pages 204-7.

Marriage Enrichment Model—Phase I

Purpose: To enable couples to discover deep love, intimacy, and joy in marriage by
—developing better communication patterns,
—learning to accept one another's strengths and weaknesses, and
—establishing mutually acceptable goals.

Friday

7:30–7:45   A Get-Acquainted Time
        I. The lead couple give following instructions:
           1. Select someone of the opposite sex whom you would like to know better. Talk for five minutes about anything that interests you or the other person.
           2. Now with the same person sit back to back on the floor or on chairs and answer the following questions on index cards.
              a. What was the color of the person's eyes?
              b. What size shoes was he or she wearing?

       c. How many rings did he or she wear?

       d. How do you think this person was feeling?

       e. What one thing did you observe about the other person that made you feel good about that person?

    3. Turn around and discuss your answers together.

  II. The total group reflects on the ability to be observant and to pick up nonverbal messages.

7:45–8:00   The film *Encounter* by Teleketics

8:00–8:15   Concentric circles

The men, who are on the inside, keep rotating with each question. The women are on the outside and do not rotate. The questions are:

1. Which scene in the film did you most identify with? Why?

2. What anxieties did you have about coming to this retreat?

3. What is unique in your relationship?

4. Is there anything of significance your mate said to you today, or in the last few days?

5. How well do you feel you communicate in your marriage?

6. What would you personally like to receive from this retreat?

8:15–9:15   Newsprint sharing by couples

Possible background music: "Never, My Love"

1. Spouses sit down together and discuss what one relationship in their marriage they ought to work on and would be willing to share with the group.

2. After they have decided upon something, ask them to draw a picture on newsprint, illustrating this area which they have chosen to share with the group.

3. Mount the pictures on the wall.

   The group members interpret what they see in the picture.

   Couples share what they were trying to communicate.

An alternate experience could be the making of a collage depicting three areas of marriage: what it was; what it is now; what it hopefully will be. Follow the same sharing process suggested for the newsprint sketch.

9:15–9:30   Worship

Instructions to the group:

1. Share with a person of the opposite sex (not your spouse) what you have learned about yourself and your relationship with your mate. This may be positive or negative. Each person take about two minutes.

2. Also share something you are still anxious about, some fear or problem or conflict. Each take about two minutes.

3. Join your spouse again. Remove your drawing from the wall. Form a large circle. The drawings will be offered on a pile in the center of the circle by each couple in turn. Both silent and audible prayer are encouraged for each couple making the offering. One of the lead couples may close in prayer.)

Saturday

9:00–10:00   Learning to accept my body
1. Body awareness exercises (see Appendix B, pp. 207-8)
2. Nonverbal forms of communication

Reflection

1. (Total group): What is your reaction to nonverbal forms of communication—your feelings? your observations?

2. (Personally): What does my sex life say about myself?
   Share your feelings with your spouse if you wish.

3. Is there anything you talked about that you would like to share with the group?

10:00–10:15   Self-selected small groups
1. Each couple select another couple with whom you feel comfortable or whom you would like to know better.

2. Each foursome select another pair of couples whom you would like to know better.

3. A lead couple should join each group of four couples, making it five couples.

10:15–10:30   Break

10:30–12:00   Small groups meet

1. The lead couple shares guidelines for participating in small group sessions. Possible questions for getting started in small groups:

a. How do you feel about your experience thus far?
b. Do you feel comfortable in this group?
c. Why did you select your couples?
d. Is there anything else you would like to share about your drawing?
e. Would you like to react to anything that has happened thus far?

2. Possible input if the questions do not create adequate interaction:

a. Use building blocks or Tinkertoys. Spouses sit back to back on the floor. One leads by building something and verbally communicating directions to the spouse for building the same thing. The one who follows cannot ask questions verbally. However, he or she can ask for clarification by pounding on the floor. Purpose: to determine the ability to give and receive verbal messages.

b. Foursome Dialogue
Two couples decide to participate in this together. The first husband and wife to dialogue select a real issue that faces them and then discuss it together for five minutes. The other couple observes the interaction between spouses. The observing couple gives feedback on who initiates conversation; who checks out what he/she thought he/she heard; who looks for alternate solutions; who seeks to move toward a decision, etc. Then the process is reversed and the other couple dialogues on an issue and the first couple provides feedback.

12:00–1:30	Lunch and free time
1:30–2:00	Communication theory input (see Appendix C, p. 209)
2:00–3:00	Communication exercises

Choose from below as time permits.

1. Fishbowl
a. Listen to the song "Nag, Nag, Nag" from *Stop the World* as introduction.
b. Women inside discuss "What barriers to communication do men create?"
c. Reverse the process. Men discuss "What barriers to communication do women create?"
d. Total group reflects on what has been heard.

2. "Word" focus—non-spouse dyad

      a. The first person shares something, in one sentence, which has emotional overtones for the other person. (It might be political, religious, or personally oriented.)

      b. The listener gives a one-word feedback which includes feelings as well as content.

      c. Reverse the process.

      d. Reflection questions and statement:

        (1) Was the feedback accurate?

        (2) Was the communication clear?

        (3) Remember, good communication usually enables accurate feedback.

3. "Sentence" focus—another non-spouse dyad

      a. Here the same exercise is repeated, but now one person expresses himself in a paragraph and the listener gives feedback in one sentence.

      b. Again, reverse the process.

      c. Let there be reflection on what you have experienced.

4. Dyads—husband and wife—nonverbal

      a. Look each other in the eyes for two minutes and, without words, try to read what the other is feeling.

      b. Share what you were feeling.

5. Dyads—husband and wife—verbal: express an ambivalence (either/or feeling)

    What you like about her. What you don't like about her.

    What you like about him. What you don't like about him.

    Illustration: Wife to husband: "I like, even sometimes envy, your aggressiveness; but sometimes it embarrasses me."

3:00–3:15   Break

3:15–4:30   Small groups meet

1. Continue the process of the morning. If there is no immediate pickup on it, you may want to introduce a marital communication inventory sheet (see Appendix C, p. 209).

2. We try to provide numerous opportunities for dialogue between husband and wife, followed by total group reflection on the dialogue. Some statements and questions we have used are:

    —"I am uncomfortable with you when . . ."

—"What feelings am I reluctant to express?"

—"I need help in . . ."

—"What are the qualities that most attracted me to you?"

—"What are my feelings about God in my marriage?"

—"Do I see you and accept you as you really are?"

—"You make me feel loved when . . ."

3. Sometimes it is good to see ourselves from another's point of view. We ask each participant to think about some changes in behavior that he/she thinks would be welcomed by his/her partner. Then the couples dialogue on this to see if they are on target.

4. A communication exercise:

Step 1. One member of each couple receives a relatively simple drawing. Spouses sit back to back. The person with the drawing describes it verbally. The other person tries to draw a replica of it. Then they compare drawings.

Step 2. The same person selects another drawing. This time spouses sit face to face and the person describing the picture is allowed to use his/her hands to communicate. The other person again tries to draw what he/she thinks has been described. Again they compare drawings.

Step 3. After they receive a third drawing, the picture is described using both words and motions as in step 2. In addition, questions and answers are allowed. After the partner has drawn his/her concept of what has been described, they compare drawings once more.

This exercise illustrates how complicated communication is, that it involves not only words but also nonverbals and is a two-way process.

After these exercises let the group discuss their feelings of frustration with the communication process.

5. Exercise for identifying feelings (see Appendix D, pp. 209-12)

   a. Wives fill in Worksheet A

   b. Husbands fill in Worksheet B

        c. Reflection by husband and wife:
           Do you feel you are sensitive to the feelings communicated by your spouse?
           Are you able to "active listen" to your spouse?

4:30–7:30	Break
7:30–8:00	The film *Weekend* by Teleketics
8:00–8:30	Biblical insights on anger
	Guidelines for constructive and destructive fight patterns (see Appendix E, p. 213)
8:30–10:00	Small groups meet

Let them first reflect on the film to discover if there is personal identification with it, any learnings or questions. The following experiences may be helpful, if necessary:

1. Couples argue at a distance with backs to each other; then they turn around and continue as they are, face to face, holding hands and looking into each other's eyes. They reflect on how it felt to argue back to back, and then let them describe what they felt when it was done face to face.

2. Perhaps the lead couple can teach the simple technique of learning how to request change as related to the style of communication between husband and wife. Generally, a couple will volunteer to do this. Usually this couple is seated face to face on chairs in the center of the circle. However, before you ask someone else to do this, it is good for the lead couple to demonstrate it with a Request for Change. The process goes something like this:

   a. Statement. First party initiates a request for change in the spouse's style of communication. Some may want to initiate a major behavioral change in the spouse, but it is better to begin with a request for change in their communication style.

   b. Restatement

      1. The listener plays back the request to see if he or she has heard it correctly.

      2. The first party gives a response as to whether or not it is accurate so far as content and feeling is concerned.

      3. If the feedback is not accurate, the listener tries again to restate what he or she has

heard. If the listener doesn't feed back accurately, he or she may request the sender to repeat the request for change.

c. Agree or disagree
   1. If the listener has made the appropriate restatement, he or she must either agree or disagree with the request. There is no room for "yes, buts."
   2. If there is disagreement, the listener may want to follow through with a request for change from his spouse. Again, the same rules are applied. So the process evolves, but the same rules are enforced.

Special Instructions: The lead couple may need to be sure that the rules are applied and the process is being followed. If there is still conflict, especially if it becomes issue-oriented, it may be necessary to introduce the "problem-solving" technique to resolve the conflict.

3. The "problem-solving" process* includes these steps:

Step 1. Define the problem.
   (a) Each party tries to define the problem.
   (b) Try to verbalize the other person's side of the conflict.

Step 2. Generate possible solutions.
   (a) Brainstorm at least a dozen possible solutions, if possible.
   (b) Avoid being evaluative or critical during the brainstorming time.
   (c) List the possible solutions on paper.

Step 3. Evaluate and test the various solutions.
   (a) Will it work?
   (b) Is it fair to both?
   (c) Will it be too hard to implement?

Step 4. Decide on a mutually acceptable solution.
   (a) Don't push or persuade the other into a solution.
   (b) State a possibly acceptable solution and make certain both parties understand.
   (c) Sometimes writing out the solution

---

*More information on handling rough spots in a marriage relationship may be found in Richard H. Klemer, *Marriage and Family Relationships* (New York: Harper & Row, 1970), p. 318.

clarifies it and eliminates later misunder-
standings.

Step 5. Implement the solution.

(a) Who is to do what and by when?

Step 6. Evaluate the solution.

(a) Are you still happy with the solution?

(b) Does it need revision? Decisions are
always open for revision, but the revisions
need to be mutually agreed upon in the
same way as the initial decision.

4. Close the evening session by suggesting that
individual members may want to give gifts of
affirmation to one another. Each reflects on what
he or she sees as a positive strength in the other
person and shares it with him or her, either on a
one-to-one basis or in the midst of the small group.

Sunday

9:00–9:30   Trust walk

Spouses take turns leading each other—leaders with
eyes open and followers with eyes closed. This
encourages the use of the other senses—hearing,
smelling, tasting, feeling.

Reflection: Dialogue on the trust walk experience with
your spouse.

Share one word which describes it with the total
group.

9:30–10:30   Building on marriage strengths (small groups)

1. Husband and wife work separately.

a. Each list on index cards the strengths that you
contribute to the marriage.

b. Compare lists. Dialogue on this as long as
necessary.

c. Together make a list of your marriage strengths,
drawing from the lists you have just made and
adding others.

d. Discuss together what you have learned from
this experience.

2. Selective sharing of strengths with the small
group.

10:30–11:30   Goal-setting (small groups)

1. Husband and wife work together.

a. What would you like your marriage to be in the
next years?

    b. What two immediate, measurable goals can you set for your continued growth in marriage. Write on index cards.

  2. Share your goals with the group if you wish.

11:30–12:00 Closing and evaluation (total group)

  1. Complete the written evaluation form (see Appendix F, p. 214). Let individuals express how they felt about the experience by sharing one word.

  2. The lead couples devise an appropriate way to close.

Sometimes we use the Sunday morning for a very informal service of worship. When we do, we incorporate the exercises on strengths as a part of our affirmation of faith in God and in each other. For the confessional part of the service, couples are asked to write down one thing in their marriages for which they would seek forgiveness. The papers are burned in the fireplace. Often forgiveness is expressed by the marriage partners. Appropriate Bible readings are read. We also give our newly set goals as an offering to God.

Appendix A

The Model Itself

Any design which is structured with a time schedule is going to appear rigid and fixed. This is not the intention of the marriage enrichment experience. As lead couples, skilled facilitators will know when the interaction among the group members and between couples is adequately dynamic to allow the current dialogue to continue, and when, on the other hand, it is time to move on with the agenda.

Sometimes we have enabled the group, on the basis of their drawings or collages, to set their own agenda. Usually there are vast areas of need that become apparent as couples share. These areas may include self-identity versus togetherness, self-worth, intimacy, barriers to communication, sex, conflict, money, identification of feelings, faith, clarification of roles, appropriate use of time and leisure, goal-setting, and learning how to affirm each other. Again, skilled facilitators will know how best to handle these areas in an experiential way to provide a new level of intimacy for the participating couples.

Limited time will be spent on cognitive information. A meaningful marriage enrichment experience is dependent on skilled facilitators who are able to be flexible, active listeners, and know how to move on with the needs of the group rather than following a rigid time schedule.

The Lead Couples—The Facilitators

The lead couples should be known as "facilitators." This implies that leadership is not obtrusive or authoritarian. They are there to facilitate and to see that things happen. They provide a setting in which a new level of relationship between couples can evolve. We recommend one lead couple for every four to six couples. A maximum number of couples is fifteen to eighteen with three lead couples. In this setting some things are done in a total group, but most of the time is spent in small groups under the leadership of a lead couple.

A primary prerequisite for a lead couple is that they be open and willing to work on their own marriage. They are participants in all the events. They share with the group their personal pilgrimage in marriage, and in particular what area or areas of growth they are working on in their own relationship. This creates identity between participants and leadership and destroys the so-called professional air that might exist if a leader were present without his or her spouse.

Lead couples, as facilitators, need some special skills in understanding group life, group dynamics, and communication skills and theory, as well as some basic understanding of the dynamics that transpire in a husband and wife relationship.

Lead couples should be sensitive to what constitutes normal behavior, and should recognize when couples need to be referred to professional marriage counselors or other appropriate professional persons.

Some Guidelines for Lead Couples, the Facilitators

(Based on several marriage enrichment experiences and collected from various unknown sources.)

1. Be sure the group realizes this is a group thing. You are not to be seen as experts or answermen. The lead couples have needs as well.
2. Each person is important as regards what happens in the group. If nothing happens, each person is responsible.
3. Facilitators have responsibility for structure, timing, and balance.
4. The facilitators must see themselves as a part of the group. They must neither become the "papa" figures nor withdrawn observers.
5. Do not put any information into the group on your own prejudgment.
6. Don't give feedback too soon. Feedback should come from within the group.

7. Husband and wife must get together. This is not primarily a personal growth lab. It's a communication process in learning to grow together.

8. Latecomers should go through the "initiation rites" to be accepted. Better still, insist that it is a total experience: every couple should begin with the group and leave when the program is completed.

9. Accept a person as he is "here and now" in the group. Forget the past and future.

10. Don't get too psychological and clinical. Work on a more conscious awareness.

11. Avoid escaping the experiential by intellectualizing.

12. Ideally, everyone talks about an equal amount. Be mindful of the nonparticipant.

13. Use methods to stimulate encounter—not as ends in themselves, or just as busy work. Don't pack the schedule.

14. Stress confidentiality.

15. Be available if couples need you privately.

> *Interaction: Some Guidelines Which Lead Couples May Want to Share with Their Small Groups*

(Based on several marriage enrichment experiences and collected from various unknown sources.)

1. Be as honest as you can possibly be with your partner and other group members.

2. Don't be anywhere you don't want to be, or cannot tolerate being. It is each group member's responsibility to let others in the group know when they are pushing too hard or stepping on toes.

3. Don't protect your partner; he/she can take care of himself/herself. It is a natural instinct to be protective, but it often impedes the process of growth in honest communication.

4. The group makes a contract to abide by these rules as far as possible, especially not pushing someone if he cries "halt!."

5. The facilitator will sometimes have to point out when group members forget and are not able to keep their rules, and this may be more often than you think.

6. Don't argue with another person's feelings! You may, however, challenge people to define their feelings more accurately.

7. Effective listening is not passive, but losing yourself to try to understand. Drop your defense and delay your reactions.

8. Remember that love is caring for the other person more than you care for yourself. You must be willing to risk in order to grow!

The Setting

Sensitive lead couples will know how to make participating couples comfortable as quickly as possible. The style of leadership in the first twenty minutes will determine whether or not couples will feel free to participate in a manner that is essential for enriching their marriages.

Appropriate facilities, such as a retreat center with a loungelike room and private sleeping space for couples, are absolutely essential. The lounge should have comfortable chairs, a rug on the floor, and a fireplace, if possible. If you are going to have several small groups, you will need several loungelike rooms as well as a larger lounge area.

The atmosphere of the room may be enhanced by hanging appropriate posters and mounted Andy Capp cartoons, for example. Sometimes we have used these statements on marriage and love written on large pieces of colored construction paper or tag board:

—Sounds of love don't just happen; you have to make them.
—Some women work so hard to make good husbands that they never quite manage to make good wives.
—The bonds of matrimony aren't worth much unless the interest is kept up.
—It also takes two to make up after a quarrel.
—Let all that you do be done in love. (I Corinthians 16:14 RSV)
—The greatest of these is love. (I Corinthians 13:13 RSV)

We have discovered that the continuity of a forty-eight-hour retreat experience from Friday evening to Sunday noon or afternoon is much more effective than three-hour evening sessions held over several weeks.

Appendix B

Body Awareness

Introduction

In the past the church carefully compartmentalized Christians into mind, soul, and body. We intellectualized and spiritualized in the church, but the body was pretty much avoided. We are now convinced that God is concerned with our whole beings, the whole person. We speak of this as a new emphasis, and yet St. Augustine, centuries ago, spoke of our five senses being gateways to God—an external means to internal understanding. The psalmist wrote that our bodies are fearfully and wonderfully made, but we are rarely aware of the thousands of miles of nerve fibers and all the other intricacies of our bodies except when we have aches and pains.

Perhaps when we watch an acrobat or a ballet dancer we feel like earthbound, leaden, dull blobs.

How great instead to be aware of our bodies in an alive, vital sense!

Warm-up Exercises

Through a process of tapping the head, patting the face, gently pounding the upper torso, twisting the waist, and shaking arms, hands, fingers, legs, and feet, the nerves are awakened until the body tingles with awareness.

Follow this by ministering to your neighbor with a back rub.

Nonverbal Exercises*

(To point out how we use our bodies to communicate with each other)

Form Concentric Circles
(This could all be done with the marriage partner, or one of the circles could rotate so that there are different partners each time.)
1. Aggression with the shoulder push.
2. Express warmth and acceptance.
   Express hostility and rejection.
3. Look into each other's eyes and share what you are feeling. (Omit if done earlier.)
4. Study hands and do some of these things:
   a. Meditate on what they did as a child.
   b. Meditate on what they do now.
   c. Observe calluses, softness, hardness.
      Express affection, appreciation.
      Try to make the other person feel good.
5. Giving and receiving love with spouse.
   Feel face—touch, explore, stroke, hold that face, massage it gently, love that face.

Reflection

See the suggested questions found in the model.

When appropriate we also use an adaptation of "A Prayer for Our Bodies," adapted from Michel Quoist, *Prayers* (New York: Sheed & Ward, 1963), pp. 35-37.

---

*For more information see Herbert A. Otto, *More Joy in Your Marriage* (New York: Hawthorn Books, 1969), pp. 44-50; Howard J. Clinebell, Jr., *The People Dynamic* (New York: Harper & Row, 1972), pp. 48-52.

Appendix C

Communication Theory

Resources

Satir, Virginia. *Peoplemaking*. Palo Alto, Calif.: Science and Behavior Books, 1972.

————.*Conjoint Family Therapy*. Palo Alto, Calif.: Science and Behavior Books, 1967.

Howe, Reuel L. *The Miracle of Dialogue*. New York: The Seabury Press, 1963.

Gordon, Thomas. *Parent Effectiveness Training*. New York: Peter H. Wyden, 1971.

Miller, Sherod; Nunnally, Elam W.; and Wackman, Daniel B. *The Minnesota Couples Communication Program—Couples Handbook*. Minneapolis, Minn., 1972.

Marital Communication Inventory Sheets

1. These sheets developed by Millard J. Bienvenu, Sr., are available from The Family Life Publications, Inc., Box 6725, Durham, N. C., 27708. Order both the male and female forms.
2. "A Marriage Mirror" for husbands only and for wives only is found in Norman Vincent Peale, *The Amazing Results of Positive Thinking* (Englewood Cliffs, N. J.: Prentice Hall, 1959).

Other Helpful Resource Items

"Outline of Marriage Strengths" in Herbert A. Otto, *More Joy in Your Marriage* (New York: Hawthorn Books, 1969), pp. 71-74.

"Self-Other Fulfillment Checklist" in Howard J. and Charlotte H. Clinebell, *The Intimate Marriage* (New York: Harper & Row, 1970), pp. 84-85.

Appendix D

Exercise for Identifying Feelings

Worksheet A

(for wives)

The husband says	He is feeling
1. "That was a great party! You can sure tell his wife's well organized."	

The husband says	He is feeling
2. "You're always nagging at me to do more. What do you think I am?"	
3. "What do you mean—my mess? I do as much around here as you do."	
4. "I'm sure I could do a better job if you'd just tell me once in a while what a great guy I am."	
5. "No matter how much I try to help you, I can't seem to do anything good enough to suit you."	
6. "Hey, how come you have to spend all evening with the kids or in the kitchen?"	
7. "So what if I ate all the hors d'oeuvres in sight? She didn't serve dinner till 8:30!"	
8. "I really think I should come off O.K. in that performance review . . . I hope . . . shouldn't I? What does the boss know, anyhow?"	
9. "That speech went great! I didn't flub it up anywhere. I even got those statistics straight."	
10. "I've had a long day. I don't see much evidence of dinner around here."	
11. "Shall I take the kids to the park for a little while?"	
12. "You know, I've been looking across the back yard, and I think we've got about the neatest lawn on the block."	

Worksheet B
(for husbands)

The wife says	She is feeling
1. "I can talk and talk and he never listens to me."	
2. "When you say things like that, I wish I'd never met you!"	
3. "It's been three weeks since I asked you to fix that faucet."	
4. "Jim wouldn't forget Nancy's birthday. He's always sending her flowers or something."	
5. "You're not strict enough with the kids."	
6. "He's always griping about the messy house, but he sure doesn't help me much."	
7. "I just can't win in this family. No matter what I do, I get criticism."	
8. "If I left him and he had to hire someone to do all these things, he'd be more appreciative."	
9. "If you weren't so wrapped up in that motorcycle, we'd have some money for the things I need in the house."	
10. "I never seem to get caught up. I just can't cope with things the way other people can."	
11. "I don't know why you have to bowl as often as you do. Those guys mean more to you than I do."	
12. "Where've you been? I expected you home hours ago."	

The Scoring Key

Worksheet A	Worksheet B

1. (1) resentful
   (2) frustrated

1. (1) self-pitying
   (2) neglected
   (3) frustrated

2. (1) guilty
   (2) inadequate
   (3) angry

2. (1) angry
   (2) belligerent

3. (1) defensive
   (2) impatient

3. (1) upset
   (2) impatient

4. (1) unloved
   (2) neglected
   (3) defeated

4. (1) jealous
   (2) rejected
   (3) hurt

5. (1) resentful, hurt
   (2) "I'm no good"
   (3) defeated

5. (1) frustrated
   (2) helpless
   (3) inadequate

6. (1) jealous
   (2) neglected

6. (1) resentment
   (2) inadequacy

7. (1) defensive
   (2) belligerent

7. (1) "I'm no good"
   (2) loss of respect

8. (1) worry
   (2) fear

8. (1) self-pitying
   (2) bitter, resentful

9. (1) pride, satisfaction
   (2) relief

9. (1) angry
   (2) resentful
   (3) belligerent

10. (1) self-pity
    (2) disgruntlement
    (3) irritation

10. (1) frustrated
    (2) "I'm no good"

11. (1) understanding
    (2) sympathy

11. (1) neglected
    (2) lonely
    (3) hurt

12. (1) pride
    (2) competence

12. (1) afraid
    (2) worried

(Since feelings cover such a broad range, other feelings may be identified which also apply.)

Appendix E

Constructive Resolution of Conflict

I. What do we mean by conflict?
   "A different set of strong feelings that clash."
II. Analysis of the conflict pattern*
   a. The *destructive* conflict pattern
      1. Apologizing prematurely.
      2. Refusing to take the fight seriously.
      3. Withdrawing, evading, walking out, falling asleep, giving the silent treatment.
      4. Using intimate knowledge about the partner and hitting below the belt.
      5. Bringing in unrelated issues—chain reaction.
      6. Being a pseudo-accommodator.
      7. Attacking indirectly.
      8. Being a double-binder. Giving a rebuke rather than a compliment.
      9. Explaining someone's feeling for him—character analysis.
      10. Always demanding more.
      11. Withholding affection, sex, anything.
      12. Undermining, keeping the partner on edge: "Why don't we get a divorce?"
   b. The *constructive* conflict pattern
      1. Program fights. Allow time to handle the feelings.
      2. Be sure to define what the fight is all about.
      3. Each partner gives expression to his positive feelings.
      4. Each partner gives expression to his negative feelings.
      5. Replay the other person's feelings in your own words.
      6. Discover where the positions coincide.
      7. Discover the points of vulnerability.
      8. Determine how deeply each partner feels about the fight.
      9. Recognize the spontaneous expression which can occur.
III. Questions to help analyze the conflict pattern
      1. How do I typically pick a fight with my marital partner?
      2. How do I place my grievances with my spouse?
      3. What is my usual psychological state when I pick a fight with my marital partner?
      4. What way do I fight "dirty" with my partner?
      5. What do I especially like about my partner's fighting style?

*Adapted from Everett L. Shostrom, *Man, the Manipulator* (New York: Bantam Books [1967], 1968), pp. 132-33.

Appendix F

Marriage Enrichment Program

Evaluation

Listed below are a number of unfinished sentences we would like you to complete. We are learning together in these retreats, and your response will help us plan future M.E.R.'s. Please complete this evaluation and return it to the address below.

Check who is completing this evaluation:

( ) husband   ( ) wife

1. The most helpful experience in this retreat was

2. The least helpful experience in this retreat was

3. I would like to see _____ cut out of the program because

4. I would like to see _____ added to the program because

5. Other comments and suggestions

Thank you for your help. We have appreciated the opportunity to share with you, and you have helped us grow too in these few days we were able to be together.

YOU ARE THE KEY TO EXPANDING THIS PROGRAM. If you would like to see more programs of this kind in your area, write to the Rev. Delbert Vander Haar, Reformed Church in America, Western Regional Center, Orange City, Iowa 51041.

Appendix G

Marriage Enrichment Supplies

Checklist

1. Films: *Encounter*

    The Weekend

    Films available from Teleketics, Franciscan Communications Center, 1229 S. Santee St., Los Angeles, Calif. 90015

2. Records: *Stop The World* (London AMS 88001)

    "Nag, Nag, Nag"

    The Association, Greatest Hits

    "Never, My Love"

    "Time for Livin'"

3. Record player
4. 16mm projector
5. Name tags
6. Crayons
7. Magic Markers
8. Newsprint
9. Masking tape
10. Index cards
11. Tinkertoys
12. Evaluation sheets
13. Magazines

Appendix H

Other Resources

Clinebell, Howard, J., Jr., and Clinebell, Charlotte H. *The Intimate Marriage.* New York: Harper & Row, 1970.

Otto, Herbert A. *More Joy in Your Marriage.* New York: Hawthorn Books, 1969.

Lederer, W. J., and Jackson, D. D. *The Mirages of Marriage.* New York: W. W. Norton & Co., 1968.

Wiese, Bennard R., and Steinmetz, Urban G. *Everything You Need to Know to Stay Married and Like It.* Grand Rapids: Zondervan Publishing House, 1971.

Mace, David and Vera. *We Can Have Better Marriages, If We Really Want Them.* Nashville: Abingdon Press, 1974.

Harris, Thomas A. *I'm OK—You're OK.* New York: Harper & Row, 1967.

Rogers, Carl R. *Carl Rogers on Encounter Groups.* New York: Harper & Row, 1970.

Wright, H. Norman. *Communication—Key to Your Marriage.* Glendale, Calif.: Regal Press, 1974.

Smith, Gerald Walker, and Phillips, Alice I. *Me and You and Us.* New York: Peter H. Wyden, 1971.

Bosco, Antoinette. *Marriage Encounter, A Rediscovery of Love.* St. Meinrad, Ind.: Abbey Press, 1973.

Augsburger, David. *Caring Enough to Confront—The Love-Fight.* Glendale, Calif.: Regal Press, 1974.

Clinebell, Howard J., Jr. *Basic Types of Pastoral Counseling.* Nashville: Abingdon Press, 1966.

Bach, George R., and Wyden, Peter. *The Intimate Enemy: How to Fight Fair in Love and Marriage.* New York: Avon Books [1969], 1970.

Chapter 18

The Phase II Marriage Enrichment Lab

Bud and Bea Van Eck

Introduction

Couples for whom a Marriage Lab has had salutary results sometimes develop a hunger for additional opportunities for growth in a lab environment. Or, couples who continue to experience a struggle may have developed enough confidence in specific leadership and a specific group to agree to "try again." Further, lead couples who have had a score of Phase I experiences seek diversity in the structure of Marriage Labs. These factors have led to the development of a Phase II Marriage Enrichment Lab. This design was developed by Bea and Bud Van Eck of the Reformed Church in America and by Katie and Bill Sheek of the Moravian Church in America.

Assumptions

The following assumptions regarding the participants and the lab were developed:

1. Persons who attend this lab will have participated in at least one previous lab of three or more days.

This became a published criterion for the lab, although no attempt was made by the leadership to determine what the nature or the quality of the experience had been. Such an assumption ensured that the participants at least had a moderate understanding of an experiential approach to learning. They were somewhat convinced of the value of the laboratory method of growth. They had received and given feedback. Understanding that the lead couples did not pose as marriage experts or as having model marriages, they were developing responsibility for their own growth. This assumption appeared to be validated in the Phase II Lab. The start-up time was much shorter. Participants did build on their previous Marriage Lab experience.

2. Participants coming to Phase II will be less anxious and mystified about what will happen.

Phase I participants were often initially anxious. They had heard "stories" of what goes on in groups. The rumors had often touched a personal or relational anxiety. Faced with the possibility of disclosure, vulnerability, risk, pain, and so forth, participants in their first lab often behaved in an anxious manner.

Phase II participants were aware that they did experience pain, vulnerability, disclosure, and that these often became opportunities for growth. The process, the language, the design, the purpose were no longer "secrets" known only to the lead couples. Phase II participants still experienced some anxiety, but not to the extent that the design required extensive inclusion experiences.

3. Participants have some basic communication skills.

The Phase I design includes the theory and practice of communication skills. Some of the couples did utilize those skills in the interim and entered Phase II actively utilizing those skills.

4. Participants have been actively working on their marriage relationships.

Most of them did work on their relationships between Phase I and Phase II. The few who didn't wanted to work on their relationships and came to the lab to do just that. This experience induced a high motivation in the participants.

5. Participants came to work on the "gutsy" stuff of their marriages.

They had previously participated in a Marriage Lab. They knew the rewards of risking, of opening up, of experiencing pain. They had not paid their money to come for dressing the windows of their marriages.

6. Phase II will "permit" greater interaction among participants.

While Phase I design encouraged a maximum of spouse interaction and a minimum of intragroup interaction, Phase II was more balanced. Some sessions had a T-group or encounter group flavor. This was usually helpful to participants, but it did require group process skills on the part of the leaders.

Theoretical Base

During the initial planning by the Van Ecks and the Sheeks, a theoretical base for the Phase II design was developed. This base leaned heavily on R.K. Lifton's theory as well as Frankl's insights.[1]

Lifton's three levels were explicit in the design and in theory input They are: Confrontation, Reordering, and Renewal. The design specifically enabled spouses to engage in Confrontation if they desired. The experiential activities usually produced data which at times focused attention on divisive behavior and attitudes in the relationship. Reordering activities included personal emptying, reeducation, and experimenting with new ideas and attitudes. The Renewal level encouraged new behavior and new freedom. Participants verbalized their feelings about their renewal and often welcomed feedback from others regarding their new behavior. There was an opportunity for participants to "celebrate" both personal and relational renewal. The design of the lab did not usually follow Lifton's three levels sequentially. Rather, participants were often at different levels and sometimes returned to former levels. But the Lifton framework gave participants a "road map" for their experiences.

The design did not depend solely on eliciting data which pointed to divisiveness in the marriage relationship. The lab was potential-oriented rather than problem-oriented. At least equal time was devoted to working with bonding and esteeming behaviors. The following insights of Viktor Frankl were explicit both in the design and the process:

1. However dismal (or optimistic) a person is, he is free to choose his own attitudes and *does so choose.*
2. A person is constantly searching for personal meanings which mobilize him.
3. Further, in searching for values which give meaning to his existence a person explores *creative values,* which are associated with doing something worthwhile; *experiential values,* such as a painting, sunset, or intercourse; and *attitudinal values,* that is, making a conscious, volitional decision to develop constructive attitudes.

The utilization of Frankl's theory encouraged growth even among those who felt "trapped" in their marriages.

While the major time environment for the lab was the here and now, the present, data from the past and planning for the future would also be utilized.

The Purpose

The purpose of Phase II was to provide support and encouragement for couples who were working on their relationship, to provide time, opportunity, and handles to bring more joy and meaning to each couple's relationship. Stated another way, the purpose of Phase II was basically to enrich the marriage relationships of the participants, to enable them to be more zestful in their relationship to spouses. This was done by eliciting data for dialogue, by verbalizing and discussing the assumptions they had about marriage, by exploring various aspects and levels of intimacy, by discussing esteeming and diminishing behaviors, by considering the function of sex in their marriages, and by developing a new marriage contract if desired.

The Phase II Design

The design as finally developed for Phase II encompassed three full days beginning at 1:30 p.m. on Day 1 and continuing through lunch on Day 4. The following format is developed to provide an outline of the design, a rationale for the design, and some experiential data regarding the results of the design.

Day I

1:30 P.M. Welcome and housekeeping details
1:40 P.M. Inclusion exercises
—Name tags: Each participant created a name tag using the name he/she wanted to be called by.
—Wire sculpting: Each participant was given a length of wire and asked to form the wire to express his/her feelings at that moment. Discussions regarding the wire sculpture and associated feelings were shared with persons other than spouses in dyads.
—Repetitive questions: In non-spouse dyads persons repeatedly asked and briefly answered the question "Who are you?" In another non-spouse dyad, the repetitive question was "Why are you here?" Further repetitive questions were "What do you hope will happen?" and "What do you want for yourself?"
—Recording of do's and don'ts: Newsprint was posted around the room. Several sheets had as a heading "Do's for This Lab" and others had "Don'ts for This Lab." Persons were asked to record what they hoped would happen and what they hoped would not happen. Another sheet of newsprint was posted with "Want to know more about . . ." These sheets were available for revision and updating throughout the lab and became a major device for giving feedback to lead couples.
—Spouse dialogue: The first hour and fifteen minutes called for non-spouse dialogue. The last twenty minutes gave partners an opportunity to check with each other regarding feelings, self-discoveries, wants, and expectations for Phase II.

Rationale for "inclusion exercises." Persons coming into new groups are often asking, implicitly or explicitly, "Do I belong here? How? Will people accept me? Can I accept others?" Inclusion exercises are designed not only to provide data, but to reduce the amount of time needed for the group to jell. They also reduce the anxiety level of the participants.

Results of the "inclusion exercises." As participants shared, they began to open up to each other. By the time they entered the second element of the design, some were expressing an initial closeness through the verbal and nonverbal expression of feelings toward each other. This inclusion aspect was of considerable importance since the design included more intragroup dialogue than Phase I.

The first part of the design gave an opportunity to be specific about what participants wanted to work on. As participants shared with each other, they discovered a commonality of expectations and of feelings. They also had an opportunity to experience the lead couples as human beings who valued their marriages too and were committed to enriching them.

3:30 P.M.   Looking backward
    —Theory input: This consisted of a brief explanation of how Lifton's and Frankl's insights were relevant. Participants were also briefed on how the past, present, and future of the marriage relationship would be utilized in the lab.
    —Spouse dialogue: Each husband and wife dialogued on the question "What has happened in our marriage since the last Marriage Lab we participated in? Have there been any lasting effects and any change in behavior?" After the spouse dialogue, intragroup dialogue took place.
    —Human sculpture: Each couple engaged in a nonverbal human sculpture indicating what the relationship was like when they were first married. Following each sculpture, all participants had the opportunity to tell the couple what they saw in the sculpture.

Rationale for a "look backward." This was not a therapy session. The look at the past was designed as a review of the impact of the previous lab. The sculpturing was an opportunity for husband and wife to consider some of their earliest assumptions regarding their relationships.

Results of the "look backward." The assumption of the lead couples that persons had been working on their relationship was validated. As couples talked about the time intervening between the labs, they told of struggle, regression, fulfillment, and peak experiences.

The human sculpture was a stunning experience for several. They didn't like the form they finally assumed (as sculpture), yet they agreed as husband and wife that the early assumption was not only correctly expressed but was often still operative in the present relationship.

5:30 P.M.   Dinner and free time
7:00 P.M.   Marriage as a system
            —Theory on the value of feedback and self-disclosure:
            This theory presentation stressed the appropriateness of
            openness between husband and wife and between
            persons in groups. The Johari Window was the
            conceptual framework.[2]
            —Theory on marriage as a system.[3]
            —Spouse dialogue: Utilizing the data from the human
            sculpture exercise to initiate discussion, couples dis-
            cussed their early assumptions about marriage, how
            these assumptions had changed, what bonding and
            disruptive influence these assumptions had on the
            current relationship.
            —Group dialogue utilizing data from spouse dialogue.
            —Marriage Arch technique: Each person was asked to
            describe his/her marriage by drawing a stone arch,
            indicating the important dynamics, values, and be-
            haviors by labeling each stone with a value, behavior,
            attitude, or dynamic. The keystone was to be the
            individual's perception regarding the value, behavior,
            or attitude which was most crucial. This arch was
            shared with the spouse and then with the group.

Rationale for "marriage as a system." An ability to receive and
utilize feedback and a willingness to engage in self-disclosure are
assets in exploring the marriage relationship. Marriage is not a
collection of unrelated assumptions, behaviors, experiences, failures,
successes, and so forth. Rather, all the factors and aspects of marriage
are interlaced and mutually influential. Marriage needs to be
experienced and reflected on holistically.

Results of "marriage as s system." Some persons in the group began
to experience new energy to invest in the relationship as they were
willing to accept feedback and engage in self-disclosure. More verbal
risk-taking was reported by spouse dialogues and was evident in
group sharing. The Marriage Arch exercise produced useful data and
insights regarding the marriages of the persons present. A person
would often express surprise, sometimes affirmation, in what the
spouse had or had not placed in the Marriage Arch. Discussion of
some of the keystone concepts, such as comradeship, trust, esteem,
led to a vigorous discussion centered on the core value of each
relationship. Couples had an opportunity to process the values
which were more or less important to them.

Day 2

9:00 A.M. Being intentional

—Intentionality theory: This theory presentation emphasized the behaviors which result from unexpressed wants—that a person tends to become an isolated, "superior-acting" person who doesn't need anyone else, or to become a "doormat" type who attempts always to meet the needs of others. The theory values focused on specific statements of intentions in order that the person to whom the want was expressed could deal with a clear signal.

—Exercise on nonverbal behaviors: Each person listed five nonverbal behaviors observed in the spouse. These observations were shared with the spouse by acting out some of the nonverbal behaviors observed in him/her and followed by spouse dialogue on the power and influence of nonverbal behavior in the relationship. This was particularly related to the theory on intentionality.

—Experiencing intentionality: Each spouse verbalized several wants. Couples then negotiated some of their wants.

Rationale for "being intentional." One of the divisive dynamics in a relationship is the unstated wants and needs of the individuals. Such unstated wants often cause resentment, withdrawal, lack of vigor, and the satisfaction of such wants in other relationships.

Results of "being intentional." The intentionality theory presentation turned on "light bulbs." Some persons began to gain a clue regarding a lack of vitality in their marriages. They began to see that nonverbal behavior sometimes expressed the true feelings regarding unexpressed and unmet wants. In the exercise, couples felt "safe" about expressing and negotiating some wants. This exercise was one of the most beneficial of the lab, especially encouraging women to express career wants and encouraging a more explicit negotiation of sexual wants.

12:00 noon Lunch and free time

2:00 P.M. Intimacy session

—Input on intimacy: This input leaned heavily on the Clinebells' discussion regarding intimacy in *The Intimate Marriage.*[4]

—Marriage intimacy checkup: The instrument from

The Intimate Marriage, page 37, was filled out by
each person.
—Spouse dialogue: Discussion of the data took place,
followed by negotiation of specific action plans for
more intimacy.
—Intragroup sharing

Rationale for "intimacy session." The Clinebells view intimacy as a
key value, if not the key value, of marriage. At any rate, it is crucial to
a vital relationship. Further, perceptions regarding intimacy in
marriage are often restricted to sexual intimacy. The exercise
stressed the interdependency of various aspects of intimacy.

Results of "intimacy session." One of the issues which developed
through the intimacy dialogue was the question of companionship
and friendship in marriage. Some couples began to recognize that a
more adequate expression of intimacy in several areas of the
relationship contributed to a desired sense of companionship. They
discovered that there were intimacy areas in their relationship which
could be more fulfilling.

4:00 P.M.   Free time and dinner
7:30 P.M.   Intragroup dialogue: This unstructured session gave an
opportunity for persons to dialogue, ask for and receive
feedback, take risks, and express feelings. Role-play and
alter-ego exercises were utilized, although unplanned
for.

Rationale for "intragroup dialogue." Given a large amount of data
generated in the previous twenty-four hours, it was appropriate for
the lab to provide an opportunity for intragroup sharing.

Day 3

9:00 A.M.   Esteeming and diminishing
—Input on esteeming and diminishing: A brief presentation was given regarding the ability of a spouse to
nourish or diminish the other. A reference was also
made to the Transactional Analysis concept of stroking
and discounting.
—Writing exercise: Each spouse listed the behaviors by
which he/she esteemed the other and the behaviors by
which the spouse esteemed him/her.
—The same writing exercise was done for diminishing
behavior.

> —Spouse dialogue: There was discussion of existing
> esteeming and diminishing behaviors in the relation-
> ship and a negotiation of new behaviors.
> —Intragroup dialogue

Rationale for "esteeming and diminishing." "Nourishing" and "undernourishing" are concepts which are behaviorally understood in regard to physical well-being. The terms also readily related to "esteeming" and "diminishing" and can be behaviorally enacted.

Results of "esteeming and diminishing." This was another "light bulb" experience for couples. The consideration of esteeming and diminishing behavior gave persons operational methods of enriching their marriages. This exercise combined with the earlier exercise on intentionality enabled some participants to negotiate some new behaviors and revision of other behaviors in their relationship.

12:00 noon	Lunch and free time
3:00 P.M.	Sexuality session

     —Viewing of filmstrip on "Lovemaking,"[5] accom-
panied by selected readings on lovemaking.
     —Spouse dialogue: Couples discussed the feelings aroused in them by the filmstrip as well as the content. They were encouraged to discuss any area of sexuality in their relationship.

5:30 P.M.	Dinner and free time
7:30 P.M.	Sexuality session (continued)

     —Intragroup dialogue: Persons were invited to share in any way they felt comfortable.
     —Second viewing of the filmstrip.
     —A footrace to bed!

Rationale for "sexuality session." Sex is on the minds of many persons. As an important aspect of marriage, labs should not overlook sexuality and its genital expression.

Results of "sexuality session." An amazing amount of conflict and energy was generated. Some married people do not discuss lovemaking and intercourse, and by their admission have been "doing it" for years without giving each other any verbal feedback. This lab gave "permission" for such verbalization. This gave occasion for both tension and affirmation.

The group dialogue evidenced new freedom for some to discuss their sexual experience and expectations openly. This sometimes resulted in new energy both to express sexuality and to work on tension areas. Two couples expressed a negotiated breakthrough in their sexual behavior toward each other.

Day 4

9:00 A.M. The marriage contract
   —Intragroup dialogue: Opportunity was given to discuss the sexuality sessions as it related to the participants' marriage relationships.
   —Marriage contracting: On the basis of the data and experiences of this lab, couples were given opportunity to renegotiate the marriage contract.
   —Intragroup dialogue: Sharing of contract decisions.
   —Farewells.

Rationale for the "marriage contract." Experience reflected on and acted on contributes to growth. The last experience of the lab gave persons an opportunity to experience enrichment and to make decisions regarding the future of the relationship.

Results of the "marriage contract." With one exception, couples indicated new marriage vitality and hope for their marriages. Renegotiating marriage contracts included new levels of freedom, plans for relaxation and leisure, a commitment to therapy, new behaviors on intercourse, and opportunities for feedback.

Notes

1. Howard J. Clinebell, Jr., *Basic Types of Pastoral Counseling* (Nashville: Abingdon Press, 1966), pp. 240-41.
2. *Basic Reader in Human Relations Training*, Episcopal Church, p. 100. Available from the Rev. Kenneth J. Allen, 1220 W. 4th St., Los Angeles, Calif. 90051.
3. William J. Lederer and Donald D. Jackson, *The Mirages of Marriage* (New York: W. W. Norton & Co., 1968), chap. 14.
4. Howard J. Clinebell, Jr., and Charlotte H. Clinebell, *The Intimate Marriage* (New York: Harper & Row, 1970), chaps. 2 and 4.
5. This filmstrip is a part of the Unitarian Universalist Association's *About Your Sexuality* curriculum program (Boston: Beacon Press, 1970).

Chapter 19

The Marriage Communication Labs
Paul and LaDonna Hopkins

THE MARRIAGE COMMUNICATION LAB PROGRAM OF THE Christian Church (Disciples of Christ) was conceived in the fall of 1971 when four couples participated in a weekend experience led by Art and Bea Van Eck of the Reformed Church in America. The authors were the organizers of the marriage enrichment experience, having heard of the exciting and pioneering work being done by the Reformed Church and The United Methodist Church (under the guidance of Leon and Antoinette Smith) in this area. Our response as participants was even more enthusiastic than we imagined it might be! We found, as professionals who had participated in a number of encounter group experiences, that this enrichment approach offered most of the advantages and almost none of the threats which we had found in those experiences. And our marriage grew!

Since that first experience we have developed a basic design for Marriage Communication Labs which we have used in leading events and training leaders throughout the United States and Canada. We have already affirmed our debt to the United Methodist and Reformed Church programs, and it goes without saying that our approach has much in common with the programs of these churches. We have, however, developed our own style in many areas, which we believe gives our program some real uniqueness. In addition, we are continually revising portions of our design, remaining flexible and open to new insights and new approaches. No two labs we do are ever the same—not only because the participants are different, but also because we are different and some of the things we do are different.

Basic Presuppositions

We have some basic assumptions which guide the development of our labs and our program. These can be classified in two areas: "program assumptions" and "operational assumptions." The program assumptions guide the development of our total program in the United States and Canada. Some of the most important of these are the following:

227

An enrichment approach is the most feasable strategy for a church program. We are Christian educators, not therapists. Furthermore, we do not have the financial resources to train therapists, but we can train educators. And finally, an enrichment approach seems to be more effective and a better use of resources than an approach which works with pathology—often too late!

Focusing on the marriage relationship is the key to support of persons and families. We believe the maxim "As the marriage goes, so goes the family; as the family goes, so goes the world" to be true. Thus we concentrate our emphasis in programs with families on the marriage relationship, particularly at this time in history when marriage as an institution is undergoing intense pressures and radical changes.

Our design must be easily transferable as well as easily adaptable. Since we train leaders across the United States and Canada, we need to be able to train them as efficiently as possible. Thus we use a design which is almost "leaderless," in that the maximum potential is made of couple and small group interaction. On the other hand, the design has the potential of being adapted by leaders to their own style and to the needs of the participant couples. We have one area, for instance, which has developed the program by using the design which we suggested almost by rote. Another area, on the other hand, is using our design as a base and is doing more extensive training of leaders so that they can adapt it more easily to their own style.

Communication is the key to the relationship. We are aware that no weekend enrichment experience could deal with all the issues of the marriage relationship. But we believe that the key to all those issues is the way in which husbands and wives communicate with each other. Thus we concentrate on developing communication skills and helping couples use those skills in dealing with specific dimensions of their relationship. Because this is the focus, we chose the name Marriage Communication Lab.

It is more important and helpful to deal with process rather than content. Following closely upon the previous assumption, we believe that it is more important to help couples know how to deal with issues rather than to deal with a few specific issues or problems. Our emphasis, therefore, is not upon resolving a particular conflict, but on suggesting some processes and tools for resolving conflicts generally. We usually provide couples with an opportunity to work on particular issues, but in doing so we ask them to pay more attention in the lab to how they deal with them than to the issues themselves. These tools can then be applied to other situations outside the lab.

Couples can be more helpful to couples. We work as a leadership team and insist that couples we train for leadership do so also—although we recognize that another couple may work as a team differently than we do. But we are convinced that couple leadership is highly important. Time and again we have had, for instance, a wife say to Paul, "Somehow hearing you say it helps me hear what my husband has been saying to me for a long time." Or a wife says to LaDonna, "It's good to hear that someone else feels as I do." Of course, the converse is also true as husbands "hear" a female perspective or "identify" with a male leader.

The Christian dimension is more implicit than explicit. While we strongly affirm that we are doing "Christian" education, the Christian-ness is more a part of how we work than explicitly present. Occasionally, of course, we refer specifically to theology or Scripture, and we always close with a specifically Christian celebration or worship experience. But we believe that our affirmation of marriage and our "teaching to love" in very practical ways are in themselves Christian and do not always need Christian verbal symbols attached.

We also mentioned that we have some "operational assumptions" which undergird the way in which labs are conducted. Some of our more important operational assumptions are:

The lab is couple-oriented. We assume that couples have not come in order to develop a sense of "groupness" with other couples, but to work on their own relationship. The groupness usually develops anyway, but it does so in an entirely spontaneous way. Most of the time of the lab is devoted to doing things together as a couple—whether it is working on an exercise or playing or just relaxing. Often couples will choose to spend part of that couple time with other couples, but if they do it is purely voluntary.

The basic learning model is "do/reflect/draw conclusions." The lab is experiential education and inductive in approach. On two or three occasions we may make a brief input, but this usually comes as an introduction to an experience which provides most of the learning. Most of the time we deal with specific items by asking couples to do a specific exercise, to reflect upon that experience in terms of what it says to them about their relationship, and then to determine what changes they may want to make, if any.

Each is responsible for his/her own learning. We recognize that we cannot force people to learn things. So we "offer" and "suggest," but leave the "acceptance" and "use" to the persons involved. Not only does this take a great burden off the leaders' shoulders[1] (although we do affirm that we have a great responsibility for our teaching), but we have found that the learning which persons and couples do is much more significant because they have chosen to do it.

Lead couples are facilitators and have some skills, but are not perfect models. While we cannot take responsibility for the participants' learning, we can and do take responsibility for the skills which we have and the way in which we teach. So we work at sharing some specific skills and helping couples integrate those into their own relationship if they find them helpful. But we do not pretend to be perfect models ourselves, nor do we suggest that the skills we offer will be helpful to or needed by all couples. Part of what we have to offer, in fact, is that we are constantly working on our own relationship.

Participants share and do only what they feel comfortable sharing and doing. We make it very clear at the outset, and resist any pressure by the group to change, that the norm is voluntary sharing and participation. If couples or individuals choose not to participate in a particular exercise or activity, that is their decision to make. And no one is put on the spot to share with others in the group—or even with his/her own spouse—anything which he/she does not feel comfortable sharing. We may sometimes suggest to reluctant sharers that it would be helpful to reflect on why they may not wish to share—especially with their spouses—but we do not push.

The lab is education, not therapy. Though we have referred to this assumption at a couple of points already, it is important to emphasize that we assume we are working with educational skills in a preventive fashion, rather than in a therapeutic fashion with unhealthy relationships. This assumption, when it has been clarified and bought by the group, usually precludes any group session becoming more intense than is comfortable for the participants. It does not, however, prevent couples from sharing problems and ideas with each other. The assumption is also supported by pre-lab publicity and by the design of the lab itself, which is couple-oriented and voluntary.

The Lab Design

With these presuppositions in mind, then, how does a "typical" Marriage Communication Lab go? Of course, as we said earlier, there is no "typical" Marriage Communication Lab, because the group is different, we are different, and some of the things we do are different each time. But all the labs which we conduct have some things in common. Before we begin to describe those, however, let us say a word about the pre-lab preparations and the setting.

Our labs are most often publicized through the church at the local or regional level. All couples who enroll have seen a common brochure (which describes the lab and emphasizes that it is an educational event oriented to couples with basically healthy marriages) and have received a common letter from us welcoming them, suggesting what they need to bring, and giving directions to the lab site. This ensures that all have received the same pre-lab interpretation as well as helping them feel that they are welcome and that we as leaders are persons.

Couples always pay a registration fee which varies according to the cost of the facilities and the way in which leadership costs are handled. We believe it is important for couples to pay, not only to underwrite the costs but also because of the subtle factor that what we pay for, we are more likely to use and profit from. We also require that at least half of the registration fee be paid in advance, partly in order to secure facilities and partly to guard against last-minute cold feet!

We never do a Lab with less than four couples, because any less makes the group too small. If we have more than seven couples we enlist a second lead couple with whom we share leadership. An ideal size from our perspective is eight to twelve couples with two lead couples. This size group brings a wide variety of couples together and creates a sense of excitement. Having two lead couples eases some of the burden of leadership that would fall on only one couple's shoulders.

Our preference for facilities is a retreat center (Catholic retreat centers are usually ideal) which is private and peaceful, has private bedrooms and baths for each couple, a large carpeted meeting room for plenary sessions, and good meal service. (Again our prejudice is toward Catholic retreat centers. We believe Catholics must be better cooks than Protestants!) But we have done many labs under much less than ideal conditions and find that groups and couples can be remarkably flexible and innovative. Couples have discovered, for instance, that bunk beds can be pushed together quite comfortably, that noisy junior high youths in another group can be ignored, that bathrooms can be shared, and that it is even possible to bring extra mattresses in to make sitting on the hard cement floor of a church camp building tolerable! The setting is very important, but the only things which we would not give up would be a private meeting room and private bedrooms for couples. (Of course, we are describing a weekend retreat setting. The lab design could be adapted to weekly three-hour sessions or some other such schedule. But our emphasis has been upon the retreat style, so we shall discuss only that style.)

The necessary components of a lab design, from our perspective, and the order in which they should come, are these: welcoming and housekeeping details; brief community building; sharing expectations; teaching and practicing some basic communication skills (the emphasis being on communicating feelings); dealing with some specific dimensions of the marriage relationship (the group may determine this based on their expectations, but we always deal at least with conflict, sexuality, roles, and values in some way);

evaluation; and closing. These basic components may be developed in a variety of ways, depending upon the nature of the group and the needs which participants have expressed.

In addition we seek to provide some other kinds of opportunities. For instance, we think it is important to provide plenty of free time in which couples can simply relax and enjoy themselves. While we want to offer specific guidance in various areas, we do not want to push couples so hard and fast that they cannot enjoy the weekend together. Over a forty-four to forty-eight hour weekend, therefore, we generally use eighteen to twenty hours for planned agenda.

Another resource which we usually offer is a book display. Books such as *The Joy of Sex, The Massage Book, How Can I Show You That I Love You?* and *Sense Relaxation* offer words and pictures which couples discover can heighten their sensuality. Poetry books such as the works of Hugh Prather, James Kavanaugh, Ross Snyder, and Joseph and Lois Bird offer evocative reading for free moments. And "heavier" books such as works by the Clinebells, the O'Neills, and the Maces provide stimulation for thought and reflection about Marriage and relationships. Couples often carry books off to their rooms for free-time perusing—especially *The Joy of Sex!*

We could not do a lab without music. We have selected a variety of songs from various artists and put them together on tapes. We use this music for everything from background music to dance music to worship resources to specific input. Songs such as "Do You Love Me?" (from *Fiddler on the Roof*), "I Just Wanta Be Friends with You" (Bob Dylan), "Thank Heaven for You" (from *Don't Bother Me, I Can't Cope*), "The First Time Ever" (Roberta Flack), and "Time in a Bottle" (Jim Croce), can have a message all their own or can be used to introduce or conclude larger portions.

One other resource which we often find very much appreciated is the "paired couple." Although the emphasis is upon couple interaction, we do provide the opportunity at several points in the lab for couples to interact with each other. The "paired couple" is simply two couples together working on an agenda which we suggest. On the first evening, for instance, paired couples are formed (through self-selection) as they begin to share expectations. As we deal with communication skill practice, paired couples take turns being observers for each other, feeding back to each other what they see in a couple's interaction. In some labs these pairings become highly significant, even to the point where couples make commitments to check in with each other from time to time after the lab concludes.

So what happens, specifically, in a lab? As we said, it is never exactly the same, but we usually follow a pattern as already outlined. This pattern usually works something like this:

First Day: Evening

After some introductory remarks in which we welcome the couples, give them an overview of the schedule for the weekend, and make whatever housekeeping comments need to be made, we move into a short community building exercise. Rather than go around the room giving "name, rank, and serial number" we give short questions or completion statements, and ask individuals to pair up with someone they do not know and share their answers for two to three minutes. Questions and statements such as the following are used:

—"I'm happiest when . . ."
—"Right now I'm feeling . . ."
—"What was one of the funny experiences in your marriage?"
—"What was something significant your mate said to you or did for you today?"
—"What are three reasons your spouse is a good husband/wife?"
—"What are three reasons you are a good husband/wife?"
—"What are three reasons your marriage is a good marriage?"

After several pairings have been made, we ask couples to get back together and share whatever learnings they may have had in this experience. Usually this gives couples an opportunity to get a feel for a few of the other persons there, as well as being a learning experience for them.

We then move into a period of sharing and clarifying expectations. The process for this sharing is first to ask individuals to write down expectations in two categories: "hopes" and "fears." Then paired couples are formed and asked to compile their individual lists on newsprint and post these lists on the wall. Leader couples also put up their assumptions, and then all groups share their lists with the total group. This process gives everyone an opportunity to clarify what the lab is all about as well as to voice anxieties and have them dealt with in some way. Expectations range from the deeply serious fears (that "this weekend will uncover serious problems in our marriage" and that "the leaders are incompetent") to the frivolous (that "we will go streaking"). The sharing that goes on here is important for setting the tone for the rest of the weekend as well as to allay anxieties.

Following these introductory steps, we believe it is important to begin to get into some substantive agenda the first evening, however briefly. We usually begin by dealing with feelings and the way in which we handle and communicate feelings. Most often this period begins with an experience such as mirroring (in which partners "mirror" each other) or movement to music. This experience is designed to evoke feelings in the participants; we then ask them to brainstorm these as a group and we put them on newsprint. This serves as an introduction to a brief mini-lecture on feelings, the thrust of which is that we need to be more sensitive to and accepting of feelings, both our own and those of other people.[2] Following this mini-lecture we design some experience which enables couples to talk about their feelings and the way in which they communicate those feelings. This section of the lab varies quite a bit each time we do it, depending on what the group is like. We often use as resources (adapting their use to our needs) the Communications Resource Machines games "Body Talk" and "The Feel Wheel."

By the end of the first evening, then, we have done these things: everyone has "arrived"; we have clarified ground rules for the weekend; participants have become acquainted with each other a little; and we have begun to get into the matter of communication. Because couples have usually traveled some distance, and because the environment is still a little strange, couples usually head for bed early.

Second Day: Morning

The morning session of the second day is usually the hardest and most rushed session, but it often proves to be the most productive. We concentrate on the communication process and developing communication skills in this session. What is learned here is then applied to other issues as they are dealt with.

We introduce this session in various ways. Most often we use the One-Way and Two-Way Communication exercise,[3] in which partners sit back to back and one partner gives the other instructions on how to draw a design which he or she has. The first time, the partner who is drawing may not ask questions; but the second time he or she may ask clarifying questions. This is a fun way to get into communication which also provides some learnings about the communication process.

Two of the things which are always observed in the follow-up conversation are that it is important to listen well and to send clear messages. These two observations provide a lead-in for the rest of the morning, which we devote to teaching and practicing the skills of Active Listening and I-Messages from Thomas Gordon's *Parent Effectiveness Training*. Though we always regret that we do not have more time to devote to teaching these skills, we have discovered that significant learnings occur even in this brief time. We use a combination of mini-lectures, demonstration, written exercise, role play, and actual practice in the paired couples in order to teach these skills.

Second Day: Afternoon

Noon of the second day usually marks a turning point in the lab atmosphere. Prior to that time participants are still getting acclimatized and the content is a bit heavier and more rushed. The climate usually changes in the afternoon, however, as couples become more comfortable and the morning's work begins to pay off as they work with specific dimensions of their relationship.

The afternoon is usually divided in half, with one half being devoted to dealing with conflict and the other half being free time for couples. We usually begin dealing with conflict by sharing constructive and destructive patterns of conflict, as described in George Bach's *The Intimate Enemy*. Following this initial input and some initial conversation, we give couples a specific problem-solving process or conflict resolution model and send them off for an hour or so to work on a specific problem or issue. We have used at various times both the Parent Effectiveness Training Method III and a model developed by a colleague in Illinois, Terry Foland, as handles for the couples to use in this process. The important point is that we provide the couples with a *process* for resolving conflicts and problems which may arise, as well as the communication skills to use the process. We then structure forty-five minutes to an hour for total group discussion (or subgroups, if the group is large). This time is unstructured and may be used by couples to share learnings, to ask for further clarification of anything we have discussed to that point, or to share with the group specific problems they might be having.

Second Day: Evening

The evening session is designed for relaxation, fun, and romance. The subject is sexuality, but is sometimes described by couples as sensuality. We believe it is important to affirm and celebrate the sexual dimension of the marriage relationship, and we do so with music, candlelight, pictures, affirmations, and exercises. We also recognize that this is still an area of uptightness for many people, so we have designed no total group interaction for the evening. It is all couple-oriented.

We begin the evening with candlelight and soft music, inviting couples to relax and just enjoy being together. A part of this mood-setting and initial affirmation is the reading of a poem by Joseph and Lois Bird (from *Love Is All*) affirming lovemaking as a gift of God. Also a part of this affirmation is the showing of the "Lovemaking" filmstrip and a couple of recordings describing experiences with and feelings about lovemaking from the Unitarian sex education kit, *About Your Sexuality*. (We always announce ahead of time that this will be part of the evening so that those who might be offended can excuse themselves or come late.)

We then invite participants to take a fantasy trip back in time to the earliest experience they can recall in which they became aware of their maleness or femaleness. We ask them to begin at that point and come forward in time to the present, recalling all those occasions and persons who helped them shape their understanding of what it means to be male or female. After a few minutes of silent "traveling" we give mates an opportunity to share with each other what they feel comfortable sharing about their journeys. Usually persons have affirmed the experience as helpful in discovering and dealing with some attitudes and feelings about their sexuality. We have sometimes concluded this experience with a group affirmation of sexuality read responsively. This affirmation, drawn from the University of Minnesota's Sexual Attitude Reassessment program, gives the participants an opportunity verbally to affirm their own sexuality.

An important part of the evening is giving couples time to talk about their satisfaction with their present sexual relationship. This we do next, using Herbert Otto's excellent resource, the Love Life Development Test from *More Joy in Your Marriage*. We give couples forty-five minutes to an hour to go off together, fill out the test, and discuss their responses. We emphasize that it is not to be seen by anyone else and is for their own development.

We conclude the evening by returning to candlelight and soft music and inviting participants to take a twenty-four-hour fantasy holiday with their spouses. Money is no object and they may go anywhere or do anything they wish. After a few minutes of individual fantasy, we invite mates to share their holidays with each other. This delightful fantasy has on more than one occasion become reality for couples, as we have learned from later reports! We follow up this experience by providing wine, soft drinks, cheese, crackers, and soft music for dancing and conversation.

Third Day: Morning

The morning of the third day is usually divided into three or four parts, each focusing on a particular issue. We frequently begin by asking couples to take each other on "blind walks." Mates take turns being led, eyes closed, on walks in the building and around the grounds. This short exercise can be a sensory awakening experience, and the conversation following it usually raises issues of trust and leadership in the marriage.

We like to provide time for couples to deal with values in their relationship. We usually introduce this section with a brief mini-lecture, relying heavily on Raths, Harmin, and Simon's *Values and Teaching*. We then give couples an opportunity to process this material by using a variation of the values clarification strategy

Twenty Things You Love to Do, from *Values Clarification* by Simon, Howe, and Kirschenbaum.

Roles in marriage are becoming an increasingly important issue for couples. A helpful tool in this area which we use is the role performance/expectancy cards developed several years ago on the West Coast. Participants rank their own performance of roles in order of importance and then their expectations of their spouses' performance. These rankings are then compared, and lively discussion is usually sparked. We have revised these cards somewhat, basically to remove the sexist stereotyping which we found in the original set.

If we have time, we usually end the morning with group (or subgroup) discussion. This again is unstructured time for the group to use as they wish.

Third Day: Afternoon

The final afternoon usually has three or four components. The first of these components is goal-setting. We first ask individuals to write down one or two short-term goals (within three months) and one or two long-term goals (within one year). Mates are then asked to get together, share their individual ideas, and negotiate on one or two goals for each category which they will accept and work toward. These goals usually grow out of experiences during the weekend, and we have often received feedback from couples later that the goals were accomplished in a very satisfying way. We sometimes conclude this goal-setting portion by asking participants to write down three things which their mates do which they like and would like them to do more often. Mates are then asked to take turns telling each other about these things, and making some response indicating a willingness to comply.

We often put in a quick evaluation of the lab at this point. This quick evaluation—a listing of pluses and minuses about the lab—is helpful to us as we plan for future labs. But it is also helpful to the couples as they reflect on the learnings which they have had.

As we begin to close the weekend, we ask couples to do something which they probably haven't done for some time—write love letters to each other. We then collect these letters, sealed in addressed envelopes, and mail them a month later. Provided that the postal service cooperates, this experience has proved to be a delightful one for couples (though one couple did not receive their letters on the same day, which created some anxious moments around that household until the second letter arrived.) Couples usually have fun with this letter-writing, which adds to the enjoyment. Memories sometimes fade, however, as in the case of the wife who, as a joke, numbered her two-page letter 1 and 4—and then forgot she had done so. They teased us for a while about keeping pages 2 and 3 for our own reading.

As a closing celebration for the weekend we ask participants to find, create, think up, or write a gift for their mates which symbolizes something of what the weekend has meant to them. Then this gift-giving is interwoven in a closing celebration including poetry and the sharing of Communion—an act rich in Christian and loving symbolism. This closing celebration is frequently quite touching, and the gift-giving is an important part of it. And we have found that couples can be remarkably creative in "gift-shopping" in five minutes.

Conclusion

We continue to be excited about Marriage Communication Labs. Not only do we think our emphasis in these labs is correct from a theoretical standpoint, we actually see couples change and grow in their love for each other. We always send out evaluation forms after labs, and these forms reflect a consistent and highly positive appreciation for the experience itself and the learnings it involved. Those couples whom we see from time to time after their participation in labs continue to reflect a deepened relationship and an integration of some of the skills worked on in the lab.

And what is more, our own relationship has continued to grow. Not only have we profited from having frequent weekends together as a couple, but the process of shared leadership has provided us with some insights into our own interaction. And we have learned from all the couples who have been in our labs.

We think the best way of conveying the appreciation which couples have had for the experience is to share some excerpts from a letter we received from a woman who participated in a lab. She wrote:

> Perhaps the best way to begin is to relate how surprised I was when returning home and looking in the mirror. The mirror reflected the same features as always before—somehow because of feeling so different I expected to *look* different, too! . . . I can't pinpoint exactly when it happened, but sometime during the lab I was enabled to finish the task started at birth—that of becoming (in my own mind) a *real* person. . . . I'm not kidding myself that all of life will be "tip-top" from now on, but I am sure that I'll be able to "cope" in the future. I can't thank you enough for your part in this *miracle*. Tom wants to thank you also, but he can speak for himself!

While the response has not always been quite so ecstatic, we have received many such affirmations reflecting similar feelings. We are glad to be a part of creating a situation where such growth can occur.

Notes

1. We find Hugh Prather's reflection in *Notes to Myself* (Moab, Utah: Real People Press, 1970) helpful at this point: "What an ass I made of myself.—No, I didn't make the impression. It was his impression of me. I don't come across as any one thing. I don't predetermine a set reaction. There are any number of ways a person can react to what I do. How he chooses to react is his responsibility. (This is a little harder to see if I 'make a bit hit.')"
2. Hugh Prather in *Notes to Myself* again sums it up well when he says, "Both my body and my emotions were given to me and it is as futile for me to condemn myself for feeling scared, insecure, selfish or revengeful as it is for me to get mad at myself for the size of my feet. I am not responsible for my feelings, but for what I do with them."
3. J. William Pfeiffer and John E. Jones, *A Handbook of Structured Experiences*, vol. I (Iowa City, Iowa: University Associates Press, 1969).

Resources

A packet of materials containing exercise sheets, outlines for mini-lectures, and other materials used in Marriage Communication Labs is available for $6.00 from Marriage Communication Labs, P.O. Box 1986, Indianapolis, Ind. 46206.

Prather, Hugh. *I Touch the Earth, the Earth Touches Me*. Garden City, N.Y.: Doubleday & Co., 1972.
_____. *Notes to Myself*. Moab, Utah: Real People Press, 1970.
Comfort, Alex, ed. *The Joy of Sex* (illustrated ed.). New York: Crown Publishers, 1972.
Downing, George. *The Massage Book*. New York: Random House, 1972.
Bowen, Elisa. *How Can I Show You That I Love You?* Millbrae, Calif.: Celestial Arts, 1972.
Gunther, Bernard. *Sense Relaxation*. New York: P. F. Collier, 1968.
Snyder, Ross. *Inscape*. Nashville: Abingdon Press, 1968.
Bird, Joseph and Lois. *Love Is All*. Garden City, N.Y.: Doubleday & Co., 1968.
Rogers, Carl. *Becoming Partners: Marriage and Its Alternatives*. New York: Delacorte Press, 1972.

Pfeiffer, J. William, and Jones, John E. *A Handbook of Structured Experiences for Human Relations Training.* Vols. I, II, and III. Iowa City, Iowa: University Associates Press, 1969.

Bach, George R., and Wyden, Peter. *The Intimate Enemy.* New York: Avon Books [1969], 1970.

Clinebell, Howard J., Jr., and Clinebell, Charlotte H. *The Intimate Marriage.* New York: Harper & Row, 1970.

Clinebell, Charlotte H. *Meet Me in the Middle.* New York: Harper & Row, 1973.

Otto, Herbert A. *More Joy in Your Marriage.* New York: Hawthorn Books, 1969.

O'Neill, Nena and George. *Open Marriage.* New York: M. Evans & Co., 1972.

Gordon, Thomas. *Parent Effectiveness Training.* New York: Peter H. Wyden, 1970.

Goldstein, Martin, and Haeberle, Erwin. *The Sex Book.* New York: Herder and Herder, 1971.

Simon, Sidney; Howe, Leland; Kirshenbaum, Howard. *Values Clarification.* New York: Hart Publishing Co., 1972.

Raths, Louis; Harmin, Merrill; Simon, Sidney. *Values and Teaching.* Columbus: Charles Merrill Publishing Co., 1966.

Mace, David and Vera. *We Can Have Better Marriages.* Nashville: Abingdon Press, 1974.

Lederer, William J., and Jackson, Donald D. *The Mirages of Marriage.* New York: W.W. Norton & Co., 1968.

"Body Talk." Communications Research Machines, Inc., Del Mar, Calif.

"The Feel Wheel." Communications Research Machines, Inc., Del Mar, Calif.

Kavanaugh, James. *Will You Be My Friend?* Plainview, N.Y.: Nash Publishing Corporation, 1971.

About Your Sexuality. Deryck Calderwood. Boston: Beacon Press, 1970.

Chapter 20

Developing a National Marriage Communication Lab Training Program
Leon and Antoinette Smith

Marriage Communication Lab

In the middle of our second national marriage enrichment training, one of the leaders exclaimed, "Hey, what we are doing is learning to communicate as couples. We ought to call this a *Marriage Communication Lab!*" [1]

The name stuck, for our form of marriage enrichment is basically marriage communication about major concerns. [2]

A Marriage Communication Lab provides couples with an opportunity to enrich their marriages by opening and deepening the channels of communication so that they may find ways of improving their relationships. It is an *experience* in which groups of couples, under the guidance of trained and skilled leader couples, help each other to grow in their understanding of themselves and one another, how they affect one another, and ways they may enrich and strengthen their relationships. In a lab, couples have an opportunity to become aware of what is happening in their marriages, to discover both the strengths and weaknesses in their relationships, and to set new directions for future growth.

The purpose of a Marriage Communication Lab is to make good marriages better—to assist couples who have fully satisfying marriages to improve their relationships. It is not for troubled marriages that need therapy. A Marriage Communication Lab is not a substitute for marriage counseling. But we have found that it has the potential of preventing problems and of strengthening couples to face problems when they do arise.

The "content" of a Marriage Communication Lab is the participating couples—their marriages, experiences, and feelings about the ways they relate to each other; their growing awareness of each other's needs and desires; their expectations of one another; and their anxieties and hopes for the future. These may be explored through considering such concerns as what is happening in our marriage, improving communication in marriage, finding sexual fulfillment in

241

marriage, marital role expectations, indentity and intimacy, facing conflicts, expressing positive and negative feelings, deepening our spiritual life, enriching companionship, and planning our future.

A variety of methods may be used to help couples explore and enrich their marriages. These may include a number of groupings such as husbands and wives confronting one another as couples; one couple helping another couple; small groups of five or six couples; "fishbowls" in which husbands observe wives, and wives observe husbands (usually not their spouses), discussing a marital issue; or men and women in separate groups.

These methods may involve verbal and nonverbal techniques such as making collages, drawing pictures, and feeding one another, or an experience in one-way communication using wooden blocks. They may include reacting to films or records, sorting marital role cards, fantasizing, or being challenged and inspired by worship experiences. Today our labs are primarily experiential. Even though leaders may dialogue about certain facts or present a theoretical framework, such inputs are mixed with opportunities for couples to experience these understandings.

But it was not always so. In the early days our marriage enrichment groups were mainly discussion groups for couples *about* marriage. As leaders we presented a great deal of information, mostly in dialogue, but there was very little sharing on a personal level, either by the participating couples or by us as leaders.

History

Historically our labs have two roots—one from husband-wife groups in local churches and the other from clergy couples. The first grew out of couple groups in local churches in Roswell and Atlanta, Georgia, in the mid- and late 1950s. After more experimentation, we developed in the early 1960s a "study course" with a *Leader's Guide* for couples groups in local churches on "Romance in Christian Marriage."

The other source of our labs was marriage counseling seminars for ministers in the late 1950s and early 1960s. In a forty-eight hour seminar we usually had a session on the relationship of the minister's marriage to the practice of marriage counseling. Occasionally wives attended these seminars, especially when they helped with premarital counseling. It was the wives who insisted that the entire forty-eight-hour experience be devoted to marriage enrichment. We led the first of these in the spring of 1964 in Fayetteville, North Carolina, with eight or ten clergy couples.

By this time we were receiving so many requests to lead marital growth groups that we were convinced of the need for a national training program. We also realized that we needed more training to prepare us for such leadership. Thus in the summer of 1965 we went to Bethel, Maine, for the National Training Laboratory's Human Relations Lab. At that time, however, they offered nothing for couples. In fact, they would not permit husbands and wives to be in the same group. Nevertheless we found this training very helpful to us individually.

National Training Program

Selection of couples for training. From the beginning, the promotion of our national training program has been directed by the leaders of the church in each Annual Conference responsible for leadership development and family life. (An Annual Conference is roughly comparable to a state-level organization.) The Annual Conference is invited to join in a three-way agreement.

First, the Board of Discipleship (the national church agency which now finances and staffs the training program) agrees (1) to provide training and (2) to help find other trained leader couples to assist the one local couple in a lab in that conference. Second, the Annual Conference agrees to select and send for training one couple, chosen by the director of the Annual Conference Council on Ministries in consultation with the conference coordinator of family ministries. Selection is on the basis of certain qualifications. One of the partners must be a professional in the helping field. Each of the partners is rated on the following criteria (on a scale from 1 to 10): (a) whether he or she has a sound, satisfying marriage; (b) whether he or she is a warm, caring person; (c) ability to communicate understandings and insights to others; (d) ability to face problems and help persons to seek solutions; (e) experience and skill in group work; and (f) experience and skill in marriage counseling.

The Annual Conference also agrees to schedule a three-day Marriage Communication Lab for ministers and wives or other couples within the next several months following training; to use as leaders in the lab the one local couple sent for training and an additional couple trained by the Board; and to evaluate the effectiveness of the lab and report to the director of education for marriage and family life.

Third, the couple agree to prepare for the training by some reading and work on communication in their marriage; to receive training at a specified time, with full-time participation; to serve in two three-day labs without further remuneration—one in their own conference and one by invitation in another conference as can be scheduled; to be available for the next few years for a reasonable number of labs with expenses and honoraria paid by the host conference; and to evaluate the training at each lab and report to the director of education for marriage and family life.

The above method of selection of couples for training has proved very satisfactory. It has resulted in couples being chosen who already have group-work and helping skills, which we help them apply to marriage enrichment. This is absolutely necessary, for it is unthinkable that unskilled couples could be trained in five days. At the end of the training nine out of ten report that they feel ready to lead a lab. The fact that the couples are committed to leading a lab means that they are selected primarily for leadership training rather than for their marital needs. It also means that they are highly motivated to learn.

Size. Experience has taught us that ten training couples with two leader couples is the ideal size both for training and for a Marriage Communication Lab. It is possible to train as few as eight or as many as twelve couples with two leader couples, or even to involve fifteen training couples with three leader couples. But we have found that eighteen couples is too large a group for total community sharing, and a leadership team of six persons makes decision-making too slow and difficult. Further, we believe it is best to model the size, procedures, etc., in our training that we recommend for a lab.

Even though we have led groups with thirty or forty couples, using many of the experiences in a lab, we have found that the absence of small groups of five or six couples is a crucial loss. Of course, the interaction between spouses is our main concern, but in most of our labs what happens in the small groups is the heart of the experience.

Leader Preparation. Before the training couples arrive, the leadership team of two couples meets for one or two days to learn to work together as a team and to plan various segments of the training. The improvement in our labs through the years has been due to the creative work of many persons, mostly the other leader couples who team up with us. By the time the training couples arrive the leadership team has prepared an overview of the entire training experience, planned the first day in detail, and explored possibilities for ten or twelve marriage concerns from which four or five will be chosen after the couples indicate their needs and expectations.

Outline of a "Typical" Training Week

Full participation in the training session is required—from the first meal Monday noon through the noon meal on Friday. In fact, the leader couples take part in each experience just as the training couples do. We train for and model a *participatory style* of leadership.

Every training session is different because of the various skills of the leaders and the particular needs of the couples. But what follows is a sketchy description of a "typical" training session.

Orientation. After a word of welcome, the couples are invited to fantasize their preparation for leaving home, their trip and arrival—with their anxieties and hopes. This recognizes their mixed feelings and helps them to be fully present.

In a brief orientation an overview of the leadership team's proposals for the week is presented. The group is asked to agree to *experience* a Marriage Communication Lab for the first forty-eight hours and to reserve the last forty-eight hours for reflecting on their experiences in preparation for designing and leading their own labs. All groups have agreed to this kind of experiential learning, and have expressed appreciation for it.

This orientation also includes the leadership team's proposals for the Marriage Communication Lab itself, to cover six major blocks of time, each approximately three hours long. Each block of time is divided so that roughly half is given over to total community experiences and half to the small groups of five or six couples each. This alternation provides a change of pace, place, and purpose from input in the total community to mere free-flowing, couple-oriented small group work.

Possible areas of concern are mentioned, such as those listed at the beginning of this chapter. And some of the guidelines for the lab are reviewed: for example, couples are responsible for their own marriages and their own learning, and decide to what extent they wish to share in total community or small group; and the leadership team agrees to give complete instructions for each experience so that couples will not be made to think they are sharing something only with each other and are then surprised to be asked to share it with the total community. Such guidelines lower anxiety.

Experiencing a Lab

With the above background, we plunge into the lab by getting acquainted as *persons.* Each person is asked to tear out of an assortment of magazines three or four pictures (or series of words) saying something about the kind of person he is which he wishes to share with the group. These pictures are pasted on a piece of cardboard and hung around the neck with yarn for others to observe. Couples take turns going around the circle, with one spouse introducing the other by interpreting each picture or word. Then the partners may exchange whatever comments are desired.

To further the get-acquainted process and to focus on *marriage,* we ask spouses to talk over one of the most important things happening in their marriage at the present time which they would like to share with the group and to decide how to present it on newsprint—by drawing a picture, or with symbols, or colors, or however they choose. The newsprint is posted around the walls, and the group tries to verbalize what each husband and wife intend to say to us about their marriage. (No psychoanalyzing is permitted!) Then the couple explain what they actually intended to share. This process usually moves us into some meaningful material, often at a deep level. It gives the leadership team an idea of where each couple is at the present time. It demonstrates to the couples the guidelines just enumerated and is thus a freeing experience.

Small Groups. From the total community we move into two small groups for a brief time for three reasons: (1) to begin to establish the small group as a trust community for more sharing and processing of total community experiences among couples; (2) to invite the couples to share their anxieties and expectations regarding marriage enrichment (their expectations in order to guide the leadership team in planning the other sessions); and (3) to agree on ground rules for the small group, such as that each couple will decide what they want to share, we will share from our own experiences rather than from books or others or asking probing questions, and confidentiality will be respected.

Back in the total community, the leadership team sit in an inner circle, surrounded by the other couples, and list in generalized terms the marriage concerns they heard in the small groups as possible agendas for future sessions. The couples add other concerns if they wish.

Improving Communication in Marriage

The concern for "improving communication in marriage" has been included in every training we have led and usually comes in the second session as basic to the remainder of the lab.

As input, a leader couple dialogues about some of the main elements of communication (illustrating on chalkboard) with couples experiencing each element as presented: (1) two persons—sender and responder; (2) two levels—rational content and emotional feeling; (3) two kinds—verbal and nonverbal; (4) two dimensions—sharing and privacy.

Fishbowl. Fishbowling has proved very productive in helping persons to begin to share real concerns, to get in touch with some personalized enrichment possibilities, and to learn from one another.

The total community is divided into two equal groups of men and women, who are not spouses, to meet in different rooms. (1) Women sit in a tight inner circle, sharing, brainstorm fashion, "What I wish my spouse would do to improve communication in our marriage."

Men are in an outer circle, silently listening intently to learn all they can. (2) Men in center, responding to same statement as women—but *not* reacting to women, starting fresh with their own ideas. Women in outer circle, silently learning all they can. (3) Men and women in one circle, clarifying and confronting if they wish. A half-hour break allows couples to begin to share their learnings with one another.

In the small groups following, couples may want to process the previous input and experiences in the fishbowl. This is the first opportunity for "open time" for couples. Often at least one couple is ready to go. The leader couple may model if they have something real to work on, but they must be careful not to dominate the group or to forget their leadership responsibilities.

Leaders' Proposals for Remainder of Lab

After adjournment the leadership team meets, usually for two hours, to firm up plans for the remainder of the lab, based on needs expressed by the couples in the first session. These are presented as proposals to the total community the next morning:

1. **Tuesday morning:** Facing conflict in marriage
   Lunch as a silent shared meal
2. **Tuesday afternoon:** Identity and intimacy
   Role expectations for couples on their own
3. **Tuesday evening:** Sexual enrichment
4. **Wednesday morning:** Setting goals for growth

Facing Conflict

The morning session opens with wake-up exercises. One leader directs the group in individual stretching, bending, head-tapping, and body-slapping. These exercises energize and help one to be aware of and rejoice in one's total self, including the body, and to "thank God for me!"

In conflict management Virginia Satir's model is adapted to marriage and the stances experienced by each couple.[3] Also some destructive and constructive ways of marital fighting are identified.[4] One couple may, after adequate coaching, help another couple in working on a real conflict issue.

By this time small groups may have developed enough trust to permit depth sharing. Couples may want to make personal responses to the input conflict, or they may use the small group to complete the "one couple helping another couple" experience. Or, of course, they are free to work on whatever concerns them.

Shared Meal. For the shared meal at lunch finger food is provided.

Usually husbands are asked first to select food for their wives and to feed them silently, wives with eyes closed to emphasize dependence and to heighten awareness. Different food is provided for wives to choose and feed to husbands in like manner. This feeding lets the partners experience caring for and being cared for. The experience is processed in the total community immediately following, by sharing feelings about various aspects of the feeding.

Identity and Intimacy

After some free time, the afternoon session on identity and intimacy is structured so that most of the time is spent with men in one group and women in another discussing "How can I be me and be married?" Preparation in the total community may consist only in opening up the subject of ways to deal with tensions which often exist between autonomy and closeness, or it may include listening to the song "I've Gotta Be Me" from *The Golden Rainbow*. Summaries of the separate group discussions are presented to the total community for further processing.

Small groups are again free-flowing for couples to use as they wish. However, if the group bogs down, the leader couple may decide to introduce the wooden block-building experience in one-way communication and role performance.

Role Expectations. At the end of the small group session couples are given sets of marital role expectation cards with instructions for using these on their own. Ranking the role cards enables one to compare one's own performance with one's mate's expectations. Some couples process these further in the next small group session.

Sexual Enrichment

The purpose of the Tuesday evening session is to help spouses enrich their sexual relationship. A few introductory remarks are made by one of the leader couples about the importance of sex in marriage and the difficulty of developing wholesome attitudes toward sex because of our sex-rejecting and sex-exploiting culture. (We are still plagued with many sexual myths.)

In groups of two couples each, the trainees brainstorm some of the common false notions regarding sex in marriage today. These are reported and listed on newsprint—often twenty or thirty times. Some of them are discussed in the process, but many are answered in the film *Sexuality and Communication* (a presentation in lecture and role play of the female and male sexual responses in the context of the total marital relationship). It was made by the husband-wife team Beryl and Noam Chernick (both of whom are medical doctors) and produced by Ortho of Canada.[5]

The list of false notions suggests times for discussion in the small groups or by the couples on their own. Many couples report that these sessions help them to begin talking about the specifics of their sexual relations in more depth and detail than ever before.

Setting Goals for Growth

The Wednesday morning session begins with another wake-up exercise. The purpose this time is not only to energize and celebrate one's own body but also to increase husbands' and wives' awareness of the value of giving and receiving through physical touch. This time husbands and wives are asked to gently slap each other's arms, back, buttocks, thighs, and legs. "Thank God for one another!"

Although done in the context of the total community, setting goals for growth in marriage is an experience for couples alone. Each partner writes on a sheet of paper as many items as time allows under three headings: (1) "I want for me . . ."; (2) "I want for you . . ."; (3) "I want for us . . .". After fifteen or twenty minutes spouses share their lists with each other and discuss their meanings. Then they are asked to choose one item from each list and begin to work on ways to accomplish them.

Small Group. The final session of the small group takes care of any "unfinished business" but does not open up any new material. Closure must be definite and may be done verbally and nonverbally.

Celebration. The last meeting of the total community as a Marriage Communication Lab closes with a celebration of marriage and a renewal of our commitment to God and to one another.

Training for Leadership

In the second half of the training we make a definite shift of focus to the couples' concerns for their *leadership* of future labs. At the onset an overview of the proposed agenda for the remainder of the training is presented so that the couples can see each session in perspective and decide whether the proposed structure provides space for their questions. If not, changes can be made. The following is a typical schedule:

Wednesday afternoon: Reflection on total
   community experiences

Wednesday evening: Additional resources

Thursday morning: Reflection on small group
   leadership

Thursday afternoon: Designing a lab

Thursday evening: Report of design teams

Friday morning: Administration and evaluation

In the overview, the couples are told that in the closing session they will be asked to evaluate their own readiness to lead a lab. This procedure encourages them to make full use of the intervening sessions. The overview also alerts the couples to the fact that on Thursday afternoon each couple will choose another couple to become the design team to outline the kind of lab they would feel comfortable in leading. A guiding question for the next three sessions is: What additional information, resources, etc., do you need to be able to design your own lab?

Total Community Experiences

In reflecting on the total community experiences, we usually follow a chronological review of each of the sessions. This gives the participants a framework around which to organize their questions. Questions often include requests for such information as the purpose and basic assumptions underlying the entire lab or a particular experience, as well as clarification of the exact wording of an "assignment." At times some want to know other ways of working on the same issue which was in the schedule, or resources and experiences that might be used with other issues. Thus many additional resources are shared in the process.

Often wives of professionals are anxious about the extent of their own participation in total community leadership. They are reminded that each person, or each couple, chooses the method and extent of participation that is comfortable. But they are encouraged to share as fully as possible.

Additional Resources

Additional resources include reviews of articles, books, films, posters, records, and tapes, as well as printed descriptions of other experiences that might be used with other marriage concerns. We have most of these items on display and some for distribution and are able to provide the names and addresses of organizations supplying these materials. We try to close this session early enough for the group to go out for pizza or other refreshments, for we believe that having fun together is an important element in building community. Further, both the Marriage Communication Lab and the training are such intense experiences that a break is essential.

Small Group Leadership

When we reflect on small group leadership, the same small groups reassemble to reflect on their common experience. But attention must be focused on leadership concerns and not on reestablishing the small group. To aid in this transition the small groups meet in a different place instead of returning to their old "nest."

Concerns frequently expressed are: How can we facilitate couple participation and not be forced into a dominant role in the group? To what extent can the leader couple participate in the small group without losing sight of their leadership responsibilities? How do we keep one couple from dominating the group, especially if that couple seems to be looking for therapy instead of enrichment? How do we bridge from the total community to small group interaction? What is the wife's unique contribution to the leadership of the small group?

Designing a Lab

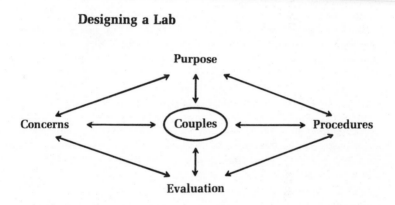

After a brief description of some of the essential elements in designing a lab—needs of the couples (the basis for the design), the purpose of each session, content concerns, methods and resources, and evaluation—the design teams are asked to develop a schedule for a lab they feel capable of leading.

A forty-eight-hour lab in a retreat setting is suggested, but they are free to describe any other format they think their groups back home need, such as six three- or four-hour evening sessions meeting once a week in a local church. We recognize that they will include many of the concerns and methods in the present training lab, but they are encouraged to include any issues or procedures from their own experiences they like. The major emphasis is on designing the kind of lab they feel ready to lead. They are asked to be ready to report—perhaps on newsprint—at the evening session.

Design Teams' Report

When the design teams report the group responds by asking questions for clarification and critiquing each proposal. Although time is quite limited for each team, it does allow for considerable learning by both the presenters and the other couples.

Administration and Evaluation

The closing session is an opportunity for questions and responses on administrative issues: the planning committee and its work, choosing the leadership team (the host couple selects another leader couple), promotion and selection of couples, preparation of the couples, finances, site selection and equipment, how to make referrals when marriage counseling is needed, evaluation and follow-up.

Sometimes couples want a comparison of the Marriage Communication Lab with other kinds of marital growth groups, such as the free-flowing Quaker marriage enrichment, the couple-centered Roman Catholic Marriage Encounter, or the more highly structured forms of marriage enrichment.

Advanced Training. Couples are encouraged to plan for advanced training in a year or so, after they have led two or more labs. At that time they will reflect on their own experiences in actually leading labs. They are also encouraged to consider further training for more specialized labs which focus on in-depth training in communication skills or in sexual enrichment. We urge them to join ACME, the Association of Couples for Marriage Enrichment (see chapter 15).

Evaluation. The training couples do their own self-evaluation, and report whether they are ready to lead a lab. If not they are asked what additional preparation—training, reading, lab experiences, etc.— they need. All are asked what kind of support, resources, etc., they want from their Conference Council or from the national office.

Celebration. Usually the closing celebration is a rejoicing not only in our own marriages and our life together in training, but also in our being a part of a growing, worldwide movement to strengthen and enrich marriage.

Notes

1. Frank Bockus at the Yokefellow Institute, Richmond, Indiana, January 27, 1967.
2. "Marriage Communication Lab" is the name of one of the major forms of marital growth groups in the United States—the one sponsored by The United Methodist Church. "Our form

of marriage enrichment" therefore refers to The United Methodist Church, even though the two of us have been involved in the program from its inception. At this writing we have helped to train more than 500 couples. These couples include a number from other denominations who have trained additional couples in their churches and developed their own Marriage Communication Lab programs. We estimate that more than 150 additional couples have been trained by others.

3. See Virginia Satir, *Peoplemaking* (Palo Alto, Calif.: Science and Behavior Books, 1972), chap. 5, "Patterns of Communication," pp. 59 ff.
4. See George R. Bach and Peter Wyden, *The Intimate Enemy* (New York: William Morrow & Co., 1969).
5. Write to Ortho Pharmaceutical (Canada) Ltd., 19 Green Belt Dr., Don Mills, Ontario, Canada, for information about the film *Sexuality and Communication*.

Chapter 21

Cassette Programs for Training and Enrichment
Howard J. Clinebell, Jr.

HOW CAN WE BEST RESPOND TO THE CHALLENGE AND opportunities with which the exciting developments in marriage and family enrichment confront us? There's a vast untapped potential in our counseling practices and in our helping agencies, both for preventing marriage disasters and for helping couples make good marriages (and even *fair* marriages) better. With the present crisis in marriage, it's obvious that there's an urgent, widespread need for this enrichment potential to be developed. But, to do this will require the creation of two things: more widely available programs for training enrichment facilitators, and more comprehensive and available marriage enrichment programs in our major people-serving institutions—particularly churches, schools, and community agencies.

A network of enrichment groups, classes, and workshops in an institution or a community provides opportunities for couples to enliven and enhance their relationships at each stage of marriage. A truly comprehensive program should begin with remote preparation for marriage (youth growth and identity groups). It should continue in premarriage growth groups, followed by enrichment experiences for young marrieds and young parents. It should include middle years marriage retread retreats, emptying nest enrichment events, and creative retirement workshops. Women's and men's consciousness raising groups, divorce recovery groups, and creative singlehood groups should all be included. The program's unifying goal is to provide encouragement, coaching, and training to help couples develop their own unique, mutually fulfilling relationship at each stage. It is a way to make marriage an ongoing growth experience, which liberates the fullest possible potential of each partner.

As the reports in this volume make clear, a fresh breeze is blowing through the institutions of marriage and the family. An encouraging variety of models and methods have been tested and are now available. Our understanding of the philosophy and psychology of growth has evolved to the point where we have a reasonably firm conceptual foundation for enrichment programs and methods. More people—professionals and trained lay enablers—are learning skills of growth facilitation and enrichment. In some institutions, innovative enrichment programs are already demonstrating their remarkable power to release couples from flat, boring, and underdeveloped marriages, by helping them learn mutual nurturing of their love.

Institutions responding to the challenges of the enrichment approach are beginning to catch a new vision of their reason for being. They see themselves as *human development centers*. There's a lift and excitement in the atmosphere of those churches, schools, and social agencies which implement this vision.

The deeper message behind all this is that we may be witnessing a major breakthrough in our society—a breakthrough to a more humanizing and potentializing life for more and more people, through all the stages of the human journey! Those involved in marriage and family enrichment are challenged to be participants in this breakthrough! The marriage enrichment movement (and the human potentials movement which is its broader context) is helping to make possible a society in which all persons have full opportunity to use their intelligence, their rich creativity, and their capacities for mutually enhancing relationships.

An Answer to Some Missing Ingredients

Think about the realities of your situation. What makes it difficult to develop a comprehensive (or even a functioning) marriage enrichment program in your institution or practice? If your situation is like many, the problem stems from one or more of three deficiencies: first, not enough well-trained leaders (enrichers); second, not enough couples who are motivated to participate in ongoing enrichment programs; third, not enough *practical* resources—lively content and/or useful processes.

It is my experience that the audio-cassette player is a device which can be of significant help in meeting each of these three needs. It isn't a panacea, of course. But, we have only scratched the surface of its possibilities as a vehicle of grass-roots training of marriage enrichers, for providing low-threat enrichment opportunities (for couples with low motivation), and as a way of providing lively input in enrichment groups. The purpose of this paper is to describe some of the productive ways in which cassettes have been used, and can be used, to meet these three basic needs. I will illustrate some of the principles by referring to experiences I have had with a series of "Growth Counseling" cassettes, with which I have been working for the past two years. At the conclusion, I will give an overview of some of the enrichment cassettes which are available.

Growth-Oriented Learning Is Essential

Cassettes are useful as enricher training tools, as resources in enrichment counseling and groups, and as a way of motivating

quality of marriages and has practical ways to help couples improve the quality of theirs. And, as a program becomes more accepted and comprehensive, *ongoing nurture of marriages* becomes increasingly normative in that social environment.

Experiential Learning Is Essential

The usefulness of cassettes, as training and enrichment tools, is increased dramatically if experiential learning is central. Learning-by-doing is basic in all enrichment work and counseling. This means that it's important to involve the learner in actually experiencing the issues, principles, and skills being discussed on the cassette. For example, in a cassette course on enhancing sexual intimacy, in the Growth Counseling series, participants are led through a series of experiences designed to help them actually *do* what the co-leaders are discussing—e.g., practicing non-demand pleasuring (including full-body caressing), creating a more sensual setting for lovemaking, communicating about what each likes most during lovemaking. During "Highlights of a Marriage Enrichment Workshop," we ask participants to invite their spouses to join them as they try the relationship-building exercises themselves. We assume that the principles of sexual enrichment or of leading a workshop probably will be understood so that they can actually be used only if they are experienced as well as talked about. Since experiencing awareness exercises or skills is both the best way to learn to help others use them and a way to enrich one's own relationships, those in training get double mileage out of experiential learning.

One aspect of experiential learning that's valuable in all marriage enrichment and training is the message communicated (nonverbally) by having a man and a woman as co-leaders or co-trainers (with equal responsibilities). With the revolution in the basic identity of women that is occurring everywhere, and the consequent profound changes in men's identities, having only one leader, or co-leaders of the same sex, impoverishes the enrichment experience of the group. Ignoring, on a leadership level, the social revolution which is having the most profound, shaking, and potentially creative impact on marriage, will truncate and may even invalidate the enrichment experience at the very point where many couples need most to change. For this reason, it is also desirable to have enrichment cassettes which include both male and female participants in facilitator roles.

Using Cassettes to Train Marriage Enrichers

Research has shown that the quality of the leader's skills and relationships is by far the most important variable in growth groups or enrichment programs.[2] This factor determines to a large extent whether a marriage enrichment group actually enriches marriages, or has indifferent or negative results. How can cassettes be useful in improving one's own enrichment skills and in training others to lead a comprehensive program? Cassette training courses have a number of assets. Since most people who do counseling have access to a tape recorder, cassettes make training easily available. They are an efficient way to augment a live trainer's impact. They allow groups of persons desiring training (but not having access to expensive or distant courses) to form small do-it-themselves learning clusters, using the person on the cassette as the instructor-facilitator, supplemented by relevant literature. Cassettes also make it possible for professionals with therapeutic supervisory-training skills, but little or no background in the enrichment approach, to upgrade their training courses and improve their skills by using the cassettes as a co-instructor.

A comprehensive enrichment program can be staffed, in most cases, only if more of the *natural growth facilitators,* who are present in every institution and community, are identified and trained. Enrichment training opportunities, strengthened by the use of cassettes, should be made available to the following:

- —counselors and mental health professionals who want to move beyond the repair model by learning growth skills;
- —ministers who want refresher courses in pastoral care and counseling (the growth approach is deeply rooted in the Hebrew-Christian tradition);
- —teachers, nurses, and other person-centered professionals who are interested in positive approaches to education and prevention;
- —seminary, social work, and counseling students in courses on methods of helping persons;
- —trained lay counselors and paraprofessionals who resonate to the growth approach;
- —lay individuals and couples, usually identified during enrichment groups and workshops, who are naturally gifted as growth enablers.

Through a program of systematic training, ongoing coaching, and the help of cassettes, lay facilitators can lead most of the enrichment events for "normal" couples in churches and schools with back-up support by professionals. Cassettes make it possible for persons with less sophisticated training to feel secure and to lead growth groups effectively. Deprofessionalizing much of the leadership of enrichment events maximizes the growth of lay persons and frees more of the time of highly trained professionals for lay training and other activities for which they have specialized skills.

When I began to try my hand at developing cassette training courses on "Growth Counseling," I found the project to be an uphill struggle. (It was much easier to write books than to communicate in any creative way via cassettes.) At one point, when I was questioning whether it was worth the effort, I was at a workshop for ministers in the Pacific Northwest. There I met a man who lives in Montana, far removed from ongoing opportunities for professional enrichment. Out of his own needs, he said, he had rounded up five or six colleagues who shared his need for tool-sharpening. Using cassettes from various sources, they were meeting each week, early in the morning in a learning group, rotating leadership among themselves. He said they had found some help in a cassette that had been made at a lecture I had given, a year before, on how to start a marriage enrichment program. From my perspective, that cassette must have been a second-rate teaching tool, being a straight lecture. Yet, even it had proved useful to this little group of self-motivated ministers. I remember returning to Claremont with a new incentive to finish the cassette project which had been kept dangling in my ineptness and struggles to learn to teach via a new medium. That minister had made me more aware of the potential usefulness of cassettes as instruments of continuing professional education.

Some Suggestions for Using Cassettes in Training and in Enrichment Groups

Feedback from persons using cassettes in enrichment work, and my own experience in this, suggest that maximal learning tends to occur when the following guidelines are followed:

1. *The best results occur when cassettes are used in small learning groups.* Interpersonal skills of any kind, including enrichment skills, are learned most readily in an interpersonal environment characterized by mutual support, openness, and willingness to risk. In enrichment workshops and in cassette courses it is important to emphasize doing "growth work" in small groups (six to eight persons), with or without a designated leader. I encourage professional counselors to invite their spouses to participate in training courses and enrichment groups with them, as important steps in preparing to co-lead enrichment events. Cassette training courses can be adapted for use as solo refresher courses, but users get more from the experience if they use the cassettes in a peer group. Of course, a husband and wife *can* constitute a learning group by themselves either for training or for enrichment. Working alone as a couple can be very valuable; this value will be enhanced if they also meet with a growth-support group of other couples regularly.

2. *It's important for the cassette learning group to have a clear,*

mutually acceptable contract with respect to its meetings. This is important in any group, but particularly so in peer-led groups. Cassettes are more apt to be helpful if the group meets regularly (preferably weekly), for a designated series of sessions, with an agreed-upon purpose. Unless the group has a clear contract and high priority for the participants, erratic attendance will reduce the potential learning opportunities for everyone. The group's contract can be renegotiated at the end of a series of sessions.

3. *A trained leader is desirable but not essential* (if the group is composed of relatively healthy individuals or couples). If a competent, growth-oriented facilitator is available to lead, a training or enrichment group usually moves faster and makes more productive use of cassettes than a peer-led group. However, many people mobilize more of their inner resources, and therefore grow more rapidly, when they must share responsibility for decisions and leadership. This distribution of the leadership functions should occur in any enrichment group, with or without a leader.

4. *Cassettes are most effective when they are used flexibly and adapted to the particular needs and interests of a group.* Cassettes are a resource and not a substitute for group and leader decisions about the unique shape of the enrichment experience in the particular situation. In peer-led groups in which no one is experienced in group methods or enrichment approaches, it may be most productive to follow a cassette course with only minor adaptations (or a book, chapter by chapter) to provide structure for the meetings. The courses which are best suited for use in this way are those which combine experiential exercises with didactic material (for example, in the list of resources at the end of this chapter, see the Malone series and the Clinebell series). Cassettes which are entirely lectures (the others on the list) can be useful to stimulate discussion and communicate important insights. In planning for their use, however, generous blocks of time should be scheduled for group interaction and experiential learning exercises between each segment of lecture input.

5. *Skill-practice or learning-by-doing is essential in all training and enrichment work.* People learn what they want to know and what they can use! This is the basic principle of experiential education. Creative teaching-learning is apt to occur if the enabler-instructor (on a cassette or in the flesh) intersperses *brief* statements about useful skills and working principles of enriching a marriage, for example, with frequent opportunities for the potential learner to practice the skills or experience the principles or insights. Frankly, I'm skeptical about the effectiveness of a thirty-minute monologue on communication, however insightful, unless the hearer has several opportunities during that time to practice skills such as responsive

listening and to receive immediate feedback from peers and/or the leader, whose role is coaching to help improve that person's skill.

6. *Modeling by the instructor of the behavior being discussed facilitates learning in both training and enrichment.* The facilitator (on a cassette or "live") should risk by showing himself or herself *in action, doing* what is being talked about. Modeling is one of the four essential ingredients in both training and enrichment, the others being *useful theory, supervised skill-practice,* and experiencing a *learning-support group.* I have found that demonstrations that are "for real"—e.g., of a couple growth session, a marriage enrichment group, a divorce recovery group, a healthy family growth interview—seem to be more useful to leaders in training than do role-played situations. The modeling in enrichment workshops is done primarily as the leaders or co-leaders or group members interact and communicate in ways that confirm or contradict the content of their statements.

7. *Provide flexible, growth-oriented structure for both training and enrichment.* At the close of a one-day enrichment retreat, one person wrote: "The most helpful thing was to tell your spouse the things you like and appreciate in him . . . also to tell him your needs. We haven't done that in twenty-three years of marriage!" The thing that made this possible for this couple was a communication exercise which we call the Intentional Marriage Method. This is a simple four-step approach by which couples can affirm their strengths, identify unmet needs, recontract to meet some of these, and check out their plan with a peer-support group. This has proved to be a meaningful experience for many couples. How they use the structure is up to them—that's the flexibility. But, the structure seems to help couples communicate and do what they haven't done without it. In general, flexible structure helps to make the use of cassette material and exercises more helpful.

8. *Provide a variety of types of learning opportunities.* People learn in various ways and relationships. In planning for the use of cassettes in an enrichment workshop, think in terms of four types of activities: *large group* (e.g., input sessions); *mini-groups* of three or four couples; *couples working alone; free time* for fun, relaxation, quiet talks, etc. Segments of cassettes can be useful in all of these. For example, they can be used as input in the whole group or in small groups. Or, couples with a special interest can gather to listen to a cassette and discuss that subject. Cassette training courses should provide for a good balance of various types of activities.

9. *"Homework" for couples or trainees is very useful.* Asking couples in an enrichment group to listen to a particular cassette and be prepared to discuss it at the next session is an excellent way to encourage them to continue their growth work at a satisfying,

sustained level. Suggesting that they record and listen to one of their skill-practice sessions is also useful homework.

10. *Encourage the participants to enjoy experimenting, experiencing, and growing in their love-nurturing skills.* Creative learning, like all creativity, seems to be related to open interaction between one's inner Adult and one's playful, experimental Child (in Transactional Analysis terms). Growth work *is* work. It does require struggle and sometimes pain to grow. But it is also deeply satisfying and a source of joy, in a profound sense, to learn how to use more of oneself in relationships. The climate created by a cassette should not be heavy or dull. The excitement of growth and the affirmation of new strengths should be experienced in enrichment events of all kinds.

I have listed the guidelines of enrichment and training together because of my conviction that the same principles of experiential learning apply, whether the primary purpose of the group is to enrich marriages or train enrichers. Furthermore, *every marriage enrichment group should also be a training group*—i.e., it should emphasize outreach to help enrich the lives and relationships of others! This outreach is integral to one's own growth. Conversely, *every training group should include enrichment of the intimate relationships of the would-be enrichers.* We can't give what we haven't got. Beyond personal growth and enrichment, the enabler needs a variety of additional training experiences to be adequately prepared—an understanding of individual and group dynamics, skills in group facilitating and enrichment methods, etc. But being a growing person is the foundation for everything else in sound training. Training cassettes should provide resources for the various aspects of training, including increased personal awareness and growth.

In his beautiful essay on education, Martin Buber, a philosopher of relationships and growth, declared, "In every hour the human race begins."[3] He went on to point out that education focuses on "the treasure of eternal possibility and the task of unearthing it."[4] In these two lines from Buber the challenge and the promise of the enrichment movement are well expressed!

Notes

1. I have discussed the methods and principles of leading growth and enrichment groups elsewhere. See *The People Dynamic: Changing Self and Society Through Growth Groups* (New York: Harper & Row, 1972).
2. See, for example, Morton A. Lieberman et al., *Encounter Groups: First Facts* (New York: Basic Books, 1973).

3. *Between Man and Man* (Boston: Beacon Press, 1955), p. 83.
4. *Ibid.,* p. 84.

Resources

Here are the cassette resources of which I am aware. There are undoubtedly others.

Experiential Learning Series

1. *Growth Counseling: Part I. Enriching Marriage and Family Life* (Abindgon Press, 201 Eighth Ave., South, Nashville, Tenn. 37203, 1973). Eight courses by Howard Clinebell, with the collaboration of Charlotte H. Clinebell. Topics include: "Growth Counseling—Basic Tools"; "Leading a Marriage Growth Group"; "Highlights of a Marriage Enrichment Workshop"; "Using Marriage Problems for Growth"; "Enriching Parent-Child Relationships"; "Enhancing Sexual Intimacy"; "Counseling for Liberation." Part II includes courses on "The Crisis of Divorce" and "The Crisis of the Mid-Years." Each series has a *User's Guide.* Courses designed for use in training marriage enrichers, counselors, and lay befrienders; most of them are also useful for couples, individually and in groups. (eight-course, four-cassette series, $27.95; separate cassettes, $7.95).
2. *Marriage Enrichment Program* (Human Development Institute, 166 E. Superior St., Chicago, Ill. 60611). Five sessions by Thomas P. Malone, an Atlanta psychotherapist. (Originally published by Bell and Howell as *Intimacy: An Encounter Program for Couples.*) Topics: "Opening Up" (communication); "Listening" (to feelings); "Paining" (dealing with the pain); "Touching"; "Risking and Growing." The sessions blend communication and awareness exercises with theory. Designed for use by individual couples, it is now adapted for use by leaders in groups. Growth-oriented. (Professional version, $89.50; couples' version, $29.50.) Closes with a philosophy of self-other fulfillment: "I hope I can help you become what you are for that is a part of my own becoming."

Lecture Series
(Useful in ways described earlier)

1. *The Family* (Family Enrichment Bureau, Escanaba, Mich. 49829). Fourteen talks by marriage counselor Urban G. Steinmetz. Designed for use in couples seminars. Topics include: "Marriage Is for Real"; "Improving Communication"; "The Complicated Me" (self-understanding); "The

Many Meanings of Sexual Intercourse"; "What Is an Adult?"; "Thoughts on Child-Rearing"; "Sex Education in the Home"; "The Church and the Home," etc. Informal conversational style. (Eight cassettes, $50.00.)

2. American Association of Marriage, Child and Family Counselors cassettes (C. Jay Skidmore, Tape Coordinator, 1425 Maple Dr., Logan, Utah 84321). Over one hundred cassettes on a wide variety of topics by leaders in the marriage and family counseling field. List available to professionals. Some cassettes could be useful in training marriage enrichers. ($5.00 to $7.00 per cassette.)

3. *Making Marriage Work* (Human Development Institute). Ten cassettes of lectures on the dynamics of premarriage, marriage, and parenting, by Carl Whitaker, University of Wisconsin, Department of Psychiatry. Topics include: "Learning the Premarital Dance"; Coming Together"; "A Marriage Is a Marriage"; "Avoiding the Deadlock"; "The Children Grow and Go." Filled with suggestions for avoiding problems and keeping a marriage growing. ($78.98.)

4. *Negotiating a Divorce* (Human Development Institute). A six-cassette lecture series by Carl Whitaker and attorney Newton Frohlich, beamed at persons experiencing divorce. Whitaker's topics include: "Prevention of Divorce Problems"; "Psychotherapy as a Divorce Facilitator"; and "Post-divorce Psychotherapy." Frohlich's include: "Choosing a Lawyer" and "Negotiating a Divorce." This insightful series could be used as a content resource in divorce growth groups. ($39.95.)

5. *Overcoming Sexual Inadequacy* (Instructional Dynamics, Inc., 166 E. Superior St., Chicago, Ill. 60611). Twelve cassettes of lectures by Stephen Neiger, Director, Behavior Therapy Clinic, Lakeshore Psychiatric Hospital, Toronto, Canada. Designed to be listened to by individual couples, they could be a useful adjunct in marriage counseling and enrichment. For couples who have difficulties in the areas of maintaining an erection, ejaculation timing, arousal, or orgasm diminution. Topics include: "Damaging Myths About Sex," "Sex Without Intercourse"; "New Findings on Sexual Responses"; "Sex Gadgets"; "Body Exploration"; "How Men Can Last Longer"; "Communicating About Sex"; "Novelty and Variety"; "Relax and Enjoy It." Sound, up-to-date information; enlightened attitudes; and helpful suggestions for couples who want to enhance their sexual pleasuring. ($89.50.)

Appendix

Additional Marriage and Family Enrichment Resources

Marriage and Family Enrichment Programs

Jerry and Elizabeth Jud, Kirkridge Shalom Retreats.
"Here we are discovering the Biblical affirmation of life, of oneself and others, in oneness of mind, body, and emotions. We are seeking to become open and free, to take the risk of sharing anger, pain, and fear which block our capacity to live and love fully, deeply, and with joy. This means our becoming newly able—in a Hebrew-Christian tradition—to give and receive love. We help each other grow, through encounter, non-verbal communication, Gestalt methods, exercises in sensory awareness, fantasy, and feedback" (free descriptive leaflet). For more information write to Dr. Jerry Jud, Kirkridge, Bangor, Pa. 18013.

Ted Bowman, *Enrichment Weekend for Total Families.*
A complete report outlining a weekend program and many helpful ideas. ($1.00 per copy.) For more information write to Ted Bowman, Coordinator, The Family Enrichment Center, 301 S. Brevard St., Charlotte, N.C. 28202.

The Family Enrichment Program of the Union College Character Research Project.
"The Family Enrichment Program is composed of three action projects for parent-child participation. These projects have been designed specifically to focus on the National Y-Guide goal of 'Strengthening Family Life' as applied to parents of children ages six through ten, who are actively involved with Y-Indian Guides, Y-Indian Princesses, and Y-Indian Maidens. In the development stage are lessonlike materials (kits) for parents to use in the home." For further information write to Dr. Ernest M. Ligon, Character Research Project, 207 State St., Schenectady, N.Y. 12305.

Urban and Jeanette Steinmetz, The Common Sense Community Program.
Marriage and family enrichment. Cassette programs and other materials with Christian emphasis. For further information write to Family Enrichment Bureau, 1615 Ludington St., Escabana, Mich. 49829.

Carl Clarke, *The Marriage Enrichment Weekend.*
Presentation of the United Methodist Church Division of Evangelism marriage enrichment program directed by Mrs. Virginia Law Shell, Dr. Carl Clarke, consultant. ($1.00 per copy.) For further information about group leader training write to Dr. Carl Clarke, Marriage Enrichment Workshops, 3304 Mathieson Dr., N.E., Atlanta, Ga. 30305.

Margaret M. Sawin, *The Family Cluster—A Process of Religious Nurturing.*
Detailed presentation of Dr. Sawin's family cluster model and leadership training program used by over 250 churches in the U.S. and Canada, Australia, and New Zealand. ($1.50 per copy.) For further information write to Dr. Margaret M. Sawin, Consultant in Family Education, P.O. Box 18074, Twelve Corners Branch, Rochester, N.Y. 14618.

Herbert A. Otto, *The Family Cluster—A Multi-Base Alternative.*
A manual for use by families who wish to develop their own family cluster. (Beverly Hills, Calif.: The Holistic Press [1970], 1975). ($3.50.) For further information write to the publisher at 8909 Olympic Blvd., Beverly Hills, Calif. 90211.

Cassettes and Other Resources

Sally Edwards, *Creative Problem Solving in the Family.*
A cassette program ($6.99 per cassette). Write to Successful Marriage Cassettes, Box 1042, Kansas City, Mo. 64141.

Gregory T. Leville, *Making Marriage Work.*
A complete and detailed program including cassettes and written materials. ($50.00 per person.)

Sidney Callahan and Eugene Kennedy, *Making Marriage Work.*
Designed to explore the personal dynamics of marriage and family relationships, includes a discussion guide. ($49.95 per cassette program.) Write to Thomas Moore Association, 180 N. Wabash, Chicago, Ill. 60601.

Elisha S. Fisch and co-authors, *The Subject Is Marriage-Aiding Growth in Marriage via Cable Television.*

Outstanding summary covering the creation of six television programs plus an evaluation. The video tape series *The Subject Is Marriage* is available on a rental basis. For information contact Dr. K. Pollock, Center for Policy Research, Inc., 475 Riverside Dr., New York, N.Y. 10027. Copies of the article "The Subject Is Marriage" are available from Publications Dept., same address. ($1.50 per copy.)

Herbert A. Otto, *The 'Now' Communication Game.*

A no win/no lose game for couples and families (children six years and up can play) designed to foster and enhance communication. ($6.50 per game.) Write to The Holistic Press, 8909 Olympic Blvd., Beverly Hills, Calif. 90211.

Successful Marriage, A Newsletter (published ten times a year).

For up-to-date, accurate reporting on the field. ($7.50 per year.) Write to Successful Marriage, 115 West Armour Blvd., Kansas City, Mo. 64141.

Biographical Notes
on the Contributors

Ramona S. Adams, Ph.D., is Associate Dean of Students and an associate professor in the Graduate School of Social Work, University of Utah, Salt Lake City, Utah.

Douglas A. Anderson, Ph.D., is Minister of Counseling of the Presbyterian Counseling Service, Seattle, Washington. He has had articles published in *Pastoral Psychology,* and *The Family Coordinator.*

Antoinette G. Bosco, M.A., is an Associate for Community Affairs at the State University of New York at Stony Brook. She has published two hundred articles in national magazines, such as *Catholic Digest, Columbia, Family Weekly, Marriage,* and *Parade.* Her books include, among others, *Joseph the Huron* (P. J. Kenedy and Sons, 1962) and *Marriage Encounter: A Rediscovery of Love* (Abbey Press, 1973).

Ed Branch, Jr., M.Ed., is a psychologist in private practice. He is the author of *I Want to Be Used* (Celestial Arts Press, 1974), and the inventor of "Two-to-One," a marriage communication game (Hyphen Consultants, 1972).

Betty Capers, B.A., is Executive Director of the San Diego Institute for Transactional Analysis, La Jolla, California.

Hedges Capers, M.Div., L.H.D., is President of the San Diego Institute for Transactional Analysis. His articles have appeared in the *Marriage and Family Counselors Quarterly,* the *Transactional Analysis Bulletin,* the *Transactional Analysis Journal,* and other publications.

Howard J. Clinebell, Jr., Ph.D., is Professor of Pastoral Counseling in the School of Theology at Claremont, California, and on the faculty of the Claremont Graduate School, Departments of Psychology and Religion. He has published some forty papers in journals such as *Pastoral Psychology* and the *Journal of Religion and Health.* Among his ten books are *Mental Health Through Christian Community* (Abingdon Press, 1965), *The Intimate Marriage,* with Charlotte H. Clinebell (Harper & Row, 1970), and *The People*

Dynamic: Changing Self and Society Through Growth Changes (Harper & Row, 1972).

Au-Deane S. Cowley, Ph.D., is an Assistant Professor of Social Work in the Graduate School of Social Work, University of Utah, and Field Work Coordinator of the undergraduate program in Social Welfare.

Herman Green, Jr., M.Div., Th.M., is Minister of Pastoral Care at First Baptist Church, El Paso, Texas. His articles have appeared in *Church Administration, Home Life,* and other church periodicals.

Don Hayward, B.S., is Vice President of the Los Angeles YMCA. He has written articles for *The Association Forum.*

Paul and LaDonna L. Hopkins are co-directors of the Association of Couples for Marriage Enrichment (ACME), Winston-Salem, North Carolina. Paul's publications include articles in *Colloquy* and *Young Children.* Together they have written articles for *Bethany Guide Education, The Christian Home,* and others.

Bernard Kligfeld, D.D., is Rabbi of Temple Emanu El, Long Beach, New York. His articles have appeared in the *Journal of Religion and Health* and *Sexology,* among others.

Julian P. Leon, M.A., is a clinical psychologist in private practice, and a consultant. He is the Chairperson of the Work-Life Program of the Gestalt Institute of Cleveland.

David R. Mace, Ph.D., is Professor of Family Sociology in the Bowman Gray School of Medicine, Wake Forest University, Winston-Salem, North Carolina. He is internationally known for his work in marrage guidance and family relations and is co-founder of the Association of Couples for Marriage Enrichment. He has published extensively in scientific and professional journals. He has written more than twenty books, including *Whom God Hath Joined* (Westminster, 1953), *Youth Considers Marriage* (Nelson, 1966), *The Christian Response to the Sex Revolution* (Abingdon, 1970).

Sherod Miller, Ph.D., is an assistant professor in the Department of Medicine, School of Medicine, University of Minnesota. His articles have appeared in *Small Group Behavior* and *The Family Coordinator.* His books include *The Minnesota Couples Communication Program Instructor's Manual; The MCCP Couples Handbook* (Interpersonal Communication Programs, 1972); and *Alive and Aware: Improving Communication in Relationships* (ICP, 1975).

Elam Nunnally, Ph.D., is an assistant professor in the School of Social Welfare, University of Wisconsin—Milwaukee. He is co-author of *Alive and Aware,* with Sherod Miller and Daniel B. Wackman.

Herbert A. Otto, Ph.D., is Chairperson of the National Center for the Exploration of Human Potential, San Diego, California. He has published over sixty articles in professional and scientific journals. Among the thirteen books of which he is author and editor are *Guide to Developing Your Potential* (Charles Scribner's Sons, 1967), *More Joy in Your Marriage* (Hawthorn Books, 1969), and *The Family in Search of a Future* (Appleton-Century-Crofts, 1970).

Roberta Otto is a group facilitator and group trainer. She is co-author with Herbert Otto of *Total Sex* (Wyden, 1972; Signet, 1973) and the soon to be published book *Positive Aspects of Divorce*.

Kenneth G. Prunty, M.A., M.Div., is Associate Secretary of the Board of Christian Education of the Church of God. His articles have appeared in such journals as *Christian Leadership,* the *Christian Education Journal,* and the *Religious Education Journal.*

Abraham Schmitt is in private practice (marriage and individual counseling). His articles have appeared in the *Journal of the Otto Rank Association* and *Christian Living,* among others.

Dorothy Schmitt, B.A., R.N., is a co-leader with Abraham Schmitt at Marriage Renewal Retreats.

Antoinette Smith, M.A., is a trainer of marriage enrichment leaders, and a marriage and family counselor. She has had various articles published in church periodicals, including *The Christian Home* and *The Church School.*

Leon Smith, Ed.D., is Director of Educational Ministries in Marriage, United Methodist Church. He has published in various church periodicals, such as *The Christian Home* and *The Interpreter.* Among his books are *Family Ministry—An Educational Resource for the Local Church* (Board of Discipleship, United Methodist Church, 1975), and *To Love and to Cherish—The Pastor's Manual on Premarital Counseling in the Methodist Church* (United Methodist Publishing House, 1970).

Delbert J. (Del) Vander Haar, is Secretary of the Western Regional Services and Family Life, General Program Council, Reformed Church in America, Orange City, Iowa. His articles have appeared in such journals as *Pioneer Christian Monthly* and *Church Herald.*

Trudy Maassen Vander Haar, A.B., presently works as a small group facilitator for marriage enrichment, family cluster workshops, pastors and wives seminars and Women's Retreats. She has written articles for *Spectrum* and the *Church Herald.*

Arthur O. (Bud) Van Eck, Ed.D., is Secretary of the Eastern Metropolitan Center, Reformed Church in America. His articles have appeared in the *Church Herald, Share,* and other periodicals.

Beatrice A. (Bea) Van Eck is a co-facilitator of marriage enrichment groups with Arthur Van Eck, and co-author with him of the tape *The Human Side of Marriage.*

Daniel B. Wackman, Ph.D., is an Associate Professor and Director of the Communication Research Division, School of Journalism and Mass Communication, University of Minnesota. Dr. Wackman's contributions have appeared in *The American Behavior Scientist* and the *Journal of Marketing Research and Journalism Quarterly.* He is co-author of *The Minnesota Couples Communication Program Instructor's Manual, The MCCP Couples Handbook* and *Alive and Aware.*

June N. Wilson, A.A., is a homemaker and nursery school teacher. She has developed a *Bibliography of Books for Children* (1974), and shares authorship in the *Leader's Manual—Family Enrichment Weekend* (United Methodist Church, 1974).

Russell L. Wilson, B.D., is Program Consultant and Coordinator of Family and Marriage Ministries, Iowa Conference, United Methodist Church. He has published articles on planning for family ministries, and is the joint author of the *Leader's Manual—Family Enrichment Weekend.*

Joseph C. Zinker, Ph.D., is a clinical psychologist in private practice. Dr. Zinker's articles have appeared in such journals as *Contemporary Psychology,* the *Journal of General Psychology,* and *Voices.* His books include *Rosa Lee: Motivation and the Crisis of Dying* (Lake Erie College Press, 1966), and *Creative Process in Gestalt Therapy* (Brunner/Mazel, 1976).